# TATTLETALE

A Two-Tour Vietnam Veteran's Combat Experiences
On the Ground and In the Air

### Charlie Palek

*7/24/01*
*To Ron*
*I hope you enjoy the book.*
*Best wishes*
*Charlie Palek*

Copyright © 2001 by Charlie Palek
All rights reserved.
No part of this book may be reproduced, stored in a retrieval system, or transmitted by any means, electronic, mechanical, photocopying, recording, or otherwise, without written permission from the author.

ISBN 0-75962-227-2

This book is printed on acid free paper.

Softlightphoto.com
Softlight@softlightphoto.com

1stBooks - rev. 3/2/01

## *Dedication*

For my mother, brother and sisters who showed me the unconditional love and support so few Vietnam veterans received.
To my dad, who died in 1997 before this book was finished. I hope he would have been proud. I considered it an honor to be his son.
To all the warriors, past, present and future, who keep this country free. I have always felt our country never cries enough or appreciates their efforts. They will always have my utmost respect and admiration.

# FOREWORD

## Tattletale
By Charlie Palek

Welcome Home, Charlie!

Thank you!

When you have been profoundly impacted by a life-changing set of episodes it is amazing the things you recall: the people, the incidents, the places, the feelings. Charlie's recollections bring all of these to life in Tattletale. This book jogs the memory of those old enough to remember. It introduces an era to those who are too young to have experienced it. Tattletale closely mirrors the experiences of thousands of young men and a nation in a state of flux and turmoil.

Tattletale provides a look at the Vietnam experience up close and personal. His naivete as a young enlistee seems much like that of our nation's leaders. As he slogged through his first tour he became keenly aware of the futility of our mired efforts. Despite wounds inflicted in combat, he chose to return for a second tour. Why? That same question arises when asking why our country's leaders chose to continue despite the clarity of the writing on the wall. Is there so much more that we do not know? Even with hindsight our comprehension is cloudy and shrouded in uncertainty and mystery.

Charlie's willingness and ability to share his poignant personal reflections are most welcomed. High school students benefit from their time with Charlie. They get a better understanding of Midwestern values and patriotism of the late fifties and early sixties. They sense the emotional highs and lows instilled into someone who has seen combat in its rawest forms. They come to respect the type of camaraderie only warrior's experience. They view the physical and mental scars of war. And, they are reminded of the awesome power and strength of friends, loved ones and family.

Having Charlie come speak to high school students is a real treat. He shares his vivid memories and his beautiful photographs of two tours. Each visit is a new and wonderful experience. Each class is unique. Every visit includes a memory recalled, a story revisited with a new twist, or an old thought dredged from the darkened corners of memory that house life's adventures. Today's youth are allowed to briefly glimpse the far-away look of someone who has seen the realities of war. With thoughtful reflection they observe someone who has learned the merits of keen attention to detail and anticipation of unexpected circumstances. If they listen closely, they hear the cries of humanity in the eternal quest for peace.

And, in all, there is the plight of youth. Ignorance clad in robes of perceived invincibility. It is joined with an unquenchable thirst for adventure that is in perpetual motion. Charlie brings these to life in <u>Tattletale</u>.

For those of us who are of Charlie's generation and who share Vietnam experiences, <u>Tattletale</u> provides a look at a world some of us did not endure. Thank goodness! We are not all made of the same mettle as Charlie and other fine warriors. You served us; you served your country. You served with dignity and honor when our leaders called. We salute you for your gallantry, courage, and conviction.

Again, thank you Charlie!

Welcome Home!


Dan Wright – high school teacher and Vietnam vet

Many of the incidents/battles in this book bring back memories because Charlie and I corresponded by letter while he was serving his two tours of duty. He was not only one of my biology students, but we became friends, a relationship you can't have with all students. Charlie was the only former student I wrote to in Vietnam. Many of his letters caused me

worry and concern as I realized some of the dangers he faced; he was my informational and emotional link to that war.
I realized how gung-ho and excited he was to go into the military after graduation, because he was the *only* student I ever had who wrote "latrine" instead of restroom when signing out of study hall. Although I couldn't understand or relate to that enthusiasm, I admired his focus and patriotism.

This book is a rare masterpiece, not only because of his excellent writing skills but also his objectivity about the war. The rarity is the way in which he matter-of-factly recalls the dedicated way he and thousands of others fought the battles they were ordered to enter. On the other hand, he was quite aware of the senseless loss of our troops by unwise decisions by their CO's, the hypocrisy of what the Pentagon and news media were telling us back home versus what was really happening. Seldom would you find an author who is this objective and yet not inject bitterness and resentment about the dismal, screwed up way they had to fight a losing war. All too often the news media shows profiles of only the homeless, bitter, psychologically damaged Vietnam vets. Charlie's letters sure changed my view of the war because they gave me a glimpse of reality versus government spin.

This book is a logical and much-needed account of the most controversial war of the twentieth century. Every Vietnam vet has a story of some kind to tell, but few write it down in the form of a book. By reading this book we can appreciate and honor the actions of *all* our vets with untold stories.

Ron Brown – high school teacher/friend

Reading Tattletale is like having lunch with a Vietnam veteran and listening to him telling tales of his personal experiences. Years gone by offer a perspective on the war, but the sights, sounds and smells remain vivid and alive in his mind-and in his telling. The account is gritty and blunt. The realism laced with humor and compassion sets it apart from other Vietnam books.

Writer Charlie Palek offers a self-deprecating account of his experiences without building himself up as a hero, martyr or survivor. He simply tells it like it was. The book leaves you grateful to the soldiers who fought and makes you marvel that Palek emerged from the experience-not only alive, but with a balanced, healthy outlook on life.

Jonathan Finck – military history buff/friend

"I am not a mooch!"

Tom Russell – former Air Cav grunt/friend

## Table of Contents

Chapter 1    THE DESIRE TO BE A SOLDIER ................................. 1

Chapter 2    LEARNING THE BASICS ......................................... 17

Chapter 3    FNG's ........................................................................ 32

Chapter 4    HOME AND FT. HOOD, TEXAS ............................. 169

Chapter 5    2nd TOUR ................................................................ 182

Chapter 6    MY FAMILY'S MEMORIES ..................................... 282

### Murphy's Law of Combat:
#45

*"Murphy was a Grunt."*

# Acknowledgements

*I must thank a few people who have helped me finish this book. First, my sister, Sherry, who translated my chicken scratching onto a neatly typed computer disc while her one-year old ran rampant through her house.*

To Melissa Smith and Sarah Messer Becking, my studio employees that typed my final drafts and helped me scan and caption the photos.

To Brett Dufur of Pebble Publishing, who helped me through the editing process of the first draft.

To my family and friends who contributed their parts. You came through for me and I will always be grateful.

And finally to Roxy, my wife of 30 years and my biggest supporter. She always had kind words and an occasional correction to make as I wrote the first draft. I love you very much.

# Chapter 1
# THE DESIRE TO BE A SOLDIER

It was only three hours after dawn, and the sun was already battering the earth. The heat pounded down in shimmering waves, and along with the cloying humidity made the simple act of breathing a chore.

Smoke from the battle the day before was still hanging in the rifts and shell craters, the air too still to dissipate it. Wisps of water vapor rising from the heated soil mixed with the smoke, turning the horizon line soft like the color of cooking caramel.

A line of infantrymen trudged across the dusty ground, the heat and humidity already staining their clothes dark with perspiration. They had moved across this same area of operations yesterday, receiving serious sniper and machine gun fire from the tree line one hundred yards ahead. Casualties were light, but they were forced to fall back and regroup that night, then hit it again this morning. There wasn't much cover, so apprehension was high. They all knew the enemy soldiers were still around, probably estimating the exact time to open fire at them again.

The men moved slowly, eyes scanning treetops and ground, left and right. They moved like veterans of previous conflicts, confident but careful, knowing full well the kind of hell that could strike them down in the blink of a muzzle flash. Their eyes were red and squinting in the white light of the day. Lips were dry. Plastic rifle stocks were slick with sweat.

Each man carried his load differently. Weapons were held ready to fire, safeties off. Machine gunners looked back to make sure their assistants were close with extra ammo ready to use. Grenades hung from their packs like lethal apples, green but deadly. Nobody was smoking-too much of a distraction.

The line slowed as the men approached yesterday's ambush area. They used what cover was available; tree trunks, shallow holes, anything that could deflect a bullet. Where there was no cover available, men knelt or flopped on their bellies to scan ahead. The platoon leader pulled out his binoculars. Squinting, he zeroed in on the ground ahead, checking the smoky shadows and dim highlights, looking for his opponent to show his hand: a glint off a rifle barrel, a slight movement in a shadow, any telltale sign of human intrusion in the forest ahead.

Charlie Palek

Every man's eyes drilled ahead, waiting. Trigger fingers flicked in and out of the trigger guards in anticipation. They'd rather be moving than presenting fat targets for every rat with a rifle or mortar. Infantrymen were never comfortable in the open. That's usually when the shit starts flying. Ambushes are sprung when a lot of chumps are in the open. When your enemies are professional soldiers, they will inflict casualties. And casualty's mean wounded men lying in an open field needing medical help. But they have to be brought back into safety first. That means some poor sap will have to drag his ass out there to get them, while his pals are laying down cover fire. All in all, the type of situation nobody likes to see happen.

With his field survey complete, the officer tucked his binoculars away and signaled the platoon to move forward. The men got up slowly, groaning under their load of food, water and ammo. A 30-meter advance brought a hailstorm of sniper fire. The snipers were just waiting for the column to stand up and present choice targets. The officer went down, as did his radioman and one of the machine gunners. High priority targets taken out first, just what they were supposed to do.

I was on the right flank, walking through the uneven ground of a shallow creek bed when the firing started. The heat had lulled me into a semi-transparent fog, the smells of cattle manure and muddy water taking my attention away from the job at hand. The buzzing insects sucking what few juices I had left became low priority when the hostile fire started. I threw myself against the creek bank rim and opened fire. My Daisy Red Ryder was firing as fast as I could cock it and point, the BB's throwing up little puffs of dust as I snapped shot at cow pies and dirt clods. My cousin Dwight, 10 meters away, was frantically sighting in on a mulberry tree that hosted a sniper in its branches.

I finally got a clean firing position and put a couple fast rounds into the tree. The enemy firing stopped and we gathered under the mulberry tree to relax and rest, the branches providing a treat of fat purple fruit. Ah, living off the land!

The date: July 1958. The place: the Shubert dairy farm, Washington County, Illinois. I was 9 years old and Dwight was 10. We had fought our way down the same pasture for years, past the pond where the big catfish lived, paralleling the creek where we gigged frogs, all the way to the end of the pasture where the two big cottonwoods stood. Once we reached them, the battle was over. We'd sit under these giants, their shade cooling us down from our campaign against the Japanese on Tarawa, Iwo or Guadalcanal. We'd discuss life, and the books we'd read about WWII, our imaginations whirling with the sounds of battle and the glory of it all.

Once we were rested, we'd begin our patrol again, back from where we came. Only this time, we'd be fighting the elite SS Divisions of the German Army in the fields of France, or the Japanese in Burma, or chasing the Desert Fox in North Africa.

When we got tired of humping the pasture, we'd pull out the plastic soldiers, find a cliff face to assault or a fortress to batter down. That one pasture provided the canvas for our vivid imaginations. We'd fight our way past the huge, lumbering milk cows that were turned out every morning after milking, their faces displaying little interest in these boys rushing back and forth, making explosive sounds and shooting at their excrement. Sometimes we'd send Dwight's younger brother Russell into the pasture to hide out and ambush us. We never used BB guns to ferret him out, but there were times we thought about it, him being just a kid and a scourge of the earth.

About the time I became interested in World War II history, I started hearing stories about some of my uncles' experiences in the war. I became extremely interested in their stories, but was reluctant to come right out and ask because I had also heard they usually didn't like discussing their wartime experiences.

My uncle Buster had served in New Guinea, and from my reading, I knew that the islands of the South Pacific had some of the worst terrain our Army had ever fought in.

New Guinea was the last island needed by the Japanese to invade Australia. The Japanese were firmly entrenched and were on their way to an invasion plan by the time the U.S., Britain and Australia got a force together to stop them. The island was one big strategic problem. Besides having to push the Japanese off the island, the terrain fought our troops every step of the way: steaming jungles, mountainous trails, impossible supply logistics, mud, ravenous insects, poisonous snakes, bloated bodies, corpse-eating rats, shortages of everything, stinking clothes, nights so dark you couldn't see anything except the cigarette butt in front of your face (if you managed to light one up and not catch a sniper's bullet in the old coconut for that nicotine fix), disease running rampant and a communications nightmare. It was the kind of place Dante would have passed up on the road to Hell.

## Charlie Palek

I got a lot of his stories second hand from his son Dwight. He told of the island natives chowing down on a dead warthog that had been killed on the road and lay bloating in the sun for a couple of days before they feasted on it. They would eat anything except a load of vinegar beets the GI's received one day. The army guys wouldn't eat them, and much to their surprise, neither would the natives. Wouldn't touch them. The GI's piled the beets in the jungle and they're probably still there. He also saw the natives fall on a nest of ants and devour them after their tree was demolished by artillery fire. Ate them like expensive after-dinner mints.

He also told of a sentinel opening up on a noise he heard in the jungle one night. The whole perimeter opened up in the direction the lookout was firing. The next morning they discovered they had wiped out a platoon of chickens. Apparently the sound of them scratching in the dirt sounded like infiltrators crawling through the jungle floor.

Uncle Buster had also brought back a few souvenirs that had always intrigued me. He had about 6 or 8 Japanese samurai swords in the corner of his stairsteps. He also had a couple Japanese rifles complete with bayonets. To my little boy eyes they looked 10 feet long. I passed them by every time I went up or down those stairs and always with a reverence that comes from knowing those rifles had been participants in a real war.

Uncle Buster was on one of the troop carriers off the coast of Japan waiting to invade when the war ended. I think he was glad he didn't have to invade Japan. New Guinea would have been a cakewalk compared to assaulting the Japanese homeland. My Uncle Rich served in the Philippines as a truck driver, but was pretty silent when it came to war stories. He did see a lot of vehicles dumped into the ocean when the outfits moved from one island to another. It was less trouble than transporting them back to the States. Being from the conservative Midwest, it seemed like an incredible waste to him.

My Uncle Les told my dad about an incident that occurred in Okinawa while he was there. There was a Japanese bomber that came over the U.S. occupied island every night and dropped a couple of bombs just to keep everyone from getting a good night's sleep. This type of harassment was typical of both sides but after several weeks of this, it started to get old. Anti-aircraft failed to find him in the dark and our fighters; ill equipped for night fighting couldn't bring him down either.

Then one day they got in a new piece of gear, a P-61 Black Widow night fighter. This bad boy was built for night patrols. It had a second crewman sitting behind and above the pilot in control of the radar and four radar-locking cannons in the turret on top of the plane. This twin engine beauty was painted jet black and built for nighttime mayhem. It didn't take long for the crew to hear about the midnight raider. Ambushing this Japanese plane was what the Black Widow was built for! So about an hour before midnight, the Widow takes off, grabs some altitude and begins a slow, wide circle over the airstrip.

The Japanese, being sticklers for schedules, showed up right at midnight like he'd done so many times before. Before the Jap plane made it over the airstrip, the low-pitched sound of its engine was interrupted by the higher pitched sound of a plane in a dive. The guys on the ground heard the four cannons pumping rounds into the dark and a fireball suddenly appeared not far from the runway. A cheer went up as the 61 landed back at their new base and a couple of new heroes were born.

Then there was Uncle Charlie, the man I was named after. He was with the "Fighting 44th" in WWII Germany as an artillery forward observer. I knew enough about that job to know he was out in front of friendly lines and probably behind enemy lines once in a while, hanging his ass out there in his camos and looking for targets. It was a hazardous job requiring good map reading skills, self-reliance and "balls."

He didn't talk to me about his escapades, but I heard some of his stories from my dad. He told dad that when his unit captured a German airfield, they walked down a long line of Focke Wulf 190's, and dropped a grenade in each cockpit, destroying every one of them. The 190 was one of my favorite model planes and I thought they could have been put to better use. It broke my heart to hear they blew them all up.

Another time one of the line units had been receiving harassment and interdiction fire from a Tiger Tank that couldn't be located. They sent Uncle Charlie out to see if he could find the firing position. Apparently he did, noticing tank tracks hidden just behind a rise overlooking the valley where the Allied lines were. On a hunch, he put a Sherman tank not far from the position, covered it with a camo net and waited for the Tiger to show up. As a bonus that night, it snowed and perfectly covered the Sherman lying in wait. The next day, the Tiger showed up exactly where he suspected. The Sherman was set up so close, the 75mm gun actually knocked the Tiger over on its side before it exploded. Mission accomplished.

Another time he anticipated where a German infantry unit would assemble before attacking. He laid in some artillery coordinates in the area and waited. When the infantry was found assembled in the exact area, he laid in what was apparently a devastating barrage. The carnage he created must have affected him quite deeply. In 1964 he committed suicide, and family members speculated that his war experiences could have been an underlying reason since no note was found. Even so, I still considered him, and all my relatives who served, to be genuine heroes.

We also had a neighbor who drove one of our school buses, but during World War II had piloted a P-38, the Fork Tailed Devil. He had told my father stories about his missions, which enthralled me. My favorite was about his escort missions over Germany keeping the B-17's and B-24's safe from German fighters. After the bombers dropped their loads and turned for the return home, the P-38's were released and allowed to low level over enemy territory looking for targets of opportunity. They apparently attacked anything that even looked military including barracks, factories, trains, truck convoys and troop concentrations.

The cool thing about the P-38 was that the guns it carried were in the nose, not on the wings. The wing guns had a point several hundred yards out where all the bullets converged into one "sweet spot." A good pilot could judge this distance and really tear up a target with 6 or 8 .50-caliber guns hitting all at once. The P-38 pilot didn't have to worry about that…since his 6 .50-caliber's and 1 20-mm cannon was in the nose, all he had to do was line up the nose with his target and kick ass. You get your plane lined up on a truck convoy and as you pass over, kick the rudder pedals slightly right and left, yawing the plane and raking those guns across the targets. Sounded like fun if you didn't think about the flesh and blood being torn to shreds under that horrendous stream of steel and tracers. My young brain soaked up these stories like a gray sponge, reliving the stories over and over, imagining myself in the cockpit or pounding the ground searching for Japanese snipers or German SS Troopers.

I can hardly remember a time when I wasn't interested in the machines, men and the battles of war. I started reading the comic books first — Sgt. Rock, Big Al, Little Al, Charlie Cigar, The Blackhawks-they started the little wires in my head to trigger. I loved the adventures of Sgt. Rock. His torn shirt, bulging muscles, sweaty brow — the only guy I knew who could hand hold a .50-caliber with a couple hundred round belt across his shoulder. He'd assault a pillbox with all this shit hanging off of him, and take out another squad of German infantry with a nifty 200-round burst from his .50. Amazing. His exploits kept my imagination running on overtime.

I also began building plastic models on a regular basis. I was especially interested in the WWII planes and military vehicles. The P-51, the P-38 and the Focke Wulf 190 were my favorites. I bought several kits of each one so I could paint different camo schemes on them or build different versions. By the time high school was out, I had a couple hundred models in my room, religiously dusting them all with a soft paint brush when they got dusty. It was a labor of love.

I eventually gravitated to paperbacks, reading every book I could get my hands on about World War I, World War II and Korea. Air combat, Naval battles, infantry assaults, and the men who fought them took up the time I would have spent getting in trouble.

Not that I was a troublemaker. I feared the consequences of getting into trouble. I was a sort of semi-geek loner, spending time by myself and enjoying it. I never suffered from boredom or loneliness. I had my circle of friends and we did a lot of stuff together. But when everybody was busy I could always find an adventure, whether it was hunting ground hogs in the pasture behind the house, taking a short bicycle trip into the countryside, or building a German ME 109 Fighter at my desk.

School was O.K. I did my work, not always brilliantly, but I got it done, and almost always on school time. By the time high school rolled around, I was doing all my homework on school time. I hardly ever brought homework home. Math was a nightmare for me. Learning the multiplication tables in grade school was agony, Algebra II like another language. I dreaded those classes like I dreaded football windsprints.

English was another matter, especially when it involved writing themes. I always got straight A's, because I wrote about what interested me: Auschwitz, The Battle of Midway, The Green Berets — I aced all my themes on such subjects. I hunkered down in study hall, did all my research and writing there and never worked at home. I couldn't — I had a new model to work on and couldn't spare the time at home for such frivolous undertakings as homework.

Then there were the girls. I was far from being a ladies man, a bit too shy and certainly not as suave as I liked to think I was. They were mysterious and confusing, but I enjoyed their company when they allowed it. The late grade school era was a time of discovery and wonder. The girls starting to blossom and the guys discussing the possibilities, as if we knew anything about it. The skirts were getting shorter and I became a newly ordained leg man. I could sit and watch them for hours. They were fascinating appendages, wrapped in nylon, crossing and uncrossing, peeking out from under those short cheerleading skirts. I was hopelessly hooked. Damned near took my attention away from the P-38 I was putting together at the time. My mind was overloaded with surging puberty and the adrenaline of battle. An explosive combination!

I did the sports trip too: basketball, track, baseball, and football in high school. I never had the drive it took to be a real competitor. I was mediocre at everything and didn't care to excel either. If we won, great. If we lost, that's the way it goes. It didn't upset my life like it did some of my teammates. I saw it as only a game. Most of my teammates saw it as a right of passage into adulthood, a yardstick on how things would go later in life. Take it too lightly — you'll be a bum — no job — living off the family and a future as dim as a hop head's eyes.

Summertime was wonderful. While a lot of my friends went to camp, I didn't feel the need to do that. I had several aunts and uncles living on dairy farms, and I would go there for a week or two; hunt, fish, and just play with the animals. My grandmother's place was old and she had a lot of acreage to wander. Her son Vernon gave me an old, rusted Daisy BB gun to use, and that was what I cut my shooting teeth on. It didn't have much of a kick anymore, but you could still bring down a sparrow if you hit him right and the range wasn't too far. Vernon kept his rifles and shotguns in the corner of the kitchen, behind the food cabinet. He let me keep my BB gun there too. It made me feel grown up.

On my 11th birthday, I went to the farm and approached the corner to get my Daisy. It wasn't there, but what replaced it was a brand new Red Ryder BB gun. I knew immediately it was for my birthday, but I played it cool, asking where that old rusty Daisy was. My dad and Vernon were standing in the kitchen, beaming like crazy, enjoying the moment. My grandma, though not too crazy about getting me a new gun, did realize the value of weaponry on the farm and tolerated the new gift. My mother on the other hand, was not enthused at all. She didn't like guns, but was out-voted on this one. I know she envisioned me putting out an eye from a bad ricochet.

I was told to take the new one out and see how it shot. I grabbed the rifle, put a whole pack of BB's down the chamber port under the barrel, and headed for the woods with my trusty collie, Shep. We walked for hours, shooting at knotholes, fence posts, and birds. I had decided at an early age that I would only shoot what was considered farm pests, and nothing more. Sparrows, blackbirds, starlings, and pigeons were fair game. Most everything else was off-limits.

Grandma's farm was a little bit of heaven for a grade school kid.

When I got a little older, I graduated to a little Remington .22 single shot, then to a Remington .22-bolt action, then finally to dad's old .22 Long Rifle Mossberg. I loved the old Mossberg. It looked like an M-1 Garand. The forearm ran up to within a half inch of the barrel. It felt like a military rifle. I put a 9-power scope on it and there wasn't a sparrow or groundhog safe within miles of where I lived.

Once the Mossberg was operational, I took it to Uncle Ray's dairy farm, where the birds were everywhere. They had lots of trees around their house and lots of places I could hunker down and snipe from. I spent hours plinking away at the bird pests, while their army of cats hauled away the carcasses. Quick, clean and efficient. As it should be.

I never was interested in shooting deer, or any other kind of game animals. I went on a couple coon hunts, but that was more to watch the dogs work. My Uncle Buster had 30-40 coon dogs on his farm at any one time, and listening to them all howl when a car drove up to the house was music to my ears. Uncle Buster would step out on the porch and yell "Shut Up!" and every dog would go silent. What control!

Life was pretty good. We never had a lot of money, but I created my own entertainment. Between my friends, hunting on the farm, and my model making, I had plenty to keep me busy. I seldom got into trouble and had no interest in doing the semi-illegal activities a lot of the kids were into.

My freshman year in high school started in 1964, about the same time as I started reading more about U.S. troops being sent to a little-known country called Vietnam. We studied *Newsweek* once a week in our history class, and I eagerly awaited reading what was going on over there. U.S. advisors were sent to help the South Vietnamese people fight the communist insurgents. The articles were small in '64, but as my high school education progressed, so did the activity of our military. The articles in *Newsweek* got longer and my interest in the conflict accelerated.

## Charlie Palek

I was playing football and basketball my freshman year, and started playing football as a sophomore, until I broke my collarbone in practice. I told the coach after the play that something was wrong, but he told me to suck it up and go back in. I played three more plays until he realized my left shoulder was sagging a bit and that I was in pain. He took me to the hospital and I came home with a shoulder brace and my left arm in a sling. My mom gave me one of her "I told you you'd get hurt" stares and I lived with the brace for six weeks.

After my sophomore year in high school, I quit all sports and got a job to make some spending cash. I never regretted it, not needing the glory like some of the other guys. I was content to sit in the stands, watch the cheerleaders and yell at the refs.

Even though I had a job, I knew I would never be able to afford a car, so I started looking at other forms of transportation. One of my friends had a Honda 50 motorcycle. It had a step through frame and was supposedly built for off-road travel. After riding it for the first time, I found my wheels. I immediately went to Mom and asked her if I could get a motorcycle. I already had the $300 in the bank and promised I would take care of it. She was predictably cold on the subject explaining to me how dangerous they were. A definite "no" from Mom. I went to Dad and asked him and he said, "That sounds like fun!" It took some heavy begging, but she finally gave in and Pop and I went to Belleville, and picked up a new Honda 50 Sport. That began my love of motorcycles, which continues to this day. I graduated later to a Honda 90 and rode that until the end of high school.

1965 rolled around and things were really heating up in Vietnam. By now, Marines had been pouring into the 1 Corp area of the northern provinces of South Vietnam. Other units, including the 173rd Airborne Brigade, elements of the 101st Airborne, and the entire 1st Air Cav, 1st Division, and elements of the 25th Division, were sent over and digging in for a fight. Troops from Australia and New Zealand were also sending combat troops. A couple of carrier groups were positioned off the coast of South Vietnam, and the Air Force was building land-based airstrips like there was no tomorrow.

I was reading about this massive buildup with great interest. The U.S. advisors sent in the early '60s were being used more and more as combat troops. The overall plan of using the U.S. advisers to train South

Vietnamese troops was obviously being scrapped. The U.S. muscle flexing seemed to be slowly becoming an American, not a Vietnamese war.

I was graduating from high school in 1967 and I started thinking about what I wanted to do. Actually, I already knew what I was going to do; I just didn't know which branch I wanted to do it in. The Air Force was trashed early on because I figured I wouldn't be able to handle the math and engineering courses to become a pilot. Being in the Air Force and not flying sounded really boring, so they were out. I thought working on the deck of an aircraft carrier would be a cool job, but swimming was never something I enjoyed, and living on the water didn't have any appeal. No salt water in my veins. The Navy was scratched.

The Marines were high on my list. Everybody knew when trouble started, the Marines were the first to go and I liked that idea. It was a tight unit with tons of history, pride, and spirit. They were getting into action early on in the northern part of the country, and since I had been reading about the infantry since I was a pup, I decided ground combat was what I wanted to do. I knew Marine training would be tough but I knew I could handle it.

The Army was also high on my list. They had more options than the Marines — Green Berets, Rangers, Airborne — it all sounded very exciting. The one thing that worried me was that if I chose a specialty that required a lot of training, I could feasibly miss the war before I got a chance to participate. Talk about a tragedy! Believe it or not, this factor was major in weighing in my options.

In 1965, becoming a Green Beret or Special Forces member required already being a certain rank with several specialties and several years of time served. The amount of time required to train for the Special Forces, I decided was too long to commit to for now. Ranger training was something that the Special Forces required anyway, but for now I didn't want to waste the 2-3 months that it would take. I was so anxious to get into the shit I couldn't even afford a couple months.

Airborne training was doable. Three weeks of training then off to one of the distinctive airborne units, 101st, 82nd, or the 173rd Airborne Brigade. They had lots of history, parachute training, assignment to a hotdog Airborne Unit. That's the ticket I wanted. I had read so much about the 101st and their battles during D-Day and later in Bastogne, France. I liked everything about the 101st …their history, their mission, their patch, everything. I wanted to be a Screaming Eagle in the worst way.

1965 came and went. 1966 ushered in a rapidly expanding war. We were hearing new terms associated with this war… search and destroy, toe poppers, recon by fire, deros, dustoff, snake 'n nape, tunnel rats, Victor Charlie, and the World.

The newsmagazines I was reading was sending more correspondents and photographers to cover the war. Much of the time reports back from the front lines were not optimistic.

The Arvins, the South Vietnamese Army that was being trained, supplied and supported by our own troops were getting their asses kicked on a regular basis. Motivation seemed to be a problem, they were mostly anti-Communist, but not pro- government. Mostly peasants, they were having a difficult time finding something to believe in powerful enough to die for. The U.S. advisers were at a standstill providing the motivation since U.S. troops were beginning to wonder about the same thing. This scourge was spreading faster than a bad rash. American troops were beginning to wonder why they were spilling their blood and filling body bags for an ally that couldn't muster the motivation to save their own country.

What most of the U.S. troops didn't know was that the typical Arvin grunt was being paid piss poor, had very little R & R, no pension if they were killed, and virtually no family support. No wonder morale was lower than whale shit. The officers were as corrupt as the government officials were and getting things done in the company and platoon levels was an act of futility.

But to the American troops slugging it out day after day with the Viet Cong and North Vietnamese Army, it didn't matter. They had their own problems. The biggest was getting out of this country in 12 months alive and with all appendages intact and functioning.

I read with fascination about the use of Spooky, the C-47 transport refitted with three 7.62 electric gattling guns. This plane was being used to support hamlets, fire support bases and outposts, pouring out 18,000 rounds per minute and turning night into day with their 200,000 candlepower flares. This firestorm in the sky could stay on station for hours, and turned out to be yet another page in the successful history of this grand old plane.

The Ho Chi Minh Trail was winding it's way down from North Vietnam through Laos and Cambodia and re-supply along the coastal routes were keeping the V.C. and the N.V.A. re-supplied at a staggering rate. Attempts to close down the trail became a full time job for the Air Force, CIA, Long Range Recon Forces and the Special Forces. The coastal areas were the responsibility of the Navy. Seal teams were running rampant in the Delta trying to shut down supply in the intercoastal waterways. It turned out to be a job bigger than anybody had anticipated.

While our troops were slugging it out in Vietnam, I stepped into my own battle, the battle of the sexes. I became infatuated over a little gal I had been going to school with since kindergarten. She had always been around; I just hadn't seen her. My eyes were on the high profile cheerleader and prom queens, unattainable since they usually were dating guy's two years older than I was.

Her name was Roxy and we approached our mutual interest in each other like a pair of black widow spiders — I moved in cautiously and she waited to see how badly I would screw up. Despite the initial "molasses in wintertime" move towards one another, we eventually became steadies and solidly devoted to each other. I could never guess just how devoted she would be until I enlisted.

1966 was the year the fighting really started to sizzle. The Marines were slugging it out in the Northern I Corp area, trying to keep the demilitarized zone (DMZ) from becoming a major infiltration route. The mountainous terrain made the work brutal and being Marines, they were usually dropped into meatgrinder situations ill equipped until the situation report got really bad.

GI hotspots in Saigon and other major cities were being indiscriminately bombed, casualties being civilian as well as soldiers. Photographs getting back to the States showed trashed street scenes of what used to be cafes and outdoor bars. Bodies and debris littered the streets while the wounded were hauled away. Not a pretty sight. It was becoming more apparent to me that someone wasn't playing fair!

Despite all the bad news, I was even more convinced I needed to be a part of this war. I had talked to the Marines and Army recruiters at our high school career day. (I think I was the only one who did.) I was still torn between the two services, but I still had time.

My parents were aware of my desire to serve. They saw this madness in different ways. Pop was proud I was willingly going to volunteer. He knew what could happen in a combat zone. We had family members serving all over the place during World War II: New Guinea, Germany, island-hopping the Pacific. Dad had heard the stories about combat but felt

*Charlie Palek*

I had to do what I wanted. Besides, he despised the guys heading for Canada. He thought they were unworthy to live in this country and Canada could have them.

Mom again took the non-adventurous path. She, like most women, didn't want to see her son marching off to war. She couldn't understand the "whys", but she knew with my interest in all things military that it was inevitable. Roxy's parents felt the same way. They knew they were going to be suffering the separation and anxieties through their only daughter. I felt like her mother resented this intrusion into their life. Her father, being the gentleman that he was, didn't lecture me, just told me to be careful.

## MURPHY'S LAW OF COMBAT
### #34

"No OPLAN survives first contact intact."

1966 ended with a hard lesson about how the war was going to be fought. Operation Attleboro involved men from 6 American units plus the ARVINS (South Vietnamese Army). The battle lasted over 2 months and both sides took it on the chin. After it was all over, the U.S. command realized that the N.V.A. had made the decision of when and where to fight — a lesson the U.S. command should have taken to heart. This tactic of choosing when to attack was to become the most frustrating form of combat the U.S. forces ever faced. The U.S. forces needed to initiate the fighting, drawing out the enemy then pounding them to dust with our massive firepower. But as the U.S. forces were finding out, the V.C. and N.V.A. were choosing the time and site of the battles. By the time we marshaled our forces, the enemy would have disappeared, melting back into the jungle or back into Cambodia. This type of action was going to become more prevalent as time went on and would eventually undermine U.S. support in the field and at home. How little we knew.

By the time 1967 arrived, I was watching with growing interest a battle forming in the I Corp area with the Marines. The place was called Con Thien. The Marines later called it the "Meatgrinder," and that's certainly the way it developed. Con Thien was two miles south of the DMZ overlooking an N.V.A. infiltration route. U.S. Intel knew N.V.A. troops were massing north of the DMZ so the Marines had to hold this outpost at all costs. The reports from the media were disturbing. The battle around Con Thien started out as a small firefight but quickly turned into a "balls to the wall" battle. The Marines had stepped on the tail of the dragon and were about to be burned.

From mid-summer 1967 to late fall, the Marines reinforced, assaulted, dug in, attacked, and fell back and the N.V.A. was on their ass the whole time, giving the Marines the conventional war the whole U.S. Command was chomping at the bit to have.

What disturbed me about this whole thing was the Marine command's apparent lack of regard for their troops. It seemed to me that they were dropping our guys into a meatgrinder. I thought their use of Korean vintage choppers and M-14 rifles was a joke... if these guys were supposed to fight a war the least they could do was equip them with modern war toys.

This convinced me that the Marines were out of the running. The idea of getting dropped onto the top of a hill to dig a bunker and get the shit pounded out of me by artillery and rocket fire was not appealing. I understood the *Espirit de Corp*, but this was ridiculous. Being one of "the Proud, the Few and the Dead" was not in my plans.

O.K., so it was the Army. I wasn't naive enough to think that the Army never screwed up, but they still offered the most options. I had read enough history to know that the Army had made some huge blunders. I also understood that war, being the fluid medium that it was, had the potential for monumental mistakes. Plans go awry in the blink of an eye. Artillery called down on friendlies, misplaced air strikes, incompetent leadership, unexpected bad weather, failed equipment... the list was endless. All I could do was hope the Army didn't take the Marines' over-zealous attitudes towards taking battle casualties.

The time came about two months before I graduated. I went to the Army recruiter and volunteered for a three-year hitch, Airborne school and Vietnam service. The recruiter smugly guaranteed all that I asked for, took my signature and sent me out the door, to return in a couple of weeks for the physical. Signing the papers set in stone that I was serious about serving. I was the only one excited about the prospect. Friends and family thought I was soft in the head. There were only a couple of other guys in my class that even discussed going into the combat arms. I suffered a few slings and arrows, looks of distaste, insanity and confusion, but I weathered it all with good humor. Young, dumb, and full of cum — that's me! The toughest part was dealing with Roxy, and both sets of parents. They didn't want to discuss the prospects or possibilities, so we avoided the subject in general.

The day of the physical came and was truly a lesson in humility. We had our eyes checked for color blindness, interviewed about childhood diseases, had all orifices checked and probed plus all the other basic tests. Standing naked with 20 other guys, bending over and spreading your ass cheeks in unison while a doctor walked down the line checking for healthy rectums was embarrassing as hell. I wondered why they didn't have private rooms for this stuff; not realizing that the Army at that time was looking for warm bodies to carry a rifle, protecting our privacy wasn't on their agenda.

So I passed the physical and was told to report to St. Louis two weeks after graduation where I would be transported to Ft. Leonard Wood, "Misery," for basic training.

I could hardly wait!

The two weeks between graduation and St. Louis were filled with anxiety and anticipation. I said my good-byes to all my relatives and friends, my high school buds threw a party in my honor, and I got my house in order.

The last night at home was tearful and emotional, especially for Roxy and I. She promised me she'd write all the time and I promised I'd be careful. Since I knew I'd be home before I shipped out overseas, I kept my anxieties to myself. This was only training for Christ's sake.

My parents took me to the bus stop at midnight. I kissed them both and told them not to worry. I climbed the steps of the bus, looked down the rows of passengers, and noticed immediately a lot of young men just like me heading for the same fate, the unknown, courtesy of the Green Machine. There were a lot of wide-eyed looks and somber faces on this bus, and I'm sure I looked just like them. It was the loneliest trip I ever took.

# Chapter 2
# LEARNING THE BASICS

Our quiet busload entered St. Louis very early in the morning. We were held there for several hours, most of us trying to catch some sleep. It came in short snatches on the bus, but by now it came more easily. Most of us were slumped down in those government chairs that defy comfortable sitting, so sleeping was a real test of our abilities to catch a few "Z's" somewhere, anywhere.

We again boarded several buses. This time, our group had grown considerably since I left Nashville. We had another 4-hour drive ahead of us, which nobody was looking forward to. This must have been our first test of sleep deprivation. Something told me I'd better get used to it.

Just before noon, we rolled into Ft. Leonard Wood, Missouri. We all dismounted amid groans, cracking bones, and sleepy eyes; hustled along by a Sergeant E-5 that obviously had command of every dirty word plus some in the English language. We lined up in our first half-assed formation, had our names read, to be sure that all were present, and headed into a building for orientation and our first lecture.

We were told we were now members of the U.S. Army, private E-1's and the lowest form of scum on the face of the earth. To prove it, we had our hair cut down to our little pointy-heads. Feeling quite naked in our burr cuts, we were ushered into our barracks, then spent the rest of our day turning in our civilian clothes and getting into our new duds: olive drab green pants, shirts, caps, t-shirts, underwear, socks, blanket and web gear. They started taking our identities immediately, getting us thinking as one unit, taking away our thoughts of individuality. It was "we" not "I" now.

Our platoon was formed and I noticed we had a real cultural mix. White, black, brown, and yellow skin every type of personality and all kinds of physical specimens. One kid in particular should have been eliminated from ever getting this far. He was a real lanky guy with big ears, buckteeth, no physical strength and the worst case of acne I'd ever seen. He had trouble keeping up with the group just carrying our duffels back to the barracks. Some recruiter probably signed him up to keep his quota up instead of turning him down like he should have. This kid should never have gotten off the bus. He was trying, but I knew the first day he wouldn't make it through basic.

We also got the good news that the first week of our training was considered "zero week" which meant it didn't count towards our 8 weeks of training! Zero Week? Nobody told us about Zero Week. Everyone was pissed about the fact this first week didn't count. Well, welcome to the U.S. Army, pal. You just got your first screwing, hope you liked it cause it most definitely won't be your last.

Zero week began as a series of lectures and training on the Army judicial system, insignias of rank, protocol, how to shine our boots, make our bunks and prepare for inspection. New friends were made and guys with natural leadership became our barrack leaders.

One evening the kid with the bad skin attempted to shave and cut every pimple on his face open, causing quite a frantic stir in the barracks. It looked like he had been hit full in the face with a blast of buckshot! We put him in this bunk with some wet towels around his face and waited for someone with authority to help us out. He was gone the next day.

Our drill instructor was a black man, about 6' 4", lean as a gazelle and had eyes that could bore through you like brown lasers. He'd stand above us during formation in front of our barracks and look down on us like someone was holding a small turd under his nose. He let us know in no uncertain terms that we did things his way or our shit would be weak forever. And we listened. He had a fierce look about him that no one wanted to see on an individual basis. So we watched, listened, and learned.

We did physical training, or PT, several times a day, rain or shine. We learned to march, throw grenades, and take care of our barracks. We did the horizontal ladder before every meal. Most of us pulled the dreaded kitchen police (or "KP"), where cleaning the grease pit was the ultimate shit job.

Our kitchen had an automatic potato peeler. It was about the size of a medium wastebasket with a very rough interior. What the KP puke would do is put the taters inside, turn it on and in about 10 minutes the interior would have scoured the peels right off. Me and a couple of the guys forgot about them one day in mid goof-off and by the time that we remembered to stop the machine, the potatoes were size of golf balls. One order of new potatoes coming up!

We were doing a lot of bayonet training, starting with the pugil sticks. They looked like giant cue tips. We donned football helmets and beat the shit out of one another with them. We were supposed to be using the bayonet moves we were taught, but the fights usually became free-for-alls, with guys swinging the sticks like Louisville Sluggers instead of a simulated rifle. It was still fun to do, and it helped us release all the built up aggression.

About three weeks into our cycle, we were issued our M-14's. It was an exciting day; we all hefted them, pulled back the bolt, dry-fired the trigger, and felt all macho just holding it in our hands. That afternoon was spent learning how to disassemble it, oil it and care for it. We were told that all formations held from now on with the rifles could have snap inspections and God help us if we were caught with a dirty weapon. If it happened you could consider the grease pit your home. We all took this bit of info to heart and cared for our 14's like we'd care for a kid sister at a sailor's reunion.

We were also getting a taste of Army life that civilians never experienced. We got our first taste of C-Rations while in the field one day. Most of the guys thought they were pretty bad, but I thought they could easily replace our mess hall food. O.K., so they had a lot of congealed fat in the meat entree, the cheese was like plastic and the crackers were stale. Considering they were canned in the 50's, it could have been worse.

Each meal consisted of a meat entree such as beef and potatoes, ham and beans or chicken and noodles. There was also a B1, B2 or B3 unit, which designated whether you got candy, cookies or cake with the meal. A foil pack with coffee, creamer, sugar, salt, pepper, spoon, can opener (called a P-38, one of the wonders of the world), and four cigarettes. Sometime you got fruit, cocktail pears, or peaches too. All in all not bad.

Army ponchos were given to everyone and we found out just how they worked in the heat and humidity of the Midwest summer. Having them on for more than 20-30 minutes in the rain kept you dry on the outside, but the moisture put off by your body coated the inside with moisture until you became just as wet from condensation as rainfall. This was before the days of Gore-Tex. Some of us would have preferred to just get wet instead putting on that stifling poncho.

We were also issued bayonets for our rifles and started spending an inordinate amount of time (I thought) on the bayonet course. We were stabbing, slashing, and butt-stroking our way into becoming killers. We still hadn't been on the range, and it worried me that we spent so much time with the bayonet. Didn't they shoot people in Vietnam? Was hand-to-hand combat more prevalent than we were told? If it was, they better teach us a few more moves than they had in our hand-to-hand combat course.

Charlie Palek

Finally, the day came to zero our rifles at the 25-yard range. Since I had zeroed my own rifle scope's at home, the concept was easy for me and I had my rifle zeroed in very little time. I was hitting a tight three round group in about 9 shots. Qualifying was going to be easy!

We ran our first PT test (physical training) consisting of five events — 100 points each. The mile run, low crawl course, grenade throw, horizontal ladder, and pushups. A score of 475 on the second scored PT test got me a weekend pass back home. I was in good shape when I enlisted so the PT test was easy to do.

The weeks ground on. We were hearing stories about Vietnam from the vets and instructors we were training with. Some of the stories were positive, some weren't. The instructors were encouraged to tell us positive experiences in Vietnam and keep the helicopter crashes, friendly fire incidents, booby traps, and other "fun" things quiet.

So we trained, learned, and did what we could to keep up a macho front.

The day finally came to qualify with our M-14's. Everybody was fired up and ready to go. O.K., we were a little nervous, but I was confident I'd do fine. We were trucked out to the range, organized into groups, and the firing commenced. We were firing at pop-up targets from 25-100 yards away. When you made a hit, the target dropped. We had a few more bullets to fire than targets to shoot, so you could fire at one target twice a few times if necessary. You became a "marksman" with a minimum number of targets hit, a "sharpshooter" for a medium score, and an "expert" for a perfect or near perfect score.

When my time came, I organized my magazines in the hole, and got ready to fire. I knew I was in trouble when I started missing the medium and long range shots. I found myself unable to hit the broadside of a barn! I was choking and couldn't correct my poor shooting! I tried settling down but the targets kept popping up, having no regard for my predicament. I realized halfway through the test that I wasn't even going to qualify for marksman, which meant I was going to have to come back and try to re-qualify again. I was humiliated and so pissed off at myself I could have volunteered for a pop-up target myself. There were guys in my company who had never fired a rifle in their life who had fired "sharpshooter," which made my situation even worse. Only one guy in our whole company fired "expert," but that was little consolation to me. I was just flat assed depressed! A fine infantryman I was going to make if I couldn't hit a target on the range. What would happen when the shit started flying in a real firefight?

Back at the barracks the guys tried to console me, explaining that I'd get another try and not to worry. I'd do it next time. It was great they were backing me up, but it provided little comfort. I still felt like shit.

A couple of days later, I went back to the range with the four other guys in our company who didn't qualify to try again. Our drill instructor watched us load up into the jeep and gave us a look of pure death — the kind of sub-human look that told us we'd better qualify this time or not come back to his company.

I did qualify, but only as a "marksman." I felt relieved, but still disappointed at my performance. I knew I could do better, I just had to learn how to control my nervousness and chill out.

So we continued to train in the muggy Missouri Ozarks in July. The Army continued its little games with us. On the hottest, driest days, they'd transport us back and forth from our training areas in 2 ½ ton trucks with the canvas cover over the bed, allowing very little air to circulate around in the back. What was allowed to circulate was dust — clouds of it swirling around our heads, gritting up our eyes and noses and making it miserable. We knew they did this on purpose.

We went to the live fire obstacle course one cold, wet day and spent the whole afternoon crawling through the mud under barbed wire entanglements and other obstacles. We had been given a class before on how to crawl and keep your weapon from getting too muddy, but by the end of the day, everybody's M-14 was pretty useless, barrels plugged with mud, sights clogged up, triggers packed with wet earth. We were all wet, dirty, and totally exhausted. So what shows up to take us back to the barracks? Open deuce and a half's. No canvas cover over the bed to break the cold wind. We rode back, freezing our asses off and sure the Army was doing it to us again.

Once we were back, cleaning our rifles was the first priority. Leaving them in their present condition was a guarantee that by the next morning they would be worthless pieces of rusting metal, sure to bring down the wrath of our Drill Instructor. Getting the mud off with rags and toothbrushes proved to be a waste of time. Then somebody got the bright idea of disassembling his rifle and taking it into the shower with him, washing off the mud, drying off each part, oiling it well and putting it back together. It was a brilliant idea, even though we were dog-tired. We all had clean and well-oiled rifles the next morning, much to the surprise of our D.I. We were becoming soldiers and probably didn't even realize it, but making sure our weapons were clean before we went to sleep was what a good soldier was all about.

I was still mulling over my failure at the range. I saw this little slice of life as a great disappointment, the kind of saddle burr that would rub me raw until I punched my last ticket. This left me with the same gut twisting feeling that I had experienced in the third grade.

Our teacher put a paper sock up on the black board that was to be used as a reward program for our math class. It was a big deal to me, because math was never my forté. We had six weeks to keep a hole from being punched in our sock. For every "E" we got in math, she'd punch a hole. Being the dimwit that I was at multiplying, I hunkered down and managed to get within one day of the deadline. But it happened, my worst nightmare. I got an "E" on a test the day before the end of the contest. Our teacher walked over to my sock and punched a hole into it with her paper punch. I never knew those punches could make so much noise. The click it made echoed in the room like a gunshot in a tunnel. She may as well have stuck an ice pick into my heart. This turned out to be one of those eternal life lessons that I never forgot. Murphy's Law, though I didn't know it at the time, was dancing on my head. "No matter how well you prepare, disappointment is always around the corner." I also learned something else.

We had a guy in our class whom I knew was a potential criminal from the first day I met him. He was a little stick of a guy that took a lot of shit from everybody and was the only guy in third grade who already knew all the dirty words and used them profusely in his conversations.

On the last day of the contest, his sock looked like somebody had stepped back with a double barrel shotgun and unloaded both barrels with number 10 shot into it. There was hardly enough paper for the thumbtack to hold up. It was nothing but holes. My lesson here — as bad as things are for you, there's always somebody out there worse off than you are. This lesson I would take to heart as I got older.

Graduation finally came and everybody was pumped about their next duty station. I was heading for Ft. Gordon, Georgia for Airborne Advanced Infantry Training. The other guys were heading for training in Army Intelligence, jungle school, artillery school, and all kinds of interesting stuff. But first — 2 weeks leave.

Those 2 weeks went by way too fast. I ate real food again, slept in past 5:30 am, and just vegged out for 14 days. I was looking forward to Advanced Infantry Training. The stories coming out of Vietnam in the fall of 1967 said we had a full-blown war going. Commanders were screaming for more U.S. troops, bays were being dredged for massive supply ships coming in, airfields were being built at an unprecedented rate, and the Hawks and Doves were drawing their battle lines. Things were definitely getting interesting.

Ft. Gordon, Georgia: Heat, humidity, and sandy red soil that got into everything. A whole new group of trainees were all heading for Airborne school and glory. We ran everywhere, singing Airborne songs to our footstep cadence and doing more pushups and sit-ups than I could count. I was put into a mortar platoon because they said I had math aptitude! Math aptitude! They must have got their wires crossed big time cause I didn't have any math aptitude. I wanted to be in the infantry — not humping a mortar tube around.

Nevertheless, I found myself learning the finer points of firing the 81-mm mortar. Declination angles, powder bags, adjusting fire. Every day was spent working in classes and in the field on firing our mortars. We humped the field and marched carrying the tube and baseplate, trying to keep up with the infantry, learning to set up the tube quickly during an ambush. I carried the baseplate on one of our training marches and I decided that mortars were not my game. It was heavy, awkward and the whole idea of carrying an 81mm mortar with a rifle platoon on a squad ambush patrol seemed ludicrous to me. What were we going to do, throw the baseplate at them? The mortar was a medium range weapon, not useful in an ambush that could have the enemy yards away instead of miles. Another exercise in futility as far as I was concerned.

We had an E-5 on the training staff who was a real little prick. He was a control freak who got off having authority over us peons. We were in formation one day when he said something particularly stupid, and I snickered a little too loudly. He singled me out, stuck his face in mine, and let me have it. His last words became prophetic, "I won't forget you, Palek." I didn't take them too seriously at the time, but that snicker was eventually going to cost me.

We started learning about Viet Cong booby traps, weapons, and tactics. Most of our instructors were Vietnam vets and we listened intently when they talked. Their experiences left us wondering what the war held for us. A couple had seen action in the II and III Corp areas, which are the central zones in the country where several "slug-it-out" battles had taken place. The instructors were quick to point out that the V.C. were tough, dedicated fighters and we should not take for granted the fact that they were generally out-gunned and under-equipped. They had a hundred ways to tear you a new asshole and if you wanted to come home in an airplane seat instead of a body bag, you'd better listen up.

We learned about trip wires, pressure release devices, toe poppers and other neat little tricks they used to take off a foot or your whole head. They also used all manners of natural materials, punji stakes smeared with shit, cans filled with nails and explosives, or bamboo whips implanted with spikes. We could only imagine what kind of damage these nasty little devices could cause. I guess you had to be there. The whole idea was more to injure than kill. If you cause enough bloody stumps and morale will suffer. Wound enough men, and the unit will be slowed down calling in medivacs and replacements. Sometimes a lot of well-placed short jabs will do more damage than that one roundhouse right to the head. That's what this war was turning into, a long bout where both fighters were trying to wear the other down.

## MURPHY'S LAW OF COMBAT
### #29
*"Remember, your weapon was made by the lowest bidder."*

We were also hearing rumors about the good ol' M-16 rifle, the mainstay weapon of our Vietnam troops. Jamming problems were the big complaint but causes we never heard about. We figured careless troopers not caring for their weapons caused the problems. Surely our military wouldn't send us out to fight a war with a substandard rifle!

The day finally came when we were issued our M-16's and started learning how to maintain them. I was impressed with them; they looked mean and efficient. Rushing out a 5.56 mm round at 1,000 meters per second provided a hard-hitting weapon that was light and used smaller ammo than the 7.62 mm M-14 so a trooper could carry more ammo. It fit you hands and shoulder exceptionally well, blending into part of your body with ease. Everything was within easy reach, even for my stubby fingers: clip release, fire control switch, charging handle- all well placed.

It broke down easy and was very simple to maintain, I thought. Little would I know what was to come down the pike a year later about this so-called "infantry" weapon. Tests had been done on this weapon in the mid sixties and as it turned out, the weapon failed miserably as an infantry weapon. However, the tests were rigged and the M-16 was sent over to Vietnam anyway. Our Pentagon was watering its garden with the blood of their children! It wouldn't be the only bloodletting to come out of this war.

We had our second PT test midway through our cycle and I passed all the events easily except the pull-ups. My dickweed E-5 changed the line he was proctoring when I came up to the bar, and flunked me, even though I gave him 10 good ones. The guys in my platoon were beginning to see what was happening, but nobody spoke up less they lose their status and not pass the test.

I finally realized that this asshole was going to flunk me no matter how many pull-ups I did. He was going to keep me from going to Airborne school and there was little I could do about it. I considered going to the Commanding Officer, but I doubted my complaint would bring any change. I could try talking to the asshole, but being in the position he was, I was sure he'd never take my plea to heart. He enjoyed having me over a barrel and short of bribery that's the way it was. I had one more chance to pass the test and I was going to try to keep him from checking my line at the bar, somehow. It looked hopeless.

The day for qualifying with the M-16 finally came. We had previously zeroed our rifles and I was determined to do better on this range than I did with the M-14. We hopped into our truck convoy and were transported to the 100-yard range. Once we arrived, we were herded into firing lines and given our ammo. The drill instructors started pushing us through the firing line way too fast. They walked up and down the line screaming at us to keep the firing up and not spend so much time aiming. They acted like they had very little time for us to qualify and were pushing us through too fast. I finally got into the pit and fired my clip at the target, hardly having the time to settle down and aim before the drill instructor was screaming at me to Fire! Fire! Fire!

Our company finished up in the late afternoon and we were told before we trucked out what we had scored. I was curtly informed that I had shot expert. I wasn't even sure I had hit the target. Most of the guys on the truck were unsure what was going on, but we felt like a shake n' bake outfit. It was obvious that they had a schedule and were behind when we entered the line. Maybe they had a sporting event to go to or something. Anyway we looked at it; we felt we had been slighted. We had just been pushed through the qualification of the infantry's primary weapon. It was a sad state of affairs, but it wouldn't be the last time we took a screwing. We plugged along, doing our training and getting leaner by the day.

Our company went on bivouac against one of the other companies in our battalion. We set up about 200 yards from our enemy and took classes on living and surviving in the great outdoors.

The evening of our first night out, our C.O. decided to send someone out to assassinate the C.O. of the other company. For some reason, I was chosen to do the job. My orders were to sneak into the lines, find my target, and eliminate him. If I got back without being captured, my mission would be claimed a success.

So we got a challenge ahead. I figured I could do this, if the other guys confirm that their C.O. was killed by me. I was going to have to get in close so there would be no doubt.

Right after sundown, while there was still ambient light illuminating the skyline, I set out with my M-14 and one clip of blank ammo. I crawled and snaked my way across no man's land until I reached the enemy lines. I lay in the shadow of some bushes watching the troopers setting up for the night. The sentries were not out yet, so I thought I'd better make my move right away.

## MURPHY'S LAW OF COMBAT
### #5
"If the enemy is within range, then so are you."

I put my face in the dirt and started for the headquarters in the middle of their camp. I had numerous holes to crawl in and around and I actually got into a foxhole right in the center of their rear area. I think I succeeded this far because the enemy troopers were incredibly lax in their security. I settled into my hole, trying to look busy and blend in, hoping the C.O. would come by before I was discovered.

Sure enough, about ten minutes later, the C.O. walked by and stopped to talk to a couple of the platoon leaders. They were 20 yards from my hole, an easy shot. But getting back out could be a problem. I'd have to take out my targets and rely on surprise and lack of readiness on their part.

*Tattletale*

In other words, "run like a ferret after a couple cups of espresso!" I weighed my options, decided to complete the mission and take my chances getting back.

I zeroed in on the targets, popped off five shots and took off like I was on fire. The shots broke the silence of the evening like a bomb, getting everybody's attention and definitely giving my position away. I ran about 30 yards when I made the mistake of trying to leap over a large hole instead of going around it. I hit the rim of the hole, fell in and by the time I was back out, I was staring at the business end of 5 M-14's.

Captured! It was a half-assed plan at best. What was I expecting, to actually get away? A trooper took my weapon and hauled my ass over to the three men I had shot. They apparently didn't realize yet that my 7.62 bullets had expertly drilled them, as they were still upright. They started asking me questions and I refused to say anything. After a couple of minutes they tired of that method of questioning. One of the officers wondered how I'd hold up under torture.

That got my attention immediately! U.S. troops don't torture people, what was he talking about? I found out. I was thrown on my back and my head tipped over the edge of a foxhole. When I again failed to answer the question, they started pouring water into my nose. Now if you've never had this done before, it's kinda like the first stages of drowning. In my position, the head cavities fill up and the water eventually starts filling your throat. That's when the gagging starts.

They poured, I'd gag and spit up, they'd question, I'd refuse to answer, they poured…this ritual went on for 10 minutes when they decided I wasn't going to squeal. They hoisted me back up and decided to send me back to my company.

My company C.O. was obviously disgusted that I had been captured. Trading me for a couple cases of beer was brought up but disregarded, as alcohol was forbidden on a field exercise. The big discussion was whether or not I had killed the three officers who I had shot at. They contended my shots were too fast and thus scattered. I contended they were doing well walking about, considering I had killed them. Our chosen leader finally decided that they had all been wounded and I was shot dead trying to escape!

Another mission accomplished! I hoped my first infantry unit in Vietnam didn't have these guys for officers. Candy-assed egomaniacs! My C.O. gave me a dirty look before dismissing me. Not even a hint of recognition for a job sorta well done. I started thinking that maybe real combat wouldn't be so bad. I was getting the impression that an E-1 was as important as a pimple on a flea in this outfit.

We spent the next few days firing a variety of weapons. The M-72 LAWS rocket (Light Anti-Tank Weapon) was a portable rocket launcher originally conceived to take out light armored vehicles, but was also being used as bunker busters and as an anti-sniper weapon. Everybody in our platoon got to fire one at an old beat up armored personnel carrier (APC) on the range. The weapon had to be unfolded so the protective caps and sights would pop off and up. It was a one-shot-wonder, disposable, and due to its clumsy sights, hard to use effectively unless the operator had fired several of them and had the experience in its use. One in twenty shots hit the APC, and we all wondered why we couldn't hit the target any more effectively.

We were told before that most of the men firing the LAW for the first time usually punched the trigger in anticipation of the noise that's coming. After all, when the tube was on your shoulder in firing position, the rocket shot through the tube just a couple of inches from your head. The heat from the rocket propellant heated up the tube and sent a warm, fuzzy kiss right into your earlobe that was quite erotic.

Anyway, because of the anticipation, punching the trigger too hard brought the front of the tube down; causing shots that fell way short of the target. Apparently this problem was common on the firing line, because our drill instructor threatened dire consequences to anyone who dropped their rocket short. The secret, like firing any other weapon, was a smooth trigger pull and a steady hand. Despite all the threats and instruction, the rusted out APC received very few new holes and we left the range shaking our heads.

The M-79 grenade launcher was, on the other hand, a very sexy weapon. The "Blooper" looked like a short, large bore shotgun that opened like a breechloader shotgun so a 40-mm explosive grenade could be inserted. This little hummer filled the gap between hand thrown grenades and the 60-mm mortars. Maximum range was about 400 meters with a kill area of five meters. Besides the high explosive grenades, the store also included buckshot, smoke, flares, CS or tear gas, and flechettes-45 small darts packed into one happy round.

Our company arrived at the M-79 range one morning and settled in for the typical lecture. Down range from the bleachers were about two dozen wooded silhouettes, about 70 yards out. Our instructor told us that after every man had fired his round, most of the targets would still be standing. We all looked around at each other and smiled. He obviously didn't know how good we were.

Several hours later, we walked away from the range shaking our heads again. A couple of the targets had fallen, but most still stood. I guess we weren't as good as we thought.

Our night navigation exercise rolled around and everybody was a little nervous about this. We were divided into teams of five, given a map of the area, a compass, and told we were to get from here to there in five hours. Between our jump-off point and our final objective were forests, a swamp and several instructors (number not known) who would be patrolling the area to try and capture us. We were to avoid the roads because they would be heavily patrolled. If we didn't make our objective in the allotted time, our ride back to the barracks would be gone and we'd be humping it back on foot. Incentive! Being captured also meant walking back to the barracks. Another incentive! Nobody wanted to walk miles back to the barracks after a night exercise.

## MURPHY'S LAW OF COMBAT
#50
"There is no such thing as the perfect plan."

Our team put down our map and planned a route. We figured we'd skirt the swamp to avoid the patrols. We thought the drill instructors wouldn't risk getting their feet wet just to find us, so we'd stay near the water before we broke free and made a mad dash for the high ground.

We shot our first azimuth and began our trek. About ½ hour later we were chest-deep in the swamp and wondering if "skirting the swamp" was such a bright idea. We hadn't seen any patrols though, so that part of our plan was sound.

We continued out of the swamp, shooting new azimuths and hoping we weren't hopelessly lost. When we finally hit the east/west road two miles from our objective, our spirits soared. The clear night and bright moon that had helped get us this far was lighting up the road like a boulevard in Vegas. We caught another group about ¼ mile down the road crossing en mass. They didn't have a problem so we scampered across the road one at a time like a mouse across a kitchen floor. No alarms were sounded so we knew we were O.K.

Four and a half hours later, our stalwart little group found our objective. We'd made it and we were definitely ready for a hot shower and a warm bunk. We felt good about what we had done, but I was still worried about our last physical test. I was still certain my favorite staffer was gunning for me.

Our last PT test came up and as I suspected, the instructor I had pissed off graded me. I gave him 8 good chin-ups, then 3 more for good measure, dropped to the ground and was told by him that the last four were not acceptable and I had flunked. I was pretty pissed by then so I ask him if he'd like to show me what 8 good chin-ups looked like. I was normally not a confrontational person, but this was too much. He looked at me and grinned, informing me that I'd better move my ass off the course to the next event or things would get ugly.

I had anticipated that I would be left with these options and, to me, I had three choices just then. I could take my case to my platoon sergeant, which I considered a lost cause. I wasn't getting any support from my barracks mates, so witnesses would be hard to find. I could get instant satisfaction and punch his lights out, but I knew I'd end up in the brig for that and that place was full of lost causes. I didn't need that.

Finally, I could take this whole episode as bad luck and let it go. After my first tour in Nam I could probably reapply to jump school. I'd hopefully have a couple stripes by then and if I kept my nose clean... so, I backed off. I drug my sorry ass to the next course and hoped that the sorry little prick that was keeping me from jump school would go to Nam and come face to nose with a V.C. bullet.

AIT ended with orders to Vietnam instead of jump school. I came home depressed, but my family got me out of my funk. Mom made all my favorite meals and Dad put on his Merchant Marine uniform, which, after over two decades, still fit him like a glove. We had our picture taken together, a retired warrior with stories to tell and a young one anxious to collect his own.

I felt I was in the best shape of my life. I was a 140 pound lean fighting machine. I was ready for anything and figured I could handle whatever the N.V.A. and Victor Charlie had to offer.

Two weeks leave blurred by, and it was off to Ft. Lewis, Washington for a couple days, then to Alaska to pick up more troops. Then on to

Hawaii, and finally to Tan Son Nhut Air Base, Republic of Vietnam. I have no memories of the long flight over, none at all.

## Chapter 3
## FNG's

Every soldier who ever flew to Vietnam has the memory of stepping off the plane onto the soil of Vietnam. My recollection was like stepping out of a meat freezer into the door of a blast furnace. The heat was breathtaking, the humidity positively suffocating. I remember thinking, "Jesus, how am I going to fight in heat like this?"

The waves of heat were shimmering down the runway, making the lines of fighters and choppers look dream-like. The noise of choppers, jets, old piston-driven fighters, vehicles, and people screaming orders was pure chaos. The smells punched you in the face like a roundhouse right. Jet fuel, oil, diesel exhaust, and the smell of the jungle all mixed into an assault of the nasal passages, one that would never go away. It would be burned into my brain as permanently as a hot iron brands a steer.

Since our flight had a mix of personnel from all services, there were reps from each that gathered us up into groups and headed us in the direction of the correct bus. God forbid that an Army guy gets sent to the Air Force!

All the Army personnel were formed up into a formation and marched to several O.D. buses with screens over the windows. We were wondering what the screens were for when our driver informed us it was to keep the V.C. from tossing a grenade into the bus. Welcome to the Nam!

We were bussed to the huge 90th Replacement Detachment in Long Binh, the place where you got your unit assignment. We arrived at this huge tent city where troops were going out, coming in, and, in some cases, in limbo. The drive through the city was an amazing trip. I never realized there could be so many different odors and fragrances coming out of one place, and they were all exotic and completely unfamiliar. It all fused into one smell that would be hard to shake. It was the same odor from one end of the country to the other — incense, cooking fish, human waste, fish sauce, general filth and diesel fumes. Bottle the smell and anyone unfamiliar with war and Vietnam in general would have a taste. They would know!

So here we were, in a new exotic land that was going to be our home for the next year. We all shuffled into a large tent with rows of benches and sat down for our first orientation lecture. We were told that the

Vietnamese had a large Buddhist population, with the Catholics running a close second. We were to observe their lifestyles and be respectful of their property, animals, possessions and particularly their young daughters. We were visitors here to help them push the Communists out of the country. We were told not to get confused and think of ourselves as conquerors. That wasn't why we were here. If we saw two young men walking hand in hand it did not mean they were homosexuals. It's the way they did things here. We all kind of snickered, wondering what kind of allies we had here — guys walking hand in hand?

We received some pamphlets and other information on how to conduct ourselves and were trooped out and assigned a tent until our unit came to get us. Our orders were issued, and I discovered I was heading for the 9th Division in the IV Corp area. Now I knew the 9th had a distinguished career fighting across Europe in WW II, but I didn't want to go to the 9th, I wanted to go to the 1st Air Cav. They had a reputation of being ass-kickers and heart breakers and that's the kind of outfit I wanted to be in. But the orders were issued and my unit designation was firmly established. Before I could begin cursing my luck, I was sent to the kitchen for 8 hours of KP. I got my ass chewed for not rinsing the soapsuds off the glasses well enough. I was hoping I'd be leaving soon. This certainly wasn't any fun!

We noticed there was a difference between us and the guys who had been in country awhile. Our faces were white as ceramic bedpans, but as we spent a few hours in the sun they became cherry red. Our jungle fatigues were a dark green, new, and still creased. I'm sure we looked pure and virginal to the old vets, fresh meat that was there to replace the happy souls going home, one way or the other.

The guys we saw on their way home were wearing the same fatigues we were, but theirs were bleached to an almost light green. Their boots had little polish on them, and many of them had the hard stares of men who had seen way too much death for their ages. Their faces were deeply tanned, cigarettes dangled from their lips like they had been smoking since age three. They walked slowly, like they lacked energy, their bodies broken in spirit and in great need to get the hell out of the country.

When they looked at us they either stared blankly or grinned ever so slightly in pity. It was scary and I didn't like it. My imagination started running on overtime. Am I going to look like that in a year? Hell's fire!

*Charlie Palek*

A couple of days at Long Binh found us on our way to Bearcat, the home of the 9th Division Jungle Training School. There were about twelve in our group, a real mix of characters. One of the guys told us his first sexual experience was with his sister. (Something I found shocking and something I really didn't need to know.) For a Midwestern boy from the middle of the Bible Belt, my education was beginning in the realm of worldly vices and the people who commit them. This was going to be a real learning experience, big time!

Bearcat was north of Saigon, another typical base camp of tents, permanent and semi-permanent buildings, an airstrip and bunkers guarding the perimeter- a standard issue Army compound. We checked into our musty smelling barracks, with its plywood floors, plywood walls and sweat-stained army cots, and unpacked our bags.

Our first day was all lectures and demonstrations by 9th Division cadre. One of the first things our instructor told us was to forget the bullshit we learned back in the States. We were in the real war now and those REMF assholes back in the World didn't know what was going on. The first thing I wanted to know was what a REMF was. It was explained to me by a guy sitting behind me that had been in country awhile that it stood for Rear Echelon Mother Fucker. No need to elaborate there. My second question was why didn't they just send us straight to Vietnam instead of going through the stateside training? I had little time to ponder that because we were going to get an earful today.

First, we were told that since we were fighting in a tropical environment, there were more than bullets and booby traps that could get us here. We were not, under any circumstances to drink water that hadn't been treated by U.S. forces. We could get deathly ill and have diarrhea for days drinking the untreated water, even the water the Vietnamese people were drinking. The Mekong River that was soon to be a major part of our lives was a sinewy, living sewer, a dumping point for all of the countries in Southeast Asia. It will eat the polish off your boots in a matter of days, stink up your body, and give you a couple dozen kinds of slimy diseases if you don't keep yourself clean.

One large, orange anti-malaria pill will be taken every Monday for the rest of your tour. The whole damn country was a breeding ground for mosquitoes, many species that hadn't been identified yet. We would be spending a lot of nights cuddled up with these little guys and malaria was one thing we did not want to catch.

There were several species of poisonous snakes, including cobras (Yow!) and a small, harmless looking guy called a krait, which had a fondness for crawling into warm, inviting little areas at night like sleeping bags, under air mattresses and next to your body. The cadre called them three steppers, because once you were bitten, that's as far as you got before the neurotoxic venom started turning your body into a non-functioning disaster.

We were to be very careful about mixing with the Vietnamese population. The Viet Cong had infiltrated every layer of society, from the top political posts to the kids selling soda. Food sold to us could be poisoned, cokes may have shards of glass in the bottle, and sweet little girls were throwing grenades into trucks filled with GIs.

The political situation is unstable and we don't know from one day to the next who our allies are. The N.V.A. are hiding in Cambodia but we can't go after them. No area is really secure, so watch your backs at all times. I thought, "Good God, is there any good news here? I'd settle for a happy thought about now."

After this verbal battering, we learned what kind of unit we were joining.

It was called the Mobile Riverine Force, an Army/Navy co-op that hadn't been tried since the Civil War. The whole contingent was TASK FORCE 117, made up of a mixed bag of Naval vessels including troopships, patrol boats, troop carriers, monitors, and a whole host of smaller support vessels.

The 9th Division's 2nd Brigade made up the Army contingent. The 3/47, 4/47, and 3/60 were the three battalions in the brigade and they rotated between working off the ships, pulling security in their base at Dong Tam, and a ready reaction force for rapid deployment wherever they were needed. This type of operation sounded a lot like what the Marines were expert at, so why weren't they down here? Oh, now I remember, they were busy getting pounded up in I Corp.

The Mekong Delta consisted of about 40,000 square kilometers of forests and swamps, but mostly rice paddies, where most of the country's rice was grown. With a population of between 7-8 million people, it was the most populated area in the country, and the most important. It was intersected from every mark on the compass by rivers and small waterways. Travel by water was preferred since there was only one major hard surface road in the Delta. Route 4 ran south from Saigon to Ca Mau.

Secondary roads were poor and hardly ever maintained. During the monsoon, the whole IV Corp area was essentially under water.

Sea tides also effected travel in all areas of the delta, especially along the coast. Naval navigators in all forms of vessels had to be very careful operating in the smaller rivers and waterways. A small river able to float small naval vessels during hightide could turn into a small ribbon of water with mud flats on each side, stranding the vessel on a bank of mud, until high tide returned. This uncomfortable position leaves the boat a sitting duck, not good in any book.

Our day of lectures ended with one last note, drug use. It was stated in no uncertain terms that drug use among the troops was illegal. I knew drugs were grown all over Southeast Asia, marijuana, heroin and opium were all here for the asking. The cadre knew that the "Demon Weed" or the harder stuff could easily take in all these young, immature soldiers, so they tried to get the message across. If you're lucky enough to get through your one-year tour intact, alive and all appendages functioning, don't take a drug habit home with you. If you do, you may wish you'd been sent home in a body bag.

We were also told the V.C. used drugs prolifically, especially prior to ground attacks. It gave them a feeling of being invincible. The story was going around about a V.C. soldier that had been stitched from throat to crotch with a long burst of M-60 fire. He continued to run another 50 yards before his brain realized his body was dead. One of the guys sitting next to me wondered out loud why they didn't put the stuff he was on in our C-rations! On that light note, our day was over and we all stumbled to the barracks trying to re-absorb all the information we had received that day. This Vietnam was going to be something else.

We had our chow and busted a few beers before turning in that night, wondering how in the hell anybody sleeps in this heat and humidity.

Morning came early, with the cadre stomping through the barracks bellowing at our group to rise up and pack, we were moving out! We looked at each other with red-rimmed eyes and faces hollow from little sleep, wondering where we were going. We still had four days of jungle school, didn't we?

We were hustled over to the chow hall, threw some food down our throats, and formed up outside, with our O.D. duffel bags, one each, at our side. One of the cadre walked up and down our formation calmly explaining that school was out, we were heading for Indian Country and the real shooting war. An element of the 3/47 had been hit hard and had taken a lot of casualties during a Riverine operation and they needed replacements.

The jaws on all our pink little faces probably dropped in unison. This kind of news, being FNG's and all, made our asses pucker so tight we thought we'd be constipated for life! We were all kind of hoping to be eased into our new unit, not thrown into the arena like so many hapless slaves. I got that coppery taste in my mouth and for the first time realized what real fear tasted like. All in all, I'd rather have a Hershey bar.

We were trucked from Bearcat to the river, then hopped aboard what looked like a real, honest to God "John Wayne and the Marines hitting the beach" type landing craft.

A couple hours later we disembarked onto a ship sitting in the middle of the river. It was called the *Benewah* and come to find out it was a barracks ship and would be our home for awhile.

We wrestled our duffels along the narrow corridors of the ship, down a level or two into a sleeping bay that contained dozens of bunks stacked to the ceiling with lockers, a huge shower area, and honest-to-goodness air conditioning! This may not be too bad after all, I thought to myself.

Since our weapons and gear had been drawn earlier, we were told to find a bunk that wasn't occupied and stow our gear. What was left of our new unit was already down in the sleeping area, cleaning their weapons and reorganizing. Their faces were tanned but drawn, the last couple of days combat etched on their faces, their eyes sad and tired. We came aboard pink-cheeked and virginal, newbies all wide-eyed and fearful, wondering what 2nd platoon, Bravo Co. 3/47 held in our future.

Our platoon sergeant, a nut-brown Hawaiian named Kalei, welcomed us rather gruffly to the 2nd platoon and we were told we would be assigned to a squad shortly and given a job. The unit had been ambushed while on the boats 2 days ago and they needed to place essential jobs on our shoulders immediately. He hoped we were quick learners.

The words had hardly left his mouth when one of the troopers walked up to one of our bigger newbies, slapped him on the shoulder and said he looked like the type of guy that could carry the "PIG" and lots of ammo, the "pig" being the M-60 machine gun. I thought, "All right! I'd like to carry one of those."

While I was fantasizing about putting down some heavy-duty cover fire to save my comrades, a tall, blond, Texan named Wiste sauntered up and introduced himself. He was the 2nd platoon RTO (Radio Telephone Operator), and he asked me if I knew the military phonetic alphabet. I assured him I did. He then stuck a piece of equipment in my face and asked me if I knew what it was. I told him it was a PRC-25 radio. He congratulated me and told me I was the 2nd platoon RTO-in-training.

Holy Shit. I didn't want to be a radio operator. I knew enough about the job to know they were considered prime targets by snipers. Wiste must have seen the disappointment in my face because he assured me I'd be a good RTO and since I was going to be with an officer in the field, we'd always be sleeping in the middle of our perimeter and probably under cover if there was any. But I was unconvinced. It didn't sound like much of a glory job to me. I didn't volunteer to come all the way to Vietnam to talk on the radio while the bullets were flying. But I had been tagged. They needed RTO's and I was it. Well KILO MIKE ALPHA! (Kiss my ass, phonetically speaking.)

I had just become our platoon's tattletale. Platoon RTO. I was going to be the one telling on our enemy. Where they were, what they were doing, how big they were, how bad they were beating us up. The bullies of my schoolyard would have been so proud.

Our bunkhouse was in the bowels of the ship, so they gave us a short tour of the ship so that we could find the essentials- mess hall, ship's store and barbershop. Smoking was not allowed on the ship unless the smoking lamp was lit. No live ammo or explosives were allowed below. There was a floating dock tied up alongside the ship where our ammo, grenades and other explosives were stored. It was also the only place where alcohol could be consumed.

Who'd have thought I'd be joining the Army and end up living on a Navy ship? Dad will be so proud. He was an old Merchant Marine veteran and he'd get a kick out of the fact that I was on the water.

The next couple of days were spent re-organizing, getting the lowdown on our new jobs and settling in. I was told the RTO's usually attended the meetings of the platoon leaders and squad leaders because they would be responsible for putting the layout grids on the maps, showing our intended movement, friendly areas, hostile area of operations, "arty" (artillery), and other support positions. We'd also be carrying an SOI, a book of "standard operating instructions." It held our radio frequencies, codes, and other highly classified information that could not fall into enemy hands. I wasn't thrilled about having that responsibility.

*Tattletale*

We also had to memorize the call signs of the units we'd be operating with. I was in the second platoon, so we were the white platoon. Our LT. was White 6, I was White 6 Oscar. Our 4 platoons were red, white and blue, green was our mortar platoon and they also carried the 60-mm recoilless rifle.

We all went down to the dock area to draw extra equipment. I wouldn't be carrying the radio yet, so I drew a rucksack frame with a pack attached, web belt for canteens and such, ammo pouches, and I pilfered a couple empty claymore bags on the way out. Ammo and grenades would be issued tomorrow morning before we loaded onto the ATC's (Armored Troop Carriers).

We were given a quick tour of the ATC's in which we'd be taken to our Area of Operation (AO). We also got a good look at the Monitors, the highly armed escort vessels traveling with us for protection. There were armed with everything from flame-throwers to 20-mm cannons. Just one of them could put out a shit storm of high explosive support fire. I was glad they were coming along.

That evening before our first sweep, I went with Wiste for the briefing. Our C.O. met with the platoon leaders and their RTO's.

We were to load up into ATC's at O dark hundred. Following a three-hour boat ride, we were to land, sweep around an area to secure an artillery support base, then dig in for its security. Wiste was given a plastic overlay and a topo map, which he laid over the correct grids so he had the AO set up on the map. We were also given information on frequencies and the call signs of our support: arty, gunships and dustoffs.

Wiste told me after the briefing that this mission was a cakewalk since they had been in a nasty fight a couple of days ago. The intention was to get the unit back into the field after a bad firefight as soon as possible, but hopefully with an easier mission.

Wakeup was going to be 03:30, so I crashed and got absolutely no sleep. This was going to be my first mission and my mind raced with mission details, anticipation, and the fear of fucking up.

Morning came fast. We chowed down in the Navy mess, had an exceptionally good breakfast, and then filed down the narrow passageways and through the hatches to the dock beside the ship. The night was stifling hot. Walking from air-conditioned comfort into the Delta night was miserable to the extreme.

We loaded up with ammo and grenades at the ammo conex. They gave me two claymores, a 200 round belt of M-60 ammo, 2 frags, 4 smoke grenades, and enough M-16 ammo to start my own insurrection.

We were also introduced to the sounds and smells that would cling to us for the rest of our lives. The low rumble of the ATC's and Monitor diesel engines resonated off of the side of the *Benewah* and surrounded us like an expensive stereo system. The smell of the diesel smoke mixed with the odor of gun oil, C-4, the river and the jungle produced a heady combo that was unforgettable. It clung to your clothes like a bad aftershave, and even when your clothes got wet, it remained like something alive.

We loaded up on the ATC, moving like zombies; our bodies stocked with 60 pounds of equipment and fire. We dropped into the ATC like we were half paralyzed, our packs throwing us off balance and our rifles banging against the guy next to us...the floor sloped to the rear, which didn't help the balance. The deck of the ATC sloped towards the back, with ribs of steel covering the deck all the way back to keep you from slipping on the cold steel. We sat down with our backs against the steel walls, some using their packs as a cushion; others found a place for their packs somewhere else. The FNG's noticed right away that sitting like we were with our legs stretched out in front of us, the slope of the floor kept your body from sitting straight. Your feet would drift towards the stern and unless your ass was able to pump itself level from one cheek to the other; you couldn't keep your body from rolling sternward. We were going to be floating around for several hours before we landed so I felt a need to get comfy.

I stuffed a flak jacket under my butt to level things out, then put my pack under my feet. It wasn't like my bed at home, but it would do. Equipment was clanging, men were cursing and a general chaos ensued while everybody settled in. Our platoon sergeant handed out 3 C-rat meals per man, picked at random when handed out. The bitching really started once everyone saw what they got to eat and a heated trading exchange ensued. Once that was over, everybody settled in, confident that the Navy would get us to our objective, safe and sound. Yeah, right!

Several hours later, a smoky magenta dawn greeted us when the ramp dropped and I started my first combat sweep. After the epileptic moves of preparing to disembark on a moving boat, we jumped ship, formed up into squads and moved out. We started out in a banana grove, laid out in rows with irrigation ditches between each row about 4 feet deep. We were moving across the grove, so we had to go down into the ditch and back up each row. Jumping from one to the other was only successful to the guys with long legs. I tried jumping from one to the other, trying to keep my feet dry, but Wiste, who I was following and observing, told me I might as well get them wet and learn to enjoy the discomfort, cause they weren't going to be dry till we got back to the ship.

So this was humping the boonies. That's exactly what we were doing, up and down, helping the man behind you up the next dike, the pack straps digging into your shoulder, boots clogged with mud, the steel pot weighing down on your head, testing the muscles in your neck. It was December, two months into the dry season and it was excruciatingly hot. Temps would vary from 90-115 degrees without any effort. The flak jackets we were told to wear weighed about 13 pounds until they sucked a couple canteens' worth of water out of your body, then they weighed more. The FNG's were told that flak jackets should be worn in the field, so we did. But we noticed few of the other guys were wearing them, except the short-timers, who had less than 90 days left. I decided that if we didn't have to wear the flak jacket, I was going to leave it on the boat — too heavy, too cumbersome, and too damned hot!

## MURPHY'S LAW OF COMBAT
### #49
### "Mines are equal opportunity weapons."

After about 40 minutes of humping the banana grove, we came to the edge of a rice paddy about 150 square meters. Since walking around the paddy on the dikes was not recommended since they were probably booby trapped, our point went straight out into the paddy to recon or act as bait.

Our forward observer for arty support was a 1st Looey and he radioed in the coordinates of the far side of the paddy, just in case. One angry shot from the tree line, and he'd call down a shit storm. I felt better about crossing but it sure seemed risky to me. Once we got into the middle of the paddy, there was nowhere to go for cover. There were no dikes to hide behind, just three feet of mud and water. Besides, I was dying from exhaustion right now, and could have cared less about hostile fire.

I thought I was in great shape when I got there, but crossing this paddy showed how woefully unprepared my body was for this kind of terrain.

The mud was over our knees with about 6 inches of water on the surface. The mud was sticky, like wet clay. You had to keep going or you'd sink deeper in the mud.

Walking through this was exhausting, and about halfway across I thought my heart would explode it was pounding so hard. I couldn't catch my breath. I couldn't stop. And the other side of the paddy looked miles away. The other guys didn't seem to be having as much trouble as I was, but I noticed the new guys were as bad off as I was. Wiste smiled when I got to the other side and told me I'd get conditioned walking in that stuff. With a pounding chest and blurry eyes, I told him I hoped to Christ that he was right. This was murder.

After rising to nearly living, we humped the rest of the day, sweeping an area around the fire support base, then settled in and dug a bunker for the night. It being the dry season did allow us to dig a couple feet into the rock hard ground. The rest of the bunker was built from banana trunks and sandbags that our re-supply chopper had brought in. We were shown how to lay our claymores out for overlapping cover, set trip flares and how to set up our M-60's for overlapping fire. I set up with Wiste in the HQ for our platoon, grabbed some chow and caught some sleep before my first radio watch.

## MURPHY'S LAW OF COMBAT
### #30
"If you can't remember, the claymore is pointed towards you."

Two a.m. rolled around and I took over guard duty. We had a full moon and night vision was very good, nice and clear. The moon lit up the landscape like a blue 50-watt bulb. I started to scan the banana grove to our front and started to see something odd. If I stared at it long enough, the moonlight shining off the banana leaves twisting in the breeze appeared like a blond gorilla sitting against a banana tree with a sombrero on. The more I stared, the more detailed the shape became. I also saw another blond gorilla later, standing against a tree. I was determined not to tell anybody about this — nobody wanted to hear an FNG telling tales about stuff like this. Thank God I didn't take a shot at them or blow a claymore.

The next morning, our Medic, Doc Hargrove, a Texan, claimed to me he saw a light colored gorilla in the grove last night. I freaked out. It was unbelievable to me we could see the same outrageous animal out there. We got a good laugh out of this, but kept it to ourselves. Our own little secret!

Four days before Christmas, 1967, and we were still pulling security at the Fire Support Base. We were part of a quick reaction force, sitting around in case somebody got in trouble. We sat around watching the Chinooks lift out the 105's and the crews, till about 3 p.m., then got the order to move out.

We spent a day back at the ship, then went out on another sweep, camped out by the river and built us a cozy little bunker for Christmas day. Santa showed up in a chopper in the afternoon on Christmas day, red suit and everything. I considered what a great target he made for a sniper, with the bright red suit, but what self-respecting V.C. sniper would shoot at Santa?

We continued sweeping through the same area and I had my first river crossing. Two of our best swimmers went across first, towing a rope. While one tied off the rope, the other provided security. Air mattresses were broken out and inflated to float our radios and rifles across on. One of the air mattresses tipped and several M-16's and M-79's fell off, but our Kit Carson Scouts dove for them and recovered them all. The canal was about 10-15 feet deep, so we used the rope to pull ourselves over with.

## MURPHY'S LAW OF COMBAT
### #27
### "Weather ain't neutral."

We were all soaked to the bone and cold that night. A cold front blew through and temps dropped in the 70's, which was damned frigid to us when 115 degrees was the norm. Supper was eaten cold out of the can, no fires allowed. Smoking was not permitted either unless you were under a poncho. Snipers knew that by aiming about 6" from the tip of a cigarette butt, a head shot was assured, and there were snipers out there. Wet, cold, and trying to keep warm inside an evil smelling poncho eating cold ham and beans. Well, I guess I asked for it, so I could hardly bitch about it.

The next morning we swept back across the same AO, crossed the same canal and set up on the edge of a large paddy. Wiste got a call that

## Charlie Palek

our battalion C.O. was in a chopper heading our way to talk to our company C.O. and the platoon leaders.

The wind was gusting badly when the H-34 bubble appeared and swooped down to land. We watched the pilot hover a few feet above the paddy, jinxing the stick back and forth so he could land as close to a paddy dike as possible. I wondered why he was working so hard to land near the dike, and my question was answered as he shut the engine down and our illustrious leader stepped out on the dike to keep his boots from getting muddy!

What kind of candy-ass was this? His fatigues were starched and creased sharp, his boots gleaming, but that little move with the chopper confirmed him in our eyes as anything but a combat soldier.

Our leaders conferred with Mr. Clean and we watched as the Colonel boarded the chopper and prepared to leave. The wind was still roaring away, and as the chopper's engine revved up, it started lifting off but only the left skid lifted. The right one was stuck in the paddy mud and wouldn't budge. Apparently the pilot didn't realize his dilemma and tried to recover, but the wind caught the underside of the bird and it tipped over.

The blades hit the mud and splintered, sending shards of composite and mud flying in all directions. It was a plain case of the fan hitting the shit. Our C.O. was standing close to the chopper when it attempted to lift off, and he was pinned under the wreckage on the outside as it tipped over. The rotor blades striking the ground caused the body of the chopper to flop around like a rock-struck sparrow, flailing the two passengers around in their seats. Since they were strapped in, they just got a hell of a ride and a dent in their pride. Our C.O. who was pinned under the chopper suffered a little indignity, but nothing serious. He was lucky. Some of his troopers pulled him out from under the bird and helped him up. His bell had been rung, that was all. The chopper was a total loss.

The company RTO called in a Huey to rescue the Battalion C.O. and the pilot. God forbid they had to spend a couple hours in the muck of the paddy. Our platoon was given the task of chopper security until it could be lifted out. We stripped it of everything valuable. Since screwdrivers and wrenches were in short supply, the radios were chopped out with a machete.

While all this was going on, our three other platoons with some Arvin Marines swept across the paddy into a tree line where 3 people were seen observing our activities. There was blue TU DIA signs everywhere, warning the locals of mines.

The Marines started hitting booby traps and mines the second they entered the woods. The American advisor with them was talking to our platoons, advising them of the booby-trapped areas. Red platoon saw three V.C. ahead of the Arvins, apparently setting booby traps as they moved in front of the Marines.

Later our guys were crossing a stream when one of the sampans they were using tipped and 2 radios, 2 M-16's, and 2 M-79's fell into the water, about $3,000 worth of gear. Red Six Oscar fell overboard and had to shuck the radio before it pulled him down. The water was moving too fast to dive for the stuff, so our C.O. called in an air strike on the area to destroy the equipment. All in all it was an expensive day for U.S. taxpayers.

Our little security force called in the Chinook to lift out the downed chopper. We only had a couple more hours of daylight left and we were getting a little antsy about getting out of there. We were in poor defensive positions and we kept seeing people in the tree line running from bush to tree, spying on us. We had high hope that some of these guys were not carrying a mortar.

About an hour before sunset, angels in the shape of Hueys got us out of there and took us back to the *Benewah*. Since we had been airlifted out, we beat the rest of the company coming back by ATC by several hours. We had all the hot water we needed in the showers and ate in a quiet mess hall. Getting back first had its advantages.

We found out later that night that the gunships that escorted our slicks worked over the tree line where we saw the spies. The gunship pilots reported seeing beaucoup V.C. down there and they looked like they were massing for an attack. The Charlie model gunships broke up their little plan and had them scattering like cockroaches in the light! I lay in my bunk with clean sheets and cooled air and thanked heaven for those gunship guys. I hoped they had good, cold beer waiting for them that night.

The next morning I woke up and discovered 28 mosquito bites on my arms and stomach, and I had used several heavy doses of repellent. They obviously love the stuff!

I wandered up to the PX, bought a tape recorder for Dad, a small color TV for Donna and Ann and had them shipped home.

Back at the bunkhouse, I found a pile of mail and dove right in, saving Roxy's letter for last.

One of the letters was from one of my favorite families, the Brune's. There was also one from one of my best friends, John Reinhardt, who told me he was going to the same school as Roxy. I felt good knowing he'd be there in case Roxy needed help.

I got a tape from the family with a drum duet pounded out by my brother while Dad played the squeezebox.

Mark Walker, one of our 60 gunners, showed me a picture of his wife, who was four months pregnant. He was a big brute from Jersey with the outrageous accent, a goofy laugh and an even goofier sense of humor. He was pissed about not being able to be home when the kid was born. I told him I needed him and his gun more than she did, and he gave me the finger! It's good to have friends.

I read a couple hot letters from Roxy, then went up on the galley deck and watched a movie. Any halfway good-looking women on the screen brought a raucous symphony of hoots, howls and whistles. Two hundred horny sailors and grunts enjoying the sight of a "round-eyed" woman was a sight quite rare to the combat troops. The Vietnamese women walked down the city streets like peacocks, heads up with dignity and grace. Frankly, I liked the way the American girls walked better — hips swinging and leg's flashing. Lots of attitude! We all missed that a lot.

Went back out the next day, occupied our old bunkers and continued security. A Chinook came in with 105 ammo during breakfast and blew out everybody's breakfast fire, and coated our croissants with dust. I learned today that mixing peanut butter with insect repellent creates a slow burning fire for simmering your dinner. The C-4 we were using to heat our food burned way too hot for slow cooking. The chef's in our squad didn't like a fire too hot when heating our 20 year old cuisine. Some of our C-rats had been packed during the Korean War, and we knew food of this type had to be handled carefully.

The Arty boys had a new round that was causing some excitement around the old campfire. It was called a beehive because it contained 7,000 tiny flechettes, or darts, in each round. It was made for repelling ground attacks. The word came down that these rounds were used to stave off a ground attack in III Corp and after it was all over, several V.C. were found pinned to the trees by the flechettes. And I thought Claymores were nasty! They were also equipping the gunships with those in their 2.75 in rockets, and we were due to get some for our green platoon's recoilless rifle.

Two of our squads were pulled off the bunker and ordered to sweep a tree line a couple klicks away after our noon tea.

About 2 hours into the sweep one of my Bearcat buds, Varvera, hit a toe popper on the side of the trail. When it blew, he fell into the side of the trail onto a nest of red ants. Even though the popper blew his boot completely off and shattered every bone in his foot, he was screaming at us to get the ants off his face and neck.

We did what we could for him while a dustoff was called in. In the meantime, an engineer with us went ahead to check for more booby traps and promptly stepped on another popper. It shattered the bones in his heel but never even broke the skin. We waited forty minutes before the dustoff arrived. By then both guys were in considerable pain and we were glad to get them out of there.

We were, not surprisingly, a little leery about these toe poppers. What they were was a .50 caliber shell with the bullet removed and a striker stick put into the shell with one end of the striker sticking above ground. All it took to set it off was to brush it with your foot. The striker set off the powder or explosive in the shell and "BOOM," you have a casualty. It wasn't intended to kill, just to maim — to slow us down and decrease morale. They certainly were doing the job. It was almost impossible to see every stick above ground as a potential striker, and that just gave us another thing to worry about.

After we regrouped, we moved on into a banana grove next to a villa. The grounds were beautifully maintained. The architecture of the main building was heavy in French influence and also in great shape. We wondered whose side they were on. We swept through the grounds and obviously interrupted the lady of the house. She stepped outside the door and watched us go by, looking at us like we were vermin in her kitchen. She held her head high, obviously mistrustful. The words "rich bitch" filtered past my ears from someone up front. It was obvious the V.C. weren't bothering her and the villa. It was in too good of shape for the middle of the war. Still, she was a handsome woman and comments about her flew fast and furious as we walked by. Boys will be boys!

I had started carrying the radio, starting out as the RTO of our platoon leader Lt. Croll. He was a fun-loving guy, always ready to laugh but took his leadership responsibilities very seriously. He was drafted and went to

Officer Training School at Ft. Benning. The guys were called "Shake and Bakes" or "90 Day Wonders" because of the 3 months it took to train them to be leaders and gentlemen. He called me Charles, and we became quite close, as officers and their RTO's often do.

I was getting to know a lot of the guys in our platoon, and we had a real mix of characters. Walker, our M-60 gunner, reminded me of Bill Cosby. He had a ton of stories he told about growing up in Jersey, and he kept us smiling. We had a Needham, a Delgado, a Takahata, a Miller, a Kostecki, a Devard, a Davis, and a Tangel.

Rick Davis was a fellow Illinois resident, from just north of my hometown. He was a platoon RTO and I asked his advice a lot. He was married to a beautiful young woman that was way too cute for him. He claimed his sexual prowess kept her endeared to him. Kostecki was a Pollock from the Windy City. He was our best point man, and he'd rather walk point than anything else. Claimed it made him nervous to be with the main body. Takahata was a bandy-legged little Japanese American and one of our best soldiers. He had a real field sense and I felt better when he was out ahead of us, keeping things in line. Tangel was a short, serious guy that had a lot of knowledge about booby traps and how the V.C. worked. He was always calm, even during a firefight, and didn't seem to have any fear.

These guys had been in the field considerably longer than I had, so I listened to what they had to say and took it to heart. Cocky FNG's who thought they knew it all didn't last long around here.

Our company had 3 Choi Hois, or Kit Carson scouts. These guys used to be N.V.A. or V.C., but for one reason or another, defected and were fighting with us. Our platoon was graced with "Ba," an absolutely fearless Vietnamese. He had been a V.C. Lieutenant until the Commies stopped paying him what they promised. He got fed up, surrendered with his AK-47, which he got an extra $30 for, and became an undercover agent. He dressed as a civilian, got close to the V.C. tax collectors and terrorists, then popped them with his .45. Any money they had on them he took and sent to his wife. After he had done this type of work for several months, he became known to the V.C. and his cover was blown. He joined the 9th Division as a scout and never looked back.

He was a wealth of information. He seemed to know everyone and everything that was going on in the Delta. He'd walk down the middle of the street in any village, waving and greeting his subjects like a King. He was certainly a comfort to have around and everyone trusted him absolutely.

Another one of the Scouts named "Bai" was older and had actually fought the French before us. He defected from the N.V.A. because the North Vietnamese government promised to care for his family while he was away fighting the new American invaders. After a couple years fighting in the South, he made it back home and found his family starving, forgotten by his government. He set his family up with relatives so they could at least survive, came all the way back down the Ho Chi Minh trail and surrendered to the South Vietnamese government, and was eventually passed on to the American 9th Division. I was showering on the *Benewah* one day when "Bai" stepped into the shower also. His skinny naked body had more wounds and scars than I had ever seen on one person. We stood there discussing his gunshot wounds, shrapnel and even bayonet scars. The fact that we were nude looking over his bod didn't even occur as strange to me; I was so fascinated by his stories. He was a supremely tough little guy and I hoped that there weren't too many more out there like him on the other side.

I had purchased a Kodak Instamatic camera to carry into the field to photograph my tour. I had tried a number of things to carry the camera and try to keep it dry. Our numerous water crossings during sweeps convinced me that the camera had to be kept somewhere above the chest. So I taped an ammo pouch on the straps of my left shoulder and put the camera in it, inside a resealable plastic bag. It worked perfectly, even when crossing a stream over my shoulder.

I had also been issued a special radio backpack that was made specifically to carry the PRC-25 radio. I felt the pack was good for static, perimeter duty, but not for humping the paddies. So I traded it in for an external backpack frame, mounted the radio on that, and still had lots of room for carrying C-rats, personal gear and I could hang a shit-load of smoke grenades on it also. Since RTO's were not required to carry M-60 ammo or claymores, I loaded up with M-16 ammo, usually about 15 magazines plus a bandoleer of zip-clip ammo and all the smoke grenades I could carry. I usually ended up giving my ammo away in a firefight anyway since I was on the radio most of the time.

After about a month in the field, us FNG's started to figure out what we needed in the field to make life a little more tolerable. I sent home for a good field knife. I had Dad buy me one and he gave it to my Uncle Rich to sharpen. I always kept a brick of C-4 in my pack for heating up the C-rats, as well as a few other necessities: a small flashlight with extra batteries, a couple of extra cartridges of film, a bottle of A-1, a toothbrush and paste, a couple of good pens, some insect repellent, a poncho (nobody wore them in the rain since we were usually wet anyway but it made a good ground cover) and a cigarette lighter (for lighting the C-4 since I didn't smoke). Poncho liners were one of the wonders of the world, but they were in short supply to the field grunts. They were excellent in keeping you warm. You could be completely wet at night, wrap yourself up in one and in a 3-4 hour period you'd be completely dry.

I visited Can Tho one day and noticed that inside an REMF barracks every bunk had a poncho liner on it, some had two. Before I left that day, I had stolen a couple of them from the barracks and took them back with me. I kept one and gave the other to one of the guys for a couple of cookies and a kiss. It pissed me off that the grunts couldn't get them because the REMF's were intercepting the supplies.

Everybody kept a bottle of rifle lubricant, called LSA, on his person. The M-16 was proving to be a real headache to keep clean in the field and during a firefight. The problem was that the ammo was excessively dirty and fouled the chamber after several magazines had been fired. Squirting LSA onto and into the bolt and chamber kept it firing, but only for awhile. Once the powder residue built up, the bolt would lock up so tight it may as well been welded shut.

The buffer spring in the stock that slammed the bolt back into the chamber proved to be weak and also caused jamming. We started seeing new buffers and chrome bolts in mid-1968, but the improvements came slowly.

The one unforgivable screw-up in this sordid little affair was the cleaning kits. They were hard to come by and to replace. They had a chamber cleaning brush in it that was shaped particularly for the M-16 chamber. Without it, the chamber was hard to clean especially when it was really dirty. Cleaning solvent was also hard to come by. This scandalous situation was unprecedented. Sending troops to fight in horrible terrain with a sub-standard rifle and no cleaning equipment made me wonder what those assholes in Washington were doing. They obviously weren't thinking about us. I fantasized about getting about a half dozen of our congressmen out in the mud and see how they like trying to break up an ambush with a piece of shit rifle. They wouldn't have lasted 2 days in the Delta.

There was a rule that troopers in the Delta shouldn't be in the field for more than three days at a time because of the skin diseases that could crop up. Since we were always wet and walking through the sewer of South East Asia, we were supposed to dry ourselves out after being in the field. We were to wear flip-flop sandals and shorts and spend as much time in the sun as possible. War being a bit unpredictable, we didn't always get to come back after three days, or get to bask in the sun as much as we liked, but it did happen once in awhile.

I also discovered the luxury of being a non-smoker. I usually put the four-pack cigarettes in my helmet band. After four or five days in the field, the smoker's were out of coffin nails and started looking at my helmet like an owl drills a mouse. The cigs became hot property — I could get anything I wanted for them — peaches or pears, snacks from home — guys would actually take an extra hour of radio watch for 4 cigarettes. I loved taking advantage of the desperate!

Our sweeps were taking us through the rice bowl of Asia. Rice production was so vast that they were actually exporting to other Asian countries, at least before the war. We got to observe these people at work, the common peasant farmer with their little plot of land, their water buffalo and their family living in a grass hooch. It had a dirt floor, small cooking area and mats on the ground for sleeping. They got up at dawn, worked all day, quit at dusk. Movement after dark was pretty much an open invitation to get shot, by either side. Since the V.C. owned the night, no self-respecting peasant family man would be out running around at night. The U.S. forces had night vision equipment mounted on sniper rifles, choppers running hunter/killer missions, jets taking infrared photos of likely infiltration routes, just dozens of ways to get yourself greased — a tiny spot on the paddy dike.

These poor folks were not politically connected in any way, but they were taking shit from both sides' 24 hours a day. The V.C. came in at night, took their food, recruited their sons and daughters and threatened them if they cooperated with the Americans.

During the day, we'd saunter through checking I.D.'s and rousting them from their homes, searching for weapons and explosives, tracking up the floor and giving them the impression we are conquerors. God forbid we find a rifle in the hooch.

Most of these folks only had one set of clothes, which were washed daily after work. They ate rice with *Nuoc mam* sauce, a delightfully aromatic concoction made by putting fish, including the guts and heads, into a vat with some homemade spices, a little vinegar, and letting it stew and brew in the sun for a couple months. What came out was a foul smelling sauce the Vietnamese poured on their rice. It permeated their bodies, and between the sauce and bathing in river water they had a very definite body odor.

The older folks would squat in the doorways of the hooch, chewing betel nut and spitting on the ground. Betel nut had a slight narcotic effect on the teeth and gums that usually had not been treated for daily dental hygiene. Their teeth were in bad shape and the nut eased the pain, no matter how horrible it looked. They had so very few possessions in their life; they considered the gift of a C-ration spoon a minor miracle. They were so grateful.

We would stop for chow around a cluster of huts once in awhile and once the C-rats came out, the kids came out of the walls it seemed like. 6 or 7 year olds would be carrying around the babies, and when you gave the kid something to eat they always fed the baby some first. The kids ate anything, too, except the chopped ham and eggs we got in our C's. I was one of the few guys who didn't mind eating C's. I had figured out that just about anything could be eaten with a dash of A-1 sauce that I lifted from the ship, except for the chopped eggs.

The contents of the eggs were kind of a gray/green color upon opening the can. I had never seen gray eggs before and I tried everything to make them palatable, but it was hopeless. Even the Viets wouldn't eat them. These are the same people that ate rotten fish sauce. Whoever packed this stuff should have been sent to Leavenworth! Somehow eating meat that had been packed in 1955 seemed reasonable, 13-year-old eggs — NO WAY!

Our platoons set up around a hooch one night and we shared our food with the family. Mamasan put some of our C's in a black pot with some cooked rice and stewed it up. She put a few fresh vegetables in it as well, and it was damned tasty.

Afterward, whatever we had left over from our C's we gave to them. The small packets of sugar and salt were highly prized. It was like we gave them a couple grams of gold. They also enjoyed the white, plastic spoons we got with the C's.

They were gracious hosts, considering we were Americans loaded down with weapons and ammo. They were Catholics, with pictures of Christ and Virgin Mary on the wall. A picture of a handsome young man in an Arvin uniform was also on the wall. He was their son, fighting further north. The family seemed comfortable around us and I enjoyed talking to them. Both mamasan and papasan were as thin as skeletons, their teeth stained by betel nut and their wrinkled skin the color of a walnut coffee table. They laughed easily and were fascinated by the pictures of our families, our gear- particularly our knives- and all the other shit GIs had a habit of carrying with them. I was reluctant to leave; it was the most pleasant evening I had spent since being here; a little taste of home. We left the next morning and gave everything we had left: fruit, gum, meat, cocoa, cookies, a real bounty for them. It was the least we could do for them since we had made their home ours, pretty much uninvited.

The first of January found us in the new base camp of the 9th Division, Dong Tam. This camp had literally sprung from the paddies. The sand foundation was dredged from the My Tho river and built up high enough to fend off the monsoon floods. On that foundation the camp was built with all the amenities — barracks, clubs, PX, motor pool, docking facilities for the boats that supported the ships, helo-pads, and a jail, with a perimeter around the whole facility.

When one of our three battalions was in Dong Tam, they were responsible for manning part of the perimeter and guarding the dredge. The dredge was a huge vacuum machine that sucked the sand from the bottom of the river and deposited it on the bank. In 1968 the dredge was working overtime to keep up with the expanding base. We'd put a squad on the dredge, one man at each corner, and a few up on the higher levels. This was 24-hour duty so we had to have a second shift for the other 12 hours. Sometimes, if we had the manpower, shifts were only 8 hours but it was still pretty boring duty. When I wasn't on duty, I read a lot of books. Daytime was spent trying to find a place out of the sun until your guard time came around. Nighttime was when HQ figured the V.C. would try to sink the thing by swimming underwater with a mine of some kind. We'd drop concussion grenades in the water at unscheduled intervals just to be sure.

We'd spend three or four days on this thing sometimes, and wish we were somewhere else. It was excruciatingly boring, but I guess it beat humping the boonies.

We also pulled Road Runner Duty, which consisted of riding APC's into the village outside Dong Tam to secure the road and secure the engineers sweeping for mines. We always rode on top of these machines, seeing how stories abounded about these steel boxes getting hit by B-40 rockets and burning the crews to crispy critters before they could get out. I had also heard of incidents where these things hit a mine and blew the driver completely out of his hatch, shearing his legs off on the way out. Our thinking was that we'd rather be on top and get blown off instead of burning up inside.

Our APC drivers had learned the Vietnamese rules of the road, rule numbers 1-10 being "there are no rules." The roads were made for the American hotrodder — Viet buses ran down the left of the road, bikes, moped traffic and people on foot ran down the right. We ran down the middle, going like a bat out of hell. We missed people and vehicles by inches, on a regular basis. It was scary shit.

The Vietnamese have a bad habit of overloading their vehicles, from motorcycles and scooters to their trucks. While pulling Road Runner one day, we came upon an accident in the road. A grossly over-loaded truck full of lumber had driven part of the way into a shell hole and had gotten stuck, in the process blocking the other lane of the narrow road. Muddy rice paddies were on each side, so we couldn't go around either.

Several officers ran out on the road to make a decision while we stayed in the truck where it was safe. The Viet truck driver was trying to get some help, so the officers hooked up the truck to one of our APC's and attempted to pull it out. The way the truck was sunk in the hole, it was obvious the load of lumber had to be taken off first because the load had shifted to the right side and threw the whole truck off balance. It didn't look like the truck could be pulled out wheels-up. The APC hooked up and tried pulling the truck out, but to no avail. It would not budge.

A couple of engineer's came by in one of the BFDT's (big fucking dump trucks). They figured they could hook up to the APC and then together they could pull the truck out. So they drove around the wreck, almost getting themselves stuck in the paddy, and hooked onto the APC. The Viet driver was hopping around like a bunny, jabbering to the American drivers, pointing and flapping his arms. He looked pissed.

The two American vehicles took the slack out of the chain and started pulling. The drivers gunned the motor and the Viet's truck started moving. Those guys saw they had some momentum going so they cranked it up. The stuck truck moved, inch by tortuous inch, until it had been pulled out of the hole onto the roadside. Unfortunately, the rear axle still remained in the hole. The engineers had pulled the truck right off the dualies. The Viet driver was stroking out right in the middle of the road.

The engineers pulled the truck into the paddy, off the road. The lumber had shifted more, breaking the right bed rack and spilling the lumber into the paddy. The Army drivers' unhooked their vehicles and headed down the road, leaving the Viet driver standing in the road, helpless. We were all watching this little drama, marveling at the Army guys' arrogance. Our C.O. called Dong Tam and told them what happened, but I don't think anybody helped the poor guy.

We came back to the same spot on the road the next morning, and the axle, the truck, and all the lumber was gone! Somehow ol' Papasan got his truck back up on the axle in less than a day and drove off. Pretty good trick. The U.S. Army could never have done that in such a short a time.

The V.C. had a hot little trick they used during convoy ambushes. They'd let the whole convoy go by on a nice straightaway, step into the middle of the highway, and fire a B-40 right down the pipe. They figured they were bound to hit something, and it worked.

The first week of January found us still honoring the Christmas Truce. We were not to fire on anyone unless we were fired on first. Defensive fire only. Everybody felt the whole thing sucked. The V.C. took full advantage of this and openly moved about during the day. We saw five black pajamas with weapons one day while running the road. They were hopping from one tree line to another, in the wide; "you can't shoot at us" open. Our APC's swung into a herringbone defense off the side of the road but all we could do was watch. They were too far off for M-16 fire, but the guys in the .50-cal rings could have tagged them right in the ear. We watched them run right by us.

The next night we set up alongside the road and saw 10 V.C. in the tree line to the west watching us. One of them even climbed a tree and watched us all night. We kept an eye on him through the night with a starlight scope, and he never left the tree. They moved out at first light the next morning. Truce indeed!

*Charlie Palek*

We stayed in the same position all day and the following night. At 2 a.m., I got off radio watch and hit the sack. At 2:30, one of the guys accidentally discharged his weapon and put everybody on alert. After the event was over, Sgt. Kalei assured the trooper that once we got back to Dong Tam, the rest of his tour would be spent on K.P. He had given his position away and that's one of the no-no's on the infantry hit parade. If they gave Purple Hearts for dishpan hands, this poor sap would have gotten one.

## MURPHY'S LAW OF COMBAT
### #39
"Calvary doesn't always come to the rescue."

On the 9th of January, a company of the 3/60th got hit while they were setting up for the night. Things got hot real fast and they shouted "RAPE" into the radio. Another company was airlifted in, smack into a hot landing zone (LZ). It was a classic ambush technique that the V.C. had perfected. They hit one unit and pinned them down with heavy fire and casualties. While the ambushing unit keeps the Americans heads down, Charlie puts several mortar and machine gun crews into the likeliest LZ used for reinforcements. If luck is with them, the Calvary rides in on their LZ and shit starts flying. It's the old "hold their nose and kick them in the ass" technique. Out of the 45 men sent in to reinforce, 19 were killed and all but four were wounded. 90% casualties was considered unacceptable to even the most hardcore Generals.

We were on dredge duty listening to the battle unfolding on our spare radio. We had been on the dredge for 8 days and were bored out of our skulls. Supper one night consisted of "mystery meat" hot dogs with mustard, ketchup, and sauerkraut. It was a vile meal and most of it was tossed into the Big Blue. We ate C's that night.

Later that night, Doc was on radio watch for two hours and when he came off, he drank a quart of Seagram's and fell asleep. He got up about 2 hours later and stepped out on an 8" ledge to take a piss. Now normally this was not a big deal, but we happened to be on the 3rd deck up, about 45 feet in the air where the radio masts and spotlights were mounted.

I was on duty and didn't realize he was going to step out on the ledge until he actually did it. I didn't yell, afraid I'd startle him and he'd do a header over the side, so I walked over and grabbed his belt behind him and held on till the deed was done. I helped him back to his bunk and realized he never knew how close he came to falling. I also hoped the guys below us were sleeping under umbrellas!

About an hour later, I was off watch and sleeping when I woke up to a warm feeling on my leg. I woke up and found Doc standing over me pissing on my leg! This was the thanks I got for saving his life! I hopped up and pointed him in a safe direction until he was done, then escorted him back to his bunk. It was close to dawn, so I stayed up and watched him for an hour or so.

That morning he woke up with a headache bigger than all outdoors. I told him about the two incidents and he didn't believe me until a couple other guys backed me up. He apologized profusely for squirting my leg and actually paled when we showed him the ledge he stepped on. We agreed that Seagram's and Doc would not get together on dredge duty anymore. We didn't tell Lt. Croll about this — we figured he had enough problems, with the war and all!

Hueys had airlifted our company a couple times in the past month and I loved flying. The air was cooler, no muddy boots, from here to there in no time. I thought I'd put in for door gunner while I was in Dong Tam. Door gunner looked like my kind of job.

I mentioned it to Lt. Croll and he told me battalion would probably turn me down because RTO's, once they were trained, were valuable and it wasn't easy to transfer out. Maybe I could extend my tour for the job once it was over and if I was still alive, I decided to wait and see; maybe try in another month or so.

I couple days later I was told I would be sent to Headquarters Company to be a permanent RTO at the base. Most of the RTO's would have jumped at the chance to get out of the field for good. I'd be working in a relatively safe environment, air conditioned, hot chow, and clean sheets every night. But the idea of being an REMF for the rest of my tour didn't appeal to me. Besides not liking the name, I knew that avoiding a lot of the chickenshit people in this outfit required that you be in the field, where the bullets were flying. A true REMF avoided the field like a hooker avoids the cops. They preferred staying in the rear, shuffling papers and biting soldiers' asses for unshined boots. I didn't like being around people like that, on or off duty, so I went to Lt. Croll and asked him to save me. He appreciated my wanting to stay. We had gotten pretty close in the last couple months.

## MURPHY'S LAW OF COMBAT
### #10
"Try to look unimportant. They may be low on ammo."

The first time we had been under fire by a sniper, I had not followed him close enough and he told me in no uncertain terms that when he stuck his hand out for the radio handset, I'd better be there. Ever since then, the guys thought we were queer for each other, because I stayed so close. We moved as one and when the shooting started we looked like one body with four legs. Even the Lt. started laughing about it after awhile. I trusted him absolutely. He had good instincts and just tried to do his job and keep his men alive. An Army career with a chest full of medals wasn't in his cards.

So he went to bat for me and convinced the HQ staff that I was needed in the field more than in the rear. They agreed and I had been saved from the life of a REMF.

One morning while in Dong Tam they gave two of our squads a night ambush assignment outside the wire. The higher ups were concerned about the V.C. mortar crews that set up at night and dropped a few rounds onto the base. They were doing some random damage but it was mostly interdiction fire to keep us from sleeping, and we all know how much a grunt enjoys an uninterrupted nights sleep. Having to get up in the middle of the night to head for a bunker makes everyone cranky.

So it was up to us to keep Dong Tam safe from the Red Stain. We packed up at mid-afternoon, set up inside the wire until dark and headed out.

I felt that our unit was not trained for this kind of mission. We had a whole shitload of long range recon people (LRRP's) that were trained for this type of mission. They could move silently and had a better grasp of what it took to complete a mission of this kind. When our unit moved in the night, it sounded louder than ball bearings rolling inside a tin can. Stealth was not our forté. We didn't know about soft hats and soft packs, taping down equipment so it didn't make any sound; the little tricks for moving stealthily in the night. I was sure the V.C. knew where we were at all times, but they never hit us that night.

We had four radios on this ambush, 3 on the company frequency, and I was on battalion. I had a dizzying array of frequencies to deal with, and it made things interesting. Langley 33 and Bravo 26 were on Battalion, Bravo 6 on Company, White 6 was our squad, India 62, Bravo 26, and Gunner 62 were on the Arty frequencies in case we ran into trouble. It was confusing, but I muddled through and made it through the night without any foul-ups. We found nothing that night, and morning found us dragging our asses back to the wire. We were tired, smelled bad and ready for chow. The only excitement we had was a B-66 flying over us while we were in the middle of a big paddy. It was taking low level recon photos and about every 10 seconds a huge flash of light went off, exposing the film. The boys at the lab probably had a good laugh when they processed the film and found a bunch of grungy GIs flipping the plane off as it went over. Those flashes lit us up like we were on a Broadway stage. So much for stealth.

A couple of nights later one of our sergeants lost a highly secret $3,700 starlite scope in a night river crossing. He got in a big heap of trouble for that one, but I never heard what Battalion did about it. The way we were losing choppers down here and planes up north, the monetary value of a starlite seemed insignificant.

January 13th found us rousted out of our snug bunks and trucked to a village at 2 a.m. Our whole company was involved, surrounding the village while the South Vietnamese National Police went in to check I.D.'s The idea was to throw a net around the village and trap the V.C. inside. Anybody without an I.D. was shipped back to Dong Tam for interrogation.

Charlie Company tripped a booby trap moving into position outside the village and dusted off 5 troopers for their efforts. About a half-hour later, they kicked another one and dusted off four more. They were obviously walking a bit too close together.

Sgt. Kalei doesn't let us forget about spacing ourselves during the sweeps. He's constantly yelling at somebody — "spread that dab of shit out!" He's seen enough casualties caused by troops walking too close together and too many casualties caused by one trap.

We spent the whole day checking I.D.'s and hanging out under the shade. We saw a beautiful young woman riding sidesaddle on the back of a scooter with a mini-skirt on and her legs crossed. She was hot and more than a few of us were willing to run down the road after her. She looked a bit expensive for us common grunts, though. There is no justice.

Some of us got a close-up look at the new Cobra Gunships this week. It's made for one thing and one thing only: to kill V.C. and N.V.A. It won't ferry supplies or troops, or do recon work. It carries enough ordinance to destroy a small town: 4 rocket pods, a 40-MM grenade launcher and a mini-gun. With a crew of two, pilot behind the gunnery officer, it has a 36" wide cockpit so its silhouette is very narrow, leaving a harder target to hit in a dive. These bad boys were suppose to be highly superior to the modified Huey gunships called "C" or Charlie models that had carried the brunt of the close air support so far. The Cobra was faster, better armed, had fewer crewmen, and was built specifically for escort and support. They looked mean and would be welcome overhead.

This first look at the Cobra got me excited about getting the doorgunner job. Helicopters in general were a real turn on to me and I wanted to be part of a chopper unit. I reapplied for the doorgunner job and was turned down again. I was told that if I extended for a year after my first tour, I'd get the doorgunner job, a 30 day leave, and after the 2nd tour was over I'd get a bonus and transportation to anywhere in the world for leave. Apparently trained RTO's were becoming more and more valuable, or so they told me. I'll continue to try.

Mid-January found us in a small village outside Dong Tam called Vinh Kim. We spent the night and nothing happened except my radio speaker went out about midnight. Nothing I did could bring it back to life, so I spent the next day on the sweep holding the handset to my ear so as not to miss any important messages. The squad liked having the speaker on the radio so they could hear the radio traffic while I did the commentary. It kept them in the know, making me feel like a walking PA system.

We stopped at noon for lunch and sat around a cluster of 12 hooches, all well built and maintained. Papasan was about 45 years old and had 10 kids, all fat and well fed.

I gave one of the little girls some gum and the other kids must have sprung from the ground 'cause they appeared from out of nowhere. After chow, the 13-year-old led us through an area that was booby-trapped. He pointed several out and we destroyed them as we moved. For his effort he received an arm load of C's.

*Tattletale*

We stopped again that night and set up around a couple of hooches again. We were using purification tabs in our water that kept it drinkable but left a high chlorine taste that even Kool-Aid couldn't cure. The hooch Mamasan offered some tea to us after we had dropped our gear and organized the night watches. We considered the tea as a change of pace and we all accepted eagerly. Our little headquarters group sat around like kids at a tea party, cross-legged on the dirt floor around a crude but efficient charcoal fire. The tea was strong and tasted like boiled oats, but it was hot and quite good. For their hospitality, we fired up some C-4 and heated up some good ol' C'Rats coffee. Papasan sniffed it, wrinkled up the hundred or so wrinkles already on his face, and claimed the beverage as #10, and added a shitload of sugar.

The six Papasans around the table were laughing and getting high on rice wine, and we were enjoying their company immensely. Mamasan graced the table with lobster, squid, and a sweetened coconut with a sugary glaze that was fantastic. I had lost my taste for seafood, but I had some lobster and ate a log of coconut. This group seemed to be eating quite well, so while the men continued to get drunk, I gave Mamasan some C's, candy and soap. She bowed several times, hands folded flat under her chin and smiled that purple-black gummy grin I was gradually getting used to, and I bowed back.

I had to go on radio watch a couple hours later, but I enjoyed the family's company a lot. Most of the old men had vanished or simply passed out at the table. Mamasan hung in until the last drunk's head hit the table, then she turned in. What a dedicated little woman she was.

It was January 24, and our company was on the *Colleton*, the other troopship in our little fleet. I spent the day trying to find a quiet spot on the ship to make a tape for my parents and Roxy. The ship's intercom was blasting about every 15 minutes, Tango boats and Monitors rumbled by, and choppers in and out provided a constant stream of realistic sound effects in the tapes background. There was no doubt that I was on a ship, my family would be sure of that.

*Charlie Palek*

# MURPHY'S LAW OF COMBAT
## #1
### "Military Intelligence can be a contradiction in terms."

Early in the morning of January 24, we were on the Tangos for a six-hour trip to secure an island believed to be a hot bed of V.C. activity. We had a typical Navy wet landing, jumping off the ramp into chest deep water, and walked in water all night long. We crossed 15 canals that night, and daybreak found us soaked and chilled right to the marrow of our creaky bones.

We had wandered too far out of our area of operations by midday, and had to walk all the way back, cross the same 15 canals right back to the point we started from. We hadn't found as much as a track, bunker, or an empty brass casing.

We set up in a banana grove and chopped down about half the trees for our bunker construction. The island seemed about 6" above the level of the river, so all construction had to be above ground. About half way through our new suburb construction project, an old Papasan came racing up to our perimeter screaming about something. One of our perimeter guards called up Ba to find out what all the fuss was about. Ba told us that the old dude was pissed about us cutting down his banana trees. Our company C.O. got involved and reparations were promised. I don't know if they promised to pay him in chickens or actual *piastres*, but he left smiling and Ba claimed he was satisfied. Knowing our government, he probably got enough money to buy a villa in the Philippines.

That night the tide came in and flooded out a couple of our newly-made bunkers. We could hear the owners cursing for miles.

The last two months in the field hadn't produced much. We found an old woman in a half-torn down hooch that was starving to death. She had no one to help her, and was nothing but a sack of bones. She was too frail to do anything herself. Ba went looking for her relatives and found them hiding from us, not because they were V.C. but because they feared us. We left them some food and moved on. Our C.O. decided against airlifting her out because she was so close to death and it would disrupt all their lives too much. We had to keep moving.

When arty or aerial bombs hit an area, the jungle can be a bitch to move through. Trees are down and have to be climbed over, large muddy craters are everywhere and the smell of cordite and napalm can almost be overwhelming. It's a dirty business- exhausting, and especially frustrating when nothing is found.

The Mekong area is vast 1,500 square miles and there aren't that many infantry troops in the IV Corp area that can do the actual "feet in the mud" sweeping. The grunts kind of assume that when we're in an area it must have had some significant activity or we wouldn't be there.

So we continued to sweep around the countryside, crossing rickety bridges across endless canals, walking in mud up to our ass, pinching leeches off the most intimate parts of our bodies, ravaged by heat, rain, humidity and insects. Not making contact after endless days of patrols put us in a catch-22 situation. We certainly didn't look forward to ducking sniper fire or mortar rounds, but after several weeks of no contact, we began hating the apparent wasted effort. Every step seemed futile. We felt our energies could be put to better use. Then when a firefight started, we felt vindicated. This is what we were out in the field for, and as much as we hated it, we felt like this is what we trained for. If we won that particular fight, so much the better. If we lived through it — even better, still.

By the end of January, the scuttlebutt was that the V.C. were building up their resources and forces for a big push. But not everyone believed it or if they did, they didn't know what the target was. Rumors were running rampant but we, being on the bottom of the info pyramid, seldom got the real truth. Army intelligence didn't believe in dispersing information to the people who really needed it until it was too late. Army Intel felt that good intelligence should be kicked around the office a few weeks. You should distill it, mull it over, discuss it, analyze it, discuss it some more, leak it to the V.C. working in the office staff, then when it's good and old and too late to use, release it to the infantry. That's probably why we had been walking into so many empty bunkers lately. It made our missions tedious.

Back out the next day for artillery fire support base security. It was January 30$^{th}$, 1968. We set up around the 105's, right in the middle of a huge rice paddy. We had to build more bunkers, above ground this time. Sgt. Kalei knows how to build bunkers. We put a lot of overhead cover on them in case we had to call arty in on our positions. Being in the position we were at, we could see a ground attack coming for miles, but I felt a bit vulnerable sitting in the middle of the paddy.

## Charlie Palek

It took us until the 31st to finish our bunker, having to haul banana logs from a far tree line. Sandbags were filled with paddy mud, no shortage of that around here.

We spent the afternoon watching the 105's lay down a pattern of VT fused defensive fire. VT or variable timed fuses could be set to fire in front of their position and explode a certain distance out, exploding in the air and sending a curtain of shrapnel straight into the ground. It was an ugly sight, unless you were on our end. It certainly provided a level of comfy security.

We were using the arty's trailer of water for drinking and cooking. About mid-afternoon, while pretty much wasting away the time, radio traffic suddenly started to sound interesting. My frequency was on the company net, but I switched to battalion off and on and noticed that voices were getting higher and things seemed to be a bit more frantic than usual. V.C. sightings and activity seemed to be picking up all over the Delta. By late afternoon, the shit was about to hit the rotor blades.

Since mid-January we had been reading about the Marines and the Khe Sahn siege. They were being pounded night and day by a large N.V.A. force that was suspected to have come down from the North specifically to wipe out the base and continue on to take the cities of Quang Tri and Hue. We began to wonder if the two events were connected. We began to think if any of our troopers hadn't received their Combat Infantry Badges yet, it wouldn't be long.

Early evening and even company radio traffic was bedlam. Lt. Croll told us after a short jog from the Headquarters bunker that we were to pack up and get ready to move out. The whole company was to be trucked to an LZ and flown to a new location. The urgency made us all curious as hell. This was supposed to be a time of truce- the Vietnamese Lunar New Year. Both sides were in a no fire situation. They don't shoot at us- we don't shoot at them. It was like Christmas and July 4th rolled up into one holiday. High command took the truce to heart and didn't suspect the N.V.A. would break it. SURPRISE!

We stuffed our packs with our essentials, formed up and hiked out of the paddy to link up with a truck convoy. The arty guys were packing up too — without us for security they weren't staying out there. All that work on our bunkers was wasted — but we couldn't leave them intact, so we stuffed some C-4 inside and blew them to hell.

## Tattletale

A 10-minute march in the paddies and I got a radio call that we were being airlifted out of the very paddy we were standing in. Somebody must have been in a big hurry to get us somewhere. While we were forming up into sticks for the upcoming lift, I was starting to feel a little woozy. It was the feeling one gets when you've ingested something bad. My stomach was queasy, head ached, and a little dizzy. "Jesus," I thought, "This is not the time to get sick!"

Lt. Croll had told us what he heard from Headquarters about the current situation report. Apparently, every V.C. and N.V.A. soldier in Southeast Asia had crawled out of their holes and was attacking every major city up and down the country, including Saigon, Da Nang, Hue, and dozens of others. Judging by the increasingly hysterical radio traffic this new offensive caught everybody off guard. The Commies had grabbed the tail of the American Eagle and were starting to pull feathers.

Now that we knew what was going on, the next really important questions were, where are we going and how will it affect us?

The Lt. told us that a major offensive had started all over Vietnam. The Communists had broken the truce and everybody's ass was in the fire. Even the base REMF's all over the country were picking up their somewhat rusty and little-used weapons and were fighting for their lives. Somehow that news actually lifted our spirits! Chaos reigned supreme and we were going right into the middle of it.

Our question — "Where are we going?" was answered while we stood in our sticks ready for pickup. Our company plus Charlie Co. were going to be airlifted outside the provincial capitol of My Tho. The V.C. had taken over the town and it was up to us to push them back out.

The thought that we were moving into My Tho to actually engage in street fighting would have been exciting to me if I hadn't really started feeling bad. There were about eight other guys in our platoon suffering from the same symptoms I was having. I started to sweat profusely but it wasn't from the heat or humidity. I was throwing up everything I had eaten in the last four hours, and when that had been expelled the dry heaves took over — violent dry heaves.

Lt. Croll started becoming concerned when I fell on my stomach across a paddy dike and dry-puked for several minutes. The choppers were on their way and he asked me if I could do the job. Considering there were around a dozen guys in the same shape I was, it was obvious we had all eaten the same stuff, but what?

I wasn't feeling good at all, but I was hoping the worst was over. I knew they needed me on this assault, so I elected to stick it out. I was having a bout of dry heaves about every 15 minutes, as were the other guys. I was feeling weak but convinced to stick it out. Lt. Croll was concerned whether or not I could keep up, especially if we ran into a hot LZ going in. I told him I'd give the radio to someone else if I couldn't keep up. He nodded, gave me a slap on the arm and went back to his work.

Our lift ships came in about sundown. We piled in and the choppers grabbed for altitude. The sunset was beautiful that night, from 3,000 feet it filled the sky with color no artist could duplicate. I vaguely remember the colors, I was busy trying to monitor and speak on the radio between dry heaving. The air was much cooler and helped my situation a little. The breeze blew though the open doors of the Huey and helped cool me down, but I was not feeling any better.

I scooted towards the open door, hanging my feet outside and letting the slipstream hit me full in the face. It helped a little more, but the wind was louder and made any traffic over the radio harder to hear. I couldn't win.

Our flight started losing altitude, signaling to us we were close to our LZ. We were told to lock and load, the LZ would probably be hot, so be ready to unass the bird fast. The pilots were not going to be on the ground for long.

My condition was bad, I could hardly sit up and the heaves were coming more often, racking my body with violent spasms. I figured if the LZ was hot I'd be lucky to be able to lift my rifle much less fire it. I figured I could stay on the radio and be of more use, if I could keep up.

Somehow the lead pilot found the LZ in the dark, and led the flight in. The door gunner's 60's were up and our assholes were all tightened up expecting the sounds of bullets hitting the ships. But, it never happened. The choppers hit the paddies running hot, flaring hard and hardly touching the ground. We leaped out into tall grass and, much to our surprise a dry paddy. I hit the ground, doubled over in mid-heave, fell, got back up, and fell again. My knees were weak and getting up was a real pain. Lt. Croll, being the jackrabbit that he was, had taken off and was yards ahead of me. A couple of the other guys hauled my ass up and helped me to where the Lt. was kneeling. I kinda humped over and dropped to both knees, panting like a coon dog running a possum. Lordy, was I sick.

Lt. Croll took the handset from me and told Headquarters that the LZ was cold and in the process of being secured. Since we were the first in, we had to secure the LZ for the remaining flights bringing in the rest of B & C companies.

I sat on the ground while the Lt. talked on the horn. My head was between my legs, waves of nausea sweeping over me. Our company C.O. was concerned about the illness that had struck down about 15 of us. A couple guys even stayed on the choppers. If they felt as bad as I did, we were going to have a heavy squad unable to do anything but barf at the enemy. Now if we had just eaten chopped eggs and could spew them out at the velocity of a Claymore, we'd have something, but that wasn't going to happen.

We were a couple klicks from My Tho, but we could hear lots of gunfire coming from town. Puff the Magic Dragon, a C-47 armed with 3 mini-guns, was working out above the town. A steady stream of red tracers was reaching down from the sky, followed by the growl of the six-barreled mini-guns. It sounded like a dragon growling. As ill as I was, it was impressive to watch. Kill them all, I thought to myself, kill them all.

Both companies finally arrived and we headed for town. Our walking sick call was not doing well; many of them required at least one man helping them to keep their feet. I was walking on my own, but pretty unsteadily. I was able to keep the radio active but the heaves had made me so weak walking became a major effort. Capt. Boice, our company C.O., didn't know what else to do with us. He couldn't leave us, so we had to stay with the company.

We reached the beat-up outskirts of My Tho early in the a.m. Automatic weapons were still cracking in the middle of town. Supposedly we were put into this side of town because the communists hadn't reached this end, so hopefully we wouldn't have to fight our way in.

Somewhere that night, somebody found a jeep and piled the sickos in it. They drove the jeep slow enough to keep pace with the healthy grunts in the outfit. I finally couldn't walk anymore. I told Lt. Croll and he had me give the radio to someone else. There was about 12 guys in the jeep, packed in like fraternity guys in a VW Bug. I flopped down on the hood of the jeep, face down and passed out. The next 3 hours are a blank.

*Charlie Palek*

## MURPHY'S LAW OF COMBAT
### #38
### "You are not Superman."

## STREETSWEEPERS

    February 1st, early morning in downtown My Tho. I woke up, sitting in a small shop doorway, my M-16 leaning against the wall. I let my vision clear, and tried to get up. My stomach muscles screamed at my brain not to bend too much too soon. I felt like I had just gone 4 rounds with Joe Louis, taking all his punches in my gut. I sat back down and caught my breath. Those dry heaves had played hell with my body.

    Using the doorway, I pushed my back up the doorway with my feet, every step hurting big time. I got upright, very unsteadily and took stock of my situation. To my right appeared to be downtown. There were all kinds of small arms fire and the occasional thud of a .50-cal. coming from that direction. To my left, there was nothing. Except for the gunfire, the town was quiet as a tomb. No people, no pets, no V.C., no U.S. grunts. It was eerie. I felt I had been dropped into a dead town. The big questions was, where were my buddies, and why had they left me in a doorway?

    I decided that walking to starboard would put me into the fighting, by myself, and that was not an option. So, I headed left, not worrying about rooftop snipers or shooters from the windows, simply because I didn't have the energy to run from door to door like I should have. I was incredibly hungry and thirsty, but I would feel better eating in the bosom of my bud's perimeter.

    I walked down the middle of a deserted street for four blocks and never saw one person. At the end of the fourth block, I ran right into our platoon. Walker was on a roof with his 60 and yelled down at me, "What in the hell are you doing out there by yourself?" I replied in no uncertain terms that my platoon had left me passed out in a doorway. Walker grinned and said he couldn't believe I was walking down the middle of the street like I owned the place. I was a bit pissed about how lightly the guys considered my predicament. I wandered into a small courtyard surrounded by villas on all sides. I found my squad loafing around waiting for orders. To do what, nobody knew. Their jaws sort of dropped when I walked up and thanked them for leaving my ass hanging out all night in a V.C. town.

Lt. Croll was horrified when I told him where I woke up. He thought I had been evacuated with the rest of the sickos. Apparently I was unconscious in a safe district. I may have looked dead, but the V.C., if they had gone by, would have at least taken my weapon and ammo. I got a few mumbled apologies but mostly dark humor ruled the day. I got called for falling asleep on war duty, to faking illness to get out of street fighting. It was all in good fun. Ha Ha!

Apparently the Jeep we were all in had stopped in the street and our medic had checked everybody for possible evac. Since I was on the hood like a whacked whitetail, they pulled me off, put me in the doorway, and forgot about me. It's nice to be needed.

We'd also heard that several of the Arty guys got sick too, and that the medics had determined that the trailer of water we were drinking was contaminated. Whether it was an accident or done deliberately, nobody knew. Seemed suspicious that it would happen the day of the Tet Offensive.

I wished all my comrades good will and I hoped they all burned in hell. I found my radio and settled back into my old job.

Our platoon was set up inside and outside of a pawnshop. It had already been ransacked, nothing much left but bits of junk and broken glass. We had our M-60's on the roof and at least one gun barrel stuck out of every door and window. Charlie Company was on our right and all we needed to get was orders to begin our sweep.

At mid-morning, I got a call from our company RTO that the V.C. had captured 4 APC's. This was cause for great concern because they had .50 caliber's mounted on those babies and everybody knew there was no place to hide from a .50. The bullets from a .50 were made to punch through 6 inches of steel. We were sitting behind four inches of plaster and tin. When the message came through that they were headed our way, preparations for our future deaths began in earnest.

We only had a few LAW's rockets, which is all we had to stop them. We positioned the LAW's ahead of our position about 2 houses down. Scouting parties looked for gas or kerosene to make Molotov cocktails, but they came up dry. We chopped holes in the wall for gunports and waited, our ears straining to hear the well-known sound of APC's rushing down the street. The pucker-factor was high on this one.

Within an hour, we found out that some Air Force jets had taken out all four APC's and for awhile, our worries were over. It was a rule of combat that not having weapons as heavy as your enemy could ruin your day. It gave us a good feeling to know the jet jockeys were in this fight too.

We sat around waiting for our orders. The sounds of battle were increasing; gunships and jets streaking over, rocket fire reverberating down the street. Mid-morning we got the order to move out, our company stretched out about three blocks with Charlie on our right, keeping in line and doing the same. We had to keep all our grunts in line to keep snipers from getting into our rear. Every building, doghouse, and outhouse had to be checked and cleared. We started down the same street I had walked up on the day before. Things in our sector were fairly calm for about four blocks, and then we started to notice the carnage. Buildings were burning or leveled by fire and high explosives, and we started to smell the first scent of death. As we advanced, we started finding bodies- lots of them; civilians, and V.C. We started receiving sniper fire and the rest of the day went to hell. The snipers seemed to be everywhere, on the rooftops, in doorways, and windows. Progress started to grind to a crawl; my job was to keep tabs on everyone else. Staying in line was crucial so we didn't start killing each other.

Dead civilians were becoming more prominent, lying in the static poses of violent death. Old men, women and children had all paid the ultimate price, killed by both sides. Wrong place at the wrong time. The dead kids really had a profound effect on me. They lay strewn around like some crazed child's broken dolls. Some were scorched or burned black. Others had died from shrapnel or gunfire. If I hadn't been so damned busy keeping up with Lt. Croll, it may have caused problems for me.

Charlie was running into machine gun fire and got stalled in their forward advance. While they were taking care of business, we were dealing with clearing buildings and taking out an abundance of rooftop snipers. We hadn't been trained in this form of combat, so everything we did was strictly "on the job training." Once a sniper was located, we covered a couple guys who raced to the building in an attempt to bring him down. Fortunately, the buildings in My Tho were seldom more than three stories high, so clearing them was not much of an uphill fight. We kicked in doors, fired into ceilings and tossed frag grenades into the rooms. We weren't worried about killing the innocent; the only living people in this area were the bad guys and us.

*Tattletale*

By mid-afternoon, we had been going flat out without food and very little water. Lt. Croll was not the kind of leader that led from the rear. He was right up in front, busting doors and chasing down snipers like everybody else. Tangel ran up the stairs of one building and actually captured a sniper alive. Tangel hauled his ass down the stairs and turned him over to the South Vietnamese troops working with us. The sniper probably never made it two blocks before being killed. It was that kind of war. No intel from that guy.

We found a couple of the APC's the jet jocks had knocked out. One was split open like a watermelon; probably a direct hit from a bomb. It was blackened and still smoking, no sign of the crew. Halfway down the block, two V.C. bodies were lying in the street. One looked like he had been hit in the eye with a 20mm cannon shell. The top of his head had been blown away, and then the body had been run over by some piece of armor. He was flat as a license plate. This really was my first encounter up close and personal of an enemy body. It was gruesome as hell, but I couldn't take my eyes off of this poor guy. His AK and ammo clips had been stripped; the magazine pouches still strapped to his chest. I stepped back and took a picture of him. That image will always represent My Tho to me.

We were finding blood trails running out of doors and windows, puddles of blood in some of the shot-up stores, and AK and SKS shells laying everywhere. We were making progress, pushing towards the other side of town, but it was a long, hot battle.

Towards the end of the first day, our company stopped and let a couple point men check ahead. I was sitting behind some rubble with the Lt., and there were about seven civilian bodies lying in the street. It appeared like they had been taken out by the same bomb blast.

I looked to my right and noticed the body of a woman lying sprawled in the street. Kneeling at her side, its head resting on the small of her back was a small child. They both looked dead, the baby covered with soot and blood. I stared at them for the longest time, but I didn't notice either of them moving, not even breathing. I turned away, got some radio traffic, and looked at them again. Something compelled me to walk over and get a closer look. I stood looking down on them, then got down on one knee. The woman was obviously dead, but the child…I wasn't sure. I ran my hand over its head and the eyes opened, ever so slowly. "Christ, this baby is still alive!" I yelled. Her breathing was so shallow as to be imperceptible. I wondered how long she had been lying there, exposed to the weather and everything else the Air Force and V.C. were shooting into the air. I scooped her up ever so gently; it was like lifting air trapped in the clothes of a baby, she was so light. She was probably suffering from starvation, exposure, and dehydration. She was too weak to do anything but look at the sky with a dull vacant stare. Ba came over, took her from me and got her back to the rear. What happened to her I never found out. She would have died lying on her mother's body if we hadn't of come along. I had to admire that kind of devotion in a 1-year-old child.

We stopped our advance towards evening, set up security and radio watches and tried to relax. We were all wound-up pretty tight, so calming down and getting the adrenaline out of our system was slow. The REMF's did send us a sundry pack to help things along. This pack was a large cardboard box filled with candy, gum, cigarettes, soap, writing material, razors, shaving cream and…Holy Shit! This one had a can of black olives in it! I grabbed those black jewels and spirited them back to our platoon. As it happened, nobody liked the things when I offered the can, so they were all mine. Really made my day!

We were all extremely dirty and bloody. Helping wounded back to the rear, dust coming from every direction, and the stink of sweat and cordite made us all look like refugees fleeing town. But no one was allowed to move out of their night position, no fires, and no cigarettes. The city was crawling with snipers just waiting for that glowing cigarette tip or silhouette in front of a fire. So, we settled in and tried to get some rest. It never came.

We were up and at it early the next morning, pushing ahead several blocks before another encounter. It was February 2nd, and My Tho was still up for grabs. We'd heard the V.C. was pulling out, the gunship companies were nailing them in the open paddies as they fled. But we still had some hard-core boys ahead of us willing to take as many Americans with them to the Promised Land.

A sniper fired at us from a rooftop across the street, and Lt. Croll headed for the building, me right behind him wondering what the hell he was doing. One of the other guys came with us, and we hit the bottom floor of the building, sweeping all the rooms, finding nothing but vacant space. We figured he was probably going to jump off the roof and head to our right, where Charlie was, and we'd be able to let them know if he was coming. We all hit the back door into a little courtyard. I was last in line and as I got into the courtyard, I turned to my left and looked up just in time to see the sniper toss a grenade at us from the roof. I yelled "grenade!" and Lt. Croll, not being close enough to get back into the building, hid behind some earthenware jars stacked along a wall. I turned around to go back into the store; the other guy and me hit the door jam at the same time…and promptly got stuck in the doorway with our asses hanging out. I heard the metallic clink of the grenade hitting the concrete but we continued our Three Stooge's routine, grunting to try and escape from this little dilemma. I knew we didn't have more than a couple seconds so I turned my shoulders inward, forcing the other guys shoulders in and broke the jam up, both of us diving into the hallway. We hit the floor hard and just had time to close our eyes and hold on to our helmets when the grenade went off.

We were lucky. No shrapnel wounds because we were behind the walls. For some unknown reason, we sat up, looked at each other and started giggling like two little girls heading for their prom. The idea of hitting that doorway together and getting stuck was just too absurd to ignore. We helped each other up, cursing and laughing like we didn't have a care in the world. The whole scene was just too much. Things got back to serious when Lt. Croll came busting through the door, heading for the stairs. He told us to keep the courtyard watch; he was going to kill that S.O.B. on the roof.

We headed back out to the courtyard, peeking up to the roof this time. Apparently this sniper was fairly confident that he'd gotten all of us with the grenade, because he started shooting again at our platoon across the street.

Lt. Croll scooted up to the roof and actually got the drop on him. For some reason, he didn't kill him. He held his M-16 on him, and took away his SKS, throwing it into the street below. He pulled off his web gear and made sure he didn't have any other ordnance on him. He brought him down from the roof to a second story window where he called down to Capt. Boice that he'd captured the sniper.

Capt Boice and his staff had gathered in the street under the window the Lt. was standing at with the sniper. Capt. Boice told Croll to bring him down. With very little hesitation, Lt. Croll tossed him out the window. I was walking back out the front door of the shop when this body whizzed past my head, hitting the ground like a bag of wet sand, face down. He didn't get up.

Boice met Croll coming out of the shop and chewed his ass out good for mistreating the prisoners or something. I only caught part of the conversation; I was laughing too hard. Tossing that guy out the window was the funniest thing I had seen all day. If Lt. Croll had killed him up on the roof, nobody would have said a word. Lt. Croll took his ass chewing like a man, then walked over to a low wall, had a seat and put his head in his hands. I walked over and ask him if he was o.k. He told me his back had been sprained when he tried going over the courtyard wall to stop the sniper. He had tried using one of the jars to get over, it crumbled and he went down hard. It became apparent that he was in real pain, but he bit the bullet and stayed with his platoon. He was an original and my respect for him hit the top of the meter.

Lt. Croll got some painkillers from the medic and we continued to advance. I knew the Lt.'s back was killing him, he couldn't walk or run without wincing, so I tried to stay as close to him as I could.

Ba caught three V.C. in an open alley as we moved forward. He killed two, one got away. In his words: "3 V.C. — ka ka dow 2, 1 di di mau." He received a watch and 2 days off for this action, plus a written commendation. The U.S. couldn't give medals to our Scouts, so he got some time off. Not a bad deal!

## MURPHY'S LAW OF COMBAT
### #32
"The only thing more accurate than incoming enemy fire is incoming friendly."

Delta Co. was on our left flank. Their nickname was "Dip-shit Delta" because they had a habit of screwing up. We stopped to regroup and Delta dropped several M-79 rounds into our area, wounding 5 guys. They knew where we were, they just weren't paying attention. We wondered if it would be better having the V.C. on our left, we'd at least know their intentions.

Sgt. Tangel captured another sniper and hauled him down from the roof. He received a Silver Star, unlike Lt. Croll. I guess it made a difference if they weren't tossed out the window.

About midday, we reached a "Y" in the road, took the right and crossed a bridge. We were what appeared to be in the middle of town.

There were actually people walking around, recovering items from their wrecked homes and looking rather zombie-like. They walked past the bodies on the street like they were blind to the carnage around them. Some of the bodies had been covered with newspaper. The smell of rotting flesh, cordite, plaster and burning wood was powerful. It seemed to seep into your skin, assaulted your eyes and left your mouth dry and foul tasting.

The first Platoon got pinned down while crossing a cemetery. The V.C. used the headstones as ambush positions. The V.C. were pulling out and could only move backward since we were moving on a several block line pushing them out of the city. Gunships were having a field day rocketing the remnants of the V.C. force that tried fleeing My Tho in the open paddies.

Ba took off his flak jacket and strolled down the middle of the street with his .45, waving at people he knew like some kind of emperor returning home. He must have been popular; everybody was waving at him.

V.C. bodies were becoming more frequent; probably the killing became easier for the arty boys and gunships when the V.C. started withdrawing. We found a V.C. medic with all his medical equipment still on. He had been hit by artillery and he was a mess, disjointed body parts pointing in all directions.

I found the bodies of the enemy more fascinating than repulsive. It amazed me what a .50-caliber shell could do to a man's chest, or how an aerial rocket could rearrange a body so violently.

The civilians caught in the middle of all this affected me. I almost stepped on what I thought was a piece of charred wood and realized it was the body of a young boy, both legs blown off and burned beyond recognition.

The carcass looked like a charred piece of wood, all black and crisp. I stood over what was once a living child, staring at it like some country farm boy seeing the city for the first time. A week ago he was playing with his friends in the streets of My Tho. Now, his own mother wouldn't be able to identify him. I thought of my own brother and three sisters, trying to shake the idea of them lying in the street. I started wondering if we were taking the right path in helping this country, or were we doing more harm than good.

We were sweeping down the city, finding more civilians wounded and lots of injured kids. One little girl about five years old had a massive shoulder wound. She wasn't crying, just walking around in deep shock. Our medics patched up as many as they could and Ba convinced some of the locals to care for the kids and take them to the rear.

We were also finding a lot of weapons in the streets — AK's, SKS's, a machine gun or two, and lots of grenades. We piled them up and destroyed some, others we kept and took with us. U.S. soldiers were always looking ahead — The Navy guys paid big bucks for war souvenirs. Free reigning, free enterprise in the middle of a city-wide firefight. Only in Vietnam!

## MURPHY'S LAW OF COMBAT
### #22
"Fortify your front and you'll get your rear shot up."

We stopped on the outskirts of town in the late afternoon. We were all dirty, smelly and hungry. Just the chance to sit down for more than 10 minutes felt like pure luxury, but it wasn't to be. We had to set up security, lay out our radio watches and organize a rear security in case we passed up any of the bad guys. There wasn't a man in the outfit that wouldn't have given a year's pay for an uninterrupted nights sleep. You could see the stress in their dusty, charcoal streaked faces. I hoped I didn't look as bad as they did.

We parked our tired bodies in the shops and homes and prepared for whatever. We hadn't eaten all day and even the guys that bitched about the C-rats didn't complain. Chopped eggs be damned!

We needed re-supply badly, especially water and ammo. Water was less of a problem — we found sources around the houses. We still had to use the purification tabs we kept, but it was better than nothing.

Ammo came later, re-supplied by choppers and hauled in. The people on watch swept the streets and rooftops for snipers with our Starlight scopes, the rest of us pulled our watches and when we came off, fell into the sleep of the dead.

The next morning, before we moved out, Lt. Croll found several watermelons and our squad dug into them like wolves on a carcass. It was the best tasting melon I had ever eaten. The night had been relatively quiet. I uncoiled my battered body from my nest on the floor and tried to straighten up. My body felt like it had been hammered like a horseshoe. Adrenaline was keeping most of us running the last couple of days. When it wore off, you felt like a hollow shell devoid of energy, with muscles sore and achy. I guess that's why they send young men to war — it's easier for them to bounce back.

We swept to the outskirts of the city on February 3rd, seeing little action. We mounted APC's and they dropped us into new areas to sweep. We found a squad of V.C. in one of our sweeps that had been hit by artillery. Concussion had killed most of them since there was very little shrapnel holes in them. We found them sitting and standing in holes and behind trees, looking like museum displays. Rigor had already set in but the bodies hadn't started decomposing yet. Recently killed. We pulled off their weapons and magazines and left them lying in the paddy like some plastic soldiers I used to get with my model military vehicles.

For four more days we APC'ed and humped all over the countryside, trying to find remnants of the V.C. force in our area. We'd been in our clothes for 8 days, ate once a day if we were lucky, and were pretty rank when we were sent back to ship.

We unloaded from the Tango's that brought us to the ship, and drug our asses up the catwalk. I figured there would be a mad dash for the showers so I elected to stay on the dock, clean my rifle and get my radio cleaned up and a new battery installed. I sat down on an ammo box and pulled maintenance. I didn't realize how tired I was until I started to relax. I barely got my rifle disassembled and I started getting real dozy. Sleep was forcing itself on my tired body but I was determined to finish the job. Our company had only got about 4-5 hours of sleep a day, adrenaline and sheer will to keep us going. Now my body needed a rest and it was fighting to get it.

I was on automatic when I reassembled the rifle. I sure don't remember doing it. The radio connections got scrubbed with an eraser, a new battery put in and the exterior cleaned up. I hosed off my boots and pants before entering the ship. I had stopped wearing socks and underwear in the field, since those items got wet, stayed wet, and instigated all kinds of rashes and diseases. My feet hurt for a while when I humped the boonies without socks, but my feet toughened up fast and after a couple weeks I didn't even notice.

I was partially asleep when I entered our berth area, when I noticed a PLAYBOY pinup on one of the bunks that stopped me dead in my tracks. It was PLAYBOY'S New Year's eve playmate and I had never seen a woman so strikingly beautiful. I couldn't take my eyes off the photo. All feelings of exhaustion disappeared as I analyzed every curve. Her name was Connie Kreske and I decided then and there that this is what I'm fighting for. She had a black sheer jacket on, pulled off her shoulder, and the party was over. Her face held a promise of things to come. My, my, my, she was a beauty! I decided to get that foldout somewhere and have it for my own. Getting that foldout was one of my life goals at the present. Not very ambitious, but I was living for the moment.

Ten minutes later I was looking at a stack of letters from Roxy and feeling like an A-1 jackass for lusting after another woman. Such is the creature man. Always thinking with the other head. Her letters perked me up, and I put sleep on hold until I read a couple of them. Grab-ass in the berths and showers were quite subdued, everybody too tired to put forth the energy. Sleep after a hot shower came easy. But a long break was not to be.

We had a 23 hour rest and were called back out to help units of the 3/60th. They had been hit bad and reinforcements were needed fast. One of their men was hit in the stomach by a B-40 rocket and was vaporized.

By the time we got to them, the fight was over. We stayed in the field and pulled a sweep into the area, even though our C.O. thought the V.C. had fled. About two hours into the sweep, Williams was on point and called in and reported finding 5 Arvins in uniform, but no weapons or ID's. As we continued forward, everybody started finding Arvin soldiers walking around goofing off. 3rd platoon found 50; we found 60, 163 total. Apparently they were supposed to be manning an outpost, but abandoned the place. We checked into the outpost and found 2 pistols and a bayonet. Where their weapons were we had no idea.

A Colonel came up on the radio and told us to tie them all up and put them under guard. While everybody busied themselves with their new task, wondering where we were going to get 163 pairs of handcuffs, I crawled to the top gun position in the outpost and took down the Vietnamese flag flying there. I decided it didn't deserve to be there.

It was obvious that these Arvins had abandoned their post and ditched their weapons. The guys were grumbling about us having to fight their battles for them. Tossing their weapons away was unforgivable especially if the Commies picked them up. This war was quickly getting on my nerves.

We took the APC low track express back to Dong Tam and then Tangos to the ship. Everybody was impressed with the number of letters and tapes I got from the family. Dad sent me another tape of him and Terry playing a duet, Ter on the drums and Dad on the accordion. It was a hot duet and I loved it. My sister Donna taped the Top 40 for me and we played the songs over and over again. Anything from home sounded good, but the music of the day was always welcome.

Back out humping the next day outside Dong Tam. A short sweep brought one of our squads into a hooch with a military-aged male. Our scouts claimed he was V.C., so they attempted to tie his hands, but he bolted and got away. Half a dozen troopers took shots at him, but apparently he ran like a rabbit and knew how to use cover to conceal his movements. He got away!

Couple hours later we ran into 5 V.C. and a .50-caliber, pounding away like they had all the ammo in the world. A .50-caliber round can go through trees, mud dikes, brick walls, and several inches of steel plating. We feared them as much as the chopper pilots. We kept our heads down and called our mortar platoon to give us some help. It took 2 minutes for the first round to come in, then another 5 minutes for the second. That's not what we'd call superior performance. We tried some 105 batteries and they laid it right on line, but the V.C. left when they realized arty was coming. Somehow those 5 V.C. humped a .51 caliber out of the tree line and got away. Still, our sniper carried an M-14 with a 4X scope on it. We saw 3 V.C. running across a paddy about 300 yards away. Still drew down on them and nailed one of them on the run — a hell of a shot. We saw his arms fly up and hit the ground. The other two never stopped running. Perfect end to a perfect day. Us: 1, Them: 0.

## MURPHY'S LAW OF COMBAT
### #41
"Sniper's motto: Reach out and touch someone."

February 14 rolled around and the day of lovers turned out to be just the opposite. We were still chasing Charlie in another nameless part of the Mekong, trying to break his back so we could all go home. It was a good thought, but the grunts on the ground had a hard-assed attitude about how things were going and there wasn't much optimism. We were hearing about the folks back home thinking the American fighting man was strung out, drugged up and reluctant to fight. Vets coming home were spit on and had dog shit thrown at them by their own countrymen. There was some hard talk on our side about what we'd do if that happened to us. Most said retribution would be swift and not very pretty. Nobody wanted to think that we would be received by a hostile crowd back in the States.

Westmoreland was spouting his bilge about "light at the end of the tunnel." We all thought he was obviously looking into a different tunnel from us. I guess it's hard to get real facts when you're sitting in an air-conditioned office with battalion C.O.'s over-estimating body counts and bird colonels climbing up your ass. He was singing the song Congress wanted to hear and it pissed us off. We were constantly being told by our officers in the higher levels that we were cutting Charlie's lifeline and killing many more troops than he was. We were wondering how these guys that we were stomping into the paddies could get enough men and ordinance together to launch a countrywide, coordinated attack over the whole country.

We seemed to be lacking a goal. There was no front lines, no objectives to take and hold. A couple weeks ago we went into an area that had tin V.C. flags nailed to all the trees. We tore them down, did our little sweep, found nothing and left. A week later we went back and all the signs were right back in the trees. It was like they were mocking us. We certainly didn't feel like we had accomplished anything. It was like catching cockroaches and putting them in a wire basket. You grab a handful, dropping them in the basket, go back for more and when you get back to the basket, it's empty. That's what it was like, chasing roaches. And we all know that roaches come out at night.

So we find ourselves back in the field on Valentines Day. The 1st and 2nd platoons are sweeping down the left side of a canal, and 3rd and 4th platoons are sweeping down the right side. I had my hands full trying to keep everybody on line. It was vital that one of the platoons did not get too far ahead of the rest. We were busting through banana groves, dikes, and canals. This type of terrain was pure exhaustion to walk in. Think of it as a giant piece of corrugated ground.

We noticed that we had a pair of the new Cobra gunships flying cover for us. They looked like lethal fireflies up there. This was the first helicopter designed for close air support and as a pure gunship. It held a pilot in the backseat, a gunnery officer in front. It carried 2.75 inch rockets, under the short stubby wings and a 7-62 mm Gatling gun and a 40 mm grenade launcher in the chin. Just one of them could bring down a shit storm on the V.C.; it felt good to have them there.

A short walk and 1st platoon received sniper fire from a tree line bunker. We had plenty of room between the sniper and us so we called in the Cobras to see their dance. They made four passes at the bunker but didn't silence the tough little sniper. Four more passes and he was still peppering away at us. A couple of our guys finally dropped some M-79 tear gas into the tree line and we watched this guy leave the bunker and run into a hooch. The 1st platoon took the hooch apart with M-79 fire and we never heard another peep out of him.

While we were checking the body in the hooch, we heard heavy fire coming from the other side of the canal. Radio chatter sounded like 3rd and 4th platoons had walked into a big ambush. It was a beauty too, textbook perfect.

## MURPHY'S LAW OF COMBAT
### #9
"If you're short of everything, except the enemy, then you are in the combat zone."

We knew we were dealing with N.V.A. troops, not V.C. after checking the body in the hooch. They had hit the left side of the canal first to get our attention. While we were dicking around with the sniper, the N.V.A. in the ambush waited till the 3rd and 4th platoons were real close, then they sprung the trap.

The enemy was pounding away with machine guns, AK's and rockets. The 3rd and 4th platoons had point men down but they couldn't get to them. The two forces were too close to call in Arty and gunship fire support was marginal. There was a two-foot dike between the wounded point men and the enemy in the tree line. We had men down that needed help so 1st and 2nd platoons headed to the other bank to help out.

There was one big problem: the canal was too deep to cross at our position without getting out the air mattresses and ropes. We also would have been badly exposed crossing straight into the opposite bank. The N.V.A. had no doubt considered that too. So we did a 180 and proceeded 1,000 meters to reinforce them. We half ran the distance and night was falling just before we reached the ambush position. We were exhausted by the time we got there and I was hoping the N.V.A. would withdraw soon. I was not looking forward to entering a night fight as tired as I was.

### MURPHY'S LAW OF COMBAT
### #6
### "Friendly fire — isn't."

My hopes were swept away by high explosives, when the 3rd and 4th, out of desperation and afraid to call in the gunships after dark, called in the Cobras to try and get the N.V.A.'s heads down. A smoke was popped showing their position and the Cobras rolled in. I was monitoring this mad house when one of the RTO's screamed into the radio to call off the guns. They had made a bad pass and dropped their rockets, mini-gun and M-79 fire right into the middle of the 2 platoons, killing 2 and wounding 12 immediately.

We got to their position right after the bad pass and things were certainly going to Hell in a hurry. Lt. Croll hopped into a canal and started firing while I tried calling off the Cobras. We were still receiving heavy fire from the tree lines. The N.V.A. were letting our wounded lie there, knowing we would try to save them. Our medics couldn't get to them because at the present, we were being outgunned. The wounded were on both sides of the dike, with open paddy between the dike and the trees. The N.V.A. had us dead to rights.

### MURPHY'S LAW OF COMBAT
### #37
### "Suppressive fire — won't."

We started laying down some suppressive fire, giving the medics a chance to pull out the wounded. To our horror, one of the wounded sat up on the dike; and I'll never forget what he looked like. Every stitch of clothing had been blown off, his naked body completely covered in blood. His legs had been severed above the knees by the mini-gun, his leg stubs bobbing up and down while he tried keeping his balance on the dike. It was the most gruesome thing I had ever seen. He was obviously in deep shock and didn't hear us screaming at him to lie back down. He collapsed and died a few minutes later, as did two others the medics managed to pull out. They probably would have lived if they hadn't been pulled through the cold canal water. It just perpetuated the shocky condition they were already in.

A dust-off had been called in and was promptly shot down. Another company of troopers was called in to secure the chopper. We got word that there would be no more choppers — period, that night. We all were tired, hungry, and cold and now we were going to have to tough it out till morning. Our wounded would have to be cared for by our medics. And rest, if we got any at all, would be fleeting. We were also low on food, water and ammo. We had been standing in cold water most of the day and when night fell, it got cold — to the bone cold. Now it might seem to you gentle readers that we were in the tropics, how could it be cold? Normally the daytime temps could get well above 120°. 126° was the hottest day I recall, with suffocating humidity. When your're used to that kind of heat, a 50° drop in temperature is extreme, especially if you have been wet all day and never dried off. It was going to be a miserable night.

## MURPHY'S LAW OF COMBAT
### #23
"When in doubt, empty your magazine."

We were still receiving fire, but it was slacking off a little. The night was black as pitch, as I hopped back into the canal and fired a couple mags into the trees. I was standing next to a soul brother and our legs were touching under the water. He was shaking so bad I wondered how he was aiming his rifle. He asked for a couple mags of ammo and I gave him three of mine. I crawled out of the canal and helped drag the dead and wounded out of the way. One of the troopers we were carrying on a stretcher died while we tried to get him to a medic.

I was tired, dirty, cold, pissed off and a big bundle of raw nerves. When my time came to grab some Z's, I found a pile of banana leaves about 4 feet tall and crawled in, hoping the leaves would keep me warm. Our KIA's were wrapped in ponchos next to my nest. I went out like a cheap light bulb, the smell of bodies and cold blood rank in the chilled night air.

Sometime in the haze of deep sleep, I felt something crawling on my face, a very light tapping on my skin. Something was walking on my face like it was booby-trapped. Still in the fog of exhaustion, I reached up and grabbed whatever it was, tossing it aside. It took my brain a couple of minutes for my mind to kick into gear and realize what I was dealing with. Whatever it was, it was soft, squishy, dry and hairy. And it was as big as my hand! The fact came to my attention that there was one humongus tarantula out there and he was probably coming back to reclaim the banana leaves I was sleeping in. Now comes the dilemma. Should I drag my ass out of the pile of leaves that had provided me with such a cozy little nest to sleep in and give in to the beast of the jungle floor? Or should I tough it out, hope he doesn't come back and face him like a man if he does? The decision took all of 15 seconds. In the famous words of Colonel Ridgeway in Bastonge, "NUTS!" I was asleep again in less time than it took to say the word.

## MURPHY'S LAW OF COMBAT
### #13
### "Shit happens."

We got up and moved out the next day licking our wounds and trying to decide if Cobra air support was something we wanted to try again. There was supposed to be an investigation into the bad pass, but I never heard the results. Just another friendly fire incident the Army will probably bury. The families of the dead men will never know our own choppers killed their son's.

We were airlifted out the next day and set-up on the bank of the Big Blue where our ships were anchored. We set-up our HQ in a hooch populated by a Papasan and three daughters. The squads got working on bunkers because we were told we'd be here for a while. I set my radio down in the hooch and found a spot on the floor to relax. I noticed Papasan looking at the radio stepping in little by little. I didn't think much of it at the time but about a half an hour later our radio frequency was jammed. This hadn't happened to me before, so we went to the alternate. One of the girls in the hooch walked by the radio and 30 minutes later our alternate is jammed. Seems like we were in the midst of V.C. sympathizers. We kicked them out of their own hooch, got on another frequency and spread the word about keeping the radio frequency covered on the radio. We checked with battalion about having these people interrogated, but they had bigger fish to fry, so we stayed the night and left the next day. We did leave them a small reminder though. A couple of the guys rigged up a tear gas grenade on a trip wire inside the hooch just to piss them off. I hoped they choked on the gas.

I had a chance to talk to Ba today, and I ask him why he Choi Hoied. He said "When ti ti GI's in Vietnam, I fight. When beaucoup GI's come, I Choi Hoi. Me no dinky dow!" He wanted to come back to the States someday.

Back to the ships. The days are running together, nobody knows what day it is. I got a tape from Donna today: Top 10 hits, bless her heart. Also, cookies from Ann, Roxy playing the piano and organ, Roxy's friend Sharon sent tapes of the Kingston Trio and Bill Cosby. Lots of entertainment tonight.

The monsoons have been stretching their wings. It has been cold, windy and wet. We never dry out in the field and ringworm is everybody's problem. Our arty forward observer came into the medic station with a solid case of ringworm from his waist down, every inch covered, even his genitalia. He was a solid red mass. The medic looked him over and shook his head. They were going to have to sheep-dip him to get rid of a case that bad. We've been told that ringworm isn't actually a worm, but a skin virus. It sets into the skin when the breeding conditions are right, which is everyday in the Delta. It itched, got infected easily if scratched, and if you got the stuff on your balls it was agonizing. This was just one of the dozens of skin problems you could come up with. We were fighting in Mother Nature's armpit, and she was wrecking our bodies!

We stayed on the ships, nursing our problems and enjoying the rest. Our next mission would be in a place nobody would believe.

The third week of February found us assaulting a place called the Rung Sat Special Zone. This area was south of Saigon on the coast and meant "Forest of Assassins." Pirates, gunrunners, slave traders, and every other kind of scum one could find on the high seas had used it as a sanctuary for centuries.

The V.C. was using the hundreds of square miles to infiltrate into the country via the coast. They had set up supply depots, fresh water wells, troop rest areas, and were enjoying the fact that the area was pretty much safe for them to operate out of. It was a nightmare of nipa palms, mangrove swamps, and jungle all interlaced with hundreds of small canals. Absolutely fucking miserable terrain.

We had heard that the Bad Boys of the Delta, the Navy Seals, were tear-assing around the Rung Sat poisoning the V.C. wells, assassinating their tax collector and attacking the V.C. at night. They were taking the war to Charlie and the V.C. didn't like it.

The guys that had been there before told us the mosquitoes were as big as Hueys and could suck you dry with one hit. On top of all this, there was the ever-present mud. Before I came into the country, a couple of troopers had jumped out of a chopper during disembarkment and were literally swallowed up by the Rung Sat mud. They sunk over their heads in the mud, suffocated and died. Pulling the bodies out was apparently a very tough operation.

Well, this place sounded like a little piece of paradise. It sounded like we'd have enough trouble just getting through the terrain. This was going to be a battle in itself.

Got up at *0 dark hundred,* and hit the Tangos. We were put in at a floodplain before we hit the jungle. I jumped off the ramp and was immediately aware of the mud I had heard about. It was the consistency of half-melted ice cream and you could not stand around in it or it would swallow you up. You had to keep moving. Each step you took had to be followed quickly by the other. It took 3 or 4 attempts to pull your foot out for the next step, each attempt sinking your other foot deeper into the mud. A 30-yard walk could be absolutely exhausting. We discovered that sliding on your belly or crawling on your knees was a little easier. Yea, this was going to be fun!

We spent the morning humping through the canals, stepping over the tangled roots of nipa palm and mangrove trees. We stopped for lunch and the C.O. called in a marking round to confirm our position.

Now after being in the field for three months, one thing that worried me was artillery support. We had a couple incidents where the first marking round we called in dropped between our point guys and the main body! I knew enough about artillery to know it wasn't an exact science. First, you had to have somebody with the infantry that knew how to read a map. Thus, our forward observer was put to use. He's been to artillery school and is an expert in map reading. I always felt better when he was with us.

The other problem is a mixed bag. Even if you get the coordinates right, a lot of physical problems can screw you up, like air density, wind, range, humidity levels, defective shells, overworked gun crews, the list is endless. I had been taught that artillery had to have a firm stance in the ground so the piece couldn't move during firing and correction. Just as I grasped the importance of this procedure, the MRF started putting 105's on barges to follow us along and give us support closer to the battle area. Well, close support is good, but what worried me was mounting a 105 on a barge on the river, a surface that was not stable in any sense of the word. Even if the barge was anchored, it seemed to me there would be enough movement under the barge to cause a significant drift. Artillery "Drift" is not good. It made me nervous.

Anyway, the marking round was fired at a specific grid coordinate, confirming to the officer on the ground where they were on the map. The problem was that when the round exploded, if it was close to the group, the shell would send out a piece of the casing about 12" long and weighing about 3 or 4 pounds. It came whizzing out of the sky like a pointy asteroid. You could hear it coming but didn't know where it would land. It was like playing roulette. It was good to know where we were, but shit — who needed this!

The round we called for exploded almost directly over our position. We were eating our C's around a small cluster of hooches. Kovac, one of the grunts in our squad, was sitting with his back to a tree, eating a can of peaches. I was about 10 yards away. We all heard the round go off, most scurried around trying to find someplace solid to hide behind. I was peeking around a large water jug next to a hooch when I saw Kovac cover his peach can with his hand. I found this priority very funny and I started laughing. This piece of shrapnel landed between me and Kovac, and it hit the ground with a lot of impact, gouging out its own little crater in the hard-pack mud. Dust and chips of mud flew everywhere. When the dust settled, there sat Kovac, protected by a small bush with no leaves, and his hand over the peaches. He obviously valued his peaches much more than his pointy little head. Strange things happen during combat sweeps, and you tend to see humor in the weirdest places.

I talked to a couple of guys during our break that had taken an R&R in Australia. It sounded like a great place. Beaches, cheap booze, girls, and nightlife — better than this. I figured I'd put in for it, rent a motorcycle and cruise the beaches. First we had to get our asses out of the Rung Sat.

## Charlie Palek

Mark Walker was bitching about our ride to the Rung Sat that morning. We were headed into the wind and the river was washing over the ramp of the Tango, draining down the canted deck and pooling at the back of the boat. Unfortunately, that was Mark's favorite spot in the Tango, so he got his ass good and wet. Listening to him bitch in his Noreastern accent was a hoot. It wasn't like he stayed dry all day. 10 seconds after he left the boat he was wet anyway. Didn't mean anything to him. Logic went over the side — all he knew was the boat ride was supposed to be dry and it wasn't. Tough titties, pal!

We also got a taste of the new C-Rats we'd been hearing about. It was overwhelming. The chocolate bars had almonds in them; spaghetti meal was real tasty. All the food was fresher and better tasting. It was great having food packaged in 1968 instead of 20 years before. Makes a big difference. Sgt. Kalei passed them out to keep it fair.

Back to the ships late in the afternoon with no contact. Up again the next day at 5 a.m. for a seven-hour Tango trip to our next AO. We turned into a narrow canal and our lead boat immediately received sniper fire. They saw several V.C. hopping around in the tree line about 50 meters off the canal. We got orders to unmass the Tangos and sweep the area. Everybody was pretty much ready to go when we heard the rifle snapping and when the Tango turned to beach and the ramp dropped, we were outta' there and on solid ground fast. Our 2 companies lined up and started sweeping towards the tree line where the V.C. was seen. We had a pair of Cobras flying cover for us. The choppers found a bunch of V.C. running like silverfish across an open paddy. They were 800 meters from us, so the Cobras rolled in and did what they did best, kick ass! They worked the group over with everything they were hauling, 2.75 inch rockets, 7.62 mini-guns and 40-mm grenades. The Cobras made runs until nothing was moving. We finally got into the kill zone and started checking bodies. The V.C. had been chopped up pretty bad — body parts and torsos were everywhere, some without heads. These guys were mostly 15-17 years old, not yet adults. Broken weapons were scattered about; mines and booby traps were being carried in canvas bags. We found 18 bodies after we tried matching up the body parts. We found seven more V.C. hiding in a tree line. Most had dropped their weapons when the Cobras rolled in and they were absolutely terrified when we coaxed them out of the bushes. I'm sure they felt we were going to kill them. Some of them were still babies, which is saying a lot since the average American infantryman's age was

19 at the time. We gathered them up, called in our find and were ordered back to the Tangos. We turned them over to military Intel where they no doubt got swallowed up by the system.

On the way back, we ran into a young woman with two small children, and she was acting hysterical! We didn't know what her problem was so Ba came over, calmed her down and talked to her. She had apparently been close to the kill zone when the snakes rolled in and thought she was witnessing the end of the world. Why she was out there was anybody's guess, but Ba felt she was in the wrong place at the wrong time and suggested we let her go. I felt really sorry for her. The kids were clinging to her like children tend to do when they're afraid. We gave her some C's, the kids some candy and set them loose.

We sloughed our way back to the boats, reboarded and continued to our original A.O. A couple more hours and our new A.O. approached. The Tangos tried nosing in to the bank before dropping the ramp, but a field of cane had grown right up to the bank, and the ramps wouldn't drop, blocked by a solid wall of green cane stems and thick as a Louisville Slugger. The boat captains had to back off, drop the ramp, then nose the boat in.

## MURPHY'S LAW OF COMBAT
### #47
"Remember, napalm is an area weapon."

We found out we couldn't go around the cane field, so we went through it, at a snail's pace. The cane was green and as tough as a walnut shell. Cutting this stuff down would have taken weeks, so we tried winding our way through, our equipment and packs getting hung up on the stems. It took hours of tough going, but we finally did break through. It was pretty much decided that walking in the paddies was preferable to the cane break. Then we got the good news!

A napalm strike ahead of us had started a fire that was rampaging right for us. The fire had reached the cane to our left, so the choppers were helping us get as far away as we could. So we turned around and walked a bit faster from whence we came. We had battered our bodies going through the cane once, now we were doing it again, and we were tired. It was a tough, hot, body-wracking trip, but we all made it back out.

We came out in a different area, what looked like a level field of waist high grass. What we didn't know was this grass had grown across a canal, forming a natural mat camouflage job. Our point guys found out about it when they stepped off the bank into about six feet of water. Curses flew as the point guys fished their steel pots and weapons out of the water. This place must not have seen the U.S. Army in a while, nothing was blown up. That's what we thought until Takahata, our short Japanese grunt stepped into a shell hole covered by a mat of grass and disappeared. One second he was there, the next second — gone! I was behind him and saw him step into the hole and it was just like he was swallowed up over his head. He came up spitting and cursing. I helped him out of the hole, trying not to laugh. Apparently this area had been blown up before; Mother Nature had just reclaimed it.

About an hour before dusk, I was crossing one of the Vietnamese bridges across a canal. Now the footbridges in this country were built specifically to harass the American presence. They were built of bamboo or wood, with support poles tied together into an X. These supports were usually about 3-4 feet apart. Running down the middle of the top of the X intersection was a pole running the length of the supports, from one end to the other. Bamboo handrails ran down each side, but they were only about 3 feet from the foot pole. Us taller Americans had to bend over, use the handrail and try and keep their balance. With all kinds of gear on our backs shifting every time we took a step, it was a comedy of errors crossing a structure like this. Most guys in country for a while just waded into the water and didn't worry about getting wet.

I figured, being the high wire artist I thought I was, I could get across this torture device without getting wet. I didn't want to spend the night wet. I was also carrying a case of C's. So I slung my rifle, balanced the case on my shoulder, and using the left handrail, plunged into the brink. I got about ½ of the way across, lost my balance, tried to catch the case as it slid off my shoulder, and fell headfirst into the canal. My helmet was recovered about 50 yards down the canal, floating to the Mekong. We recovered the C's, but I was wet and I knew the night was going to be cold and miserable. Walker was behind me and laughed about my fall for hours.

We set up our perimeter that night, sent out an ambush patrol and settled in. The mosquitoes were bad, very bad. Everybody was doped up with repellent we carried, but it had no effect…they ravaged every inch of our bodies that were exposed. The next morning found our whole troop looking like it had been laid out for a skeeter smorgasbord. My eyelids were swollen, my earlobes were covered with welts, my eyes even felt swollen from the bites. I hoped there were no malaria carriers in the group that had dined on my bod. I got up scratching and it didn't stop all day. I wondered how much blood could be sucked away before I got weak and found myself unable to move! Last night was probably real close.

March 4. We're in Dong Tam, spending time in the barracks for equipment refit and new clothes. I received my birthday box from the family. It had all the essentials: cookies, popcorn, apple butter, Mad Magazines for radio watch, and other food. We pull time on berm duty or dredge security. Security is tightening up, and Dong Tam is being mortared regularly. They received 200 rounds of mortar fire last week. Security around the base is paranoid since Tet.

I am one of the youngest guys in the platoon, and I've taken a lot of shit because I'm an R.A. (enlistee) and volunteered for the Nam. Most of the guys figure I had little to live for and decided the combat pay could help me get over my miserable existence. The battle for Khe Sanh was heating up and the Marines were gearing up to do battle with the N.V.A. 66th regiment. It was going to be a long, bloody fight.

The fact that the Marines had to draft 4,000 men in April was devastating to the all-volunteer Corp. Replacements for their I Corp. mission were becoming scarce. Losses were high and they, as well as the Army, needed warm bodies.

Our HQ set up a movie screen between two of the barracks and we waited till dark and fired up the projector. We had a mixed crowd of Army and Navy guys, and one was as sex-starved as the next. The movie starred Gina Lolabrigida, and she was looking fine. Guys were actually running up to the screen and biting her ass during the film. They got standing ovations and everybody had a good time. I decided watching a movie with all these horny guys was the only way to go. I laughed until my gut hurt. God help the round eyes when we get back home.

A couple more days and then to Can Tho. I didn't like Can Tho because of the snipers there. It never failed. We'd draw highly accurate sniper fire every time we stepped into the area. My radio antennae always seemed more conspicuous in the Can Tho area. I tried hunkering down into my helmet as I walked.

## Charlie Palek

We put in, sweeping up a canal with Charlie Co. on our left. We started receiving fire from a single sniper, and he stayed with us for two days, bugging out as we advanced and setting up farther down the path harassing and slowing our movements. The guy had balls, I had to admit.

Our companies stopped at a wide canal and it was decided to pump a little M-79 fire into the weeds just in case our V.C. pal was near. I was standing next to one of the RTO's in another platoon. This guy had caught a spent bullet in his mouth about 2 months earlier. It went through his cheek, chipped out some jawbone and knocked out a few teeth. He spit the bullet out before the medics got to him. This kind of incident creates awe in an outfit, and celebrity status is the outcome. I thought that kind of wound would get him a ticket home, but he was back in the field in no time. Giving a guy a break isn't the Army's way.

Anyway, I was standing around behind some bushes with a couple of RTO's, when an M-79 piece of shrapnel came calmly flitting out of the trees and hit another RTO right in the arm. It was still hot but nearly spent, so it buried itself just under the skin's surface and sizzled like a hamburger on a grill. I heard him say "shit" and noticed a little stream of smoke coming out of his arm. We got the medic over and he made a small, shallow incision and pulled out a piece of steel about the size of half a grain of rice. He was O.K., but the incident was so weird we had to laugh. We figured he was definitely charmed.

We moved out and ran into a machine gun nest about 500 meters down the road. He hit all four of our point men, and they all needed help. Members of the platoon managed to pull two out, one crawled back on his own, but the RTO was hurt too bad. Two guys tried going after him, but the V.C. gunner got them too. They managed to crawl back, but the RTO was left where he got hit. About midnight a couple guys crawled out and hoped to recover him alive, but he had died earlier.

Lt. Croll had the habit of wanting to be where the action was all the time, the unfortunate part being I had to go with him. He raced up front during the machine gun attack and me and three other guys followed him forward and to the left. He thought maybe we could out-flank the gun and take care of it.

We were walking in what looked like a good old-fashioned WWI trench line with about 3 feet of water in it. We were trying to be quiet, when I actually smelled the body odor of the enemy. We must have all smelled it at once, because we all stopped together and our noses started to wrinkle. The air was full of sour sweat and fish sauce. The hair was standing straight up on the back of my neck. We all stopped and listened and sure enough, we could hear them moving ahead of us in the jungle! It was getting dark fast, so Lt. Croll, much to our relief, decided to pull back out. We had already determined that we were about 50 meters past the shot-up point men. A bamboo thicket was about 20 meters ahead of us, and that's probably where the N.V.A. were. We di-died back the way we came and thanked our lucky stars we didn't get waxed out there. It was a little too close and I told the Lt. I was glad he hadn't made us rush into the bamboo. He told me he had a real bad feeling about the whole situation and that's why he pulled us out. About a half-hour later, the N.V.A. mortared the shit out of the position in the canal that we had just left. Lt. Croll had proven to me again that he was a man of exceptional instincts.

That night we got mortared and took a few casualties, but nothing life threatening. Our medics took care of them until morning, when we dusted them out. Nobody got any sleep. We were cold, wet and miserable again.

The next day became a milestone in my life, one of those "burr under the saddle" events that haunts you forever. Things happened and choices were made that I'll always wonder about. Could I have gotten away with something I would never had guessed I would ever in my whole life consider?

The morning started off well, but by 10 a.m. things heated up. One of the guys in the platoon was walking a dike when a sniper bullet hit a smoke grenade on his belt and knocked him off the dike. He landed on the safe side of the dike, but his M-16 was dropped on the exposed side, about 3 feet from reach. We were all hunkered down in chest-deep water trying to see where this guy was holed up. We figured he was at ground level, instead of an elevated position, probably in a well-camouflaged spider hole. He had our number, and if just so much as a partial head stuck over the dike it received fire. One of his bullets skipped across one of the guy's helmet, confirming to us that he had us nailed down until we found him.

*Charlie Palek*

## MURPHY'S LAW OF COMBAT
### #16
"Never draw fire — it irritates everyone around you."

    We called in to the company acting C.O., an arrogant S.O.B. that had taken over the company until a replacement could be found. He was a 1<sup>st</sup> Looey and I hadn't liked him that much. But he was in charge so I radioed to him and told him the situation. There was other sniper fire coming from our front, so he had a situation to deal with. I told him we were pinned down and trying to outflank the sniper's position as soon as we found him. He wasn't firing at us unless he had a target, and nobody in the platoon was anxious to accommodate him. When I told the C.O. about the rifle, he told us in no uncertain terms to recover it! We were also to hold our positions because there were another 1 or 2 snipers out there. Trying to outflank one might lead us into the sights of the other. Lt. Croll was chomping at the bit to get this guy, but we were pinned down and told to hold our position.

    The C.O. called us back a few minutes later and asked if we had recovered the rifle. Lt. Croll told him that we hadn't and he thought the sniper was waiting for us to make the attempt. Our C.O. told Lt. Croll that we were not leaving this area until the rifle was recovered. I was listening to this conversation and told Lt. Croll we could roll a grenade on it and destroy it, but our C.O. would have none of that either. We were to send a man over the dike and get the goddamned thing! I couldn't believe what I was hearing. This was a suicide mission and the C.O. didn't seem to care.

    Lt. Croll argued with him, and when he was done, he tossed me the handset and called him every name in the book. I called the C.O. back and tried once more to convince him this was a bad idea. He told me to get off the radio and keep the net open. By the time I was done, Lt. Croll had a plan. He stretched us across the dike, and told everybody to put just his rifle over the dike and lay down some fire. We were going to toss a couple smoke grenades for cover and send out a man. He chose a guy named Davis, a goofy looking guy with a long neck, an overbite and jug-handle ears, but he was a good soldier. Reliable, responsible and always ready to do his duty. Davis stood by the dike where the rifle lay. We tossed out three smokes, waited for them to billow, started laying down fire and Davis went over the top. He was promptly shot through the throat and died instantly.

I saw him get his shoulder over the dike when his head snapped back, his helmet flew off and he slumped into the water over his head. A couple guys pulled him up out of the water and they realized he was dead. The sniper had just waited for somebody to show himself to retrieve the rifle. The smoke and suppressing fire hadn't done a bit of good. I don't even think I heard the shot, I just saw him fall.

The guys floated his body past Lt.Croll and I grabbed the back of his shirt and saw the dirty canal water washing into his open mouth and washing out the hole in his throat, tinted with blood. I was horrified how fast this all happened. My fur was already up about the C.O.'s cavalier attitude about exposing a man to recover a fucking M-16 rifle. Now I was just flat-ass pissed.

I clumsily tried closing his dead-stare eyes as he passed by. Lt. Croll could see I was really pissed-off about this and he told me to calm down and stay on the radio. I got back on the horn and told Bravo 6 we just had a man killed trying to recover the rifle and nobody was going to try again.

He broke off my transmission with a "roger" and then we heard that a sniper up the trail had killed Vernon Miller and wounded Kovac, both walking point. I hadn't even been aware of any firing up there — I was so zoned in on our own little problems.

Bravo Co. Oscar was trying to get a dustoff in to lift out Kovac. He was still alive but barely hanging on. Miller's death plummeted me into a deeper depression, deeper than I thought possible. 15 minutes earlier I thought I'd hit bottom, but I was wrong. This killing was too much. I was depressed and outraged, not knowing who to curse first, the V.C. or our own C.O.

I helped them carry Davis to the LZ while one of the other guys watched the radio. The sniper had bugged out because we weren't receiving fire anymore. We found an LZ back down the trail, dropped the body on the ground and walked back. I was mentally drained, and still highly irritated.

I walked back to the ambush area and ran into Bravo 6 and his RTO. They were trying to get the dustoff in and 6 had his back to me. I stopped and considered killing the bastard, right where he was standing. Shoot him in the back and give him as much of a chance as he gave Davis. The RTO was looking at me, wondering what I was doing. I was running murder scenarios in my head, weighing the facts of such a chancy move. Could I get away with it? Do I want to spend 20 years in LBJ for killing an officer? Could it be pulled off later when he was alone? I wanted to do it in the worse way, but I couldn't bring myself to do it. I was too afraid of going to jail for the rest of my life, and this asshole wasn't worth that. I resigned myself to the fact that I didn't have the moxy to kill him. But he had to be taken out of the field, and there were legal ways to do it.

I got back to our platoon, found Lt. Croll and told him I was going to file a report on Bravo 6, that 1st Lieutenant prick. He told me to calm down and let him take care of it. His eyes showed the sadness that we all felt, and I knew he'd file a report because he didn't fear repercussions. He wasn't a career soldier and didn't worry about ruffling a few feathers. I told him I'd back him up 100% if he needed an additional witness.

The next day a machine gun firing 5" above the ground hit Charlie Co. He was putting out a deadly grazing fire and he killed and wounded several Charlie Co. guys while they were crossing a canal. One of our platoons flanked the gunner and turned him into guava jelly with a couple of frags while he pounded away on Charlie Co. I was ready to leave this area. Can Tho was not good. Being picked off one at a time somehow felt worse than being in a full-blown battle.

I was starting to appreciate the value of a well-placed, disciplined sniper. They could demoralize and slow down a large force while expending a few cents worth of bullets. Being on the business end of a sniper's rifle was one of my least favorite places, but you had to admire the precision. We were dropping tons of bombs on guys hauling food and ammo on bicycles along Uncle Ho's trail, and nobody really knew how much damage was being done. It was one of the all-time great jerk offs.

We moved out of Can Tho the next morning, and not a moment too soon as far as I was concerned. We sailed back to Dong Tam and set up shop at the base for…who knew how long.

Doc Hargrove, our medic, sat back on his bunk and was listening to country western music and started catching a lot of crap about it. Most of the guys were Rock & Roll fans, or in the case of the brothers, Motown was king — But C & W, no way! Doc was batting the shit right back at us until some smart-ass mentioned that President Johnson came from Texas and they should be kicked out of the union for siring such an impotent imbecile. Since Doc was from the Lone Star State too, we expected a sharp riposte, but Doc had nothing to say. He didn't like Johnson either.

On March 9, 1968, we piled out of the barracks in the morning to find out we were going to walk the outer perimeter of Dong Tam for a couple days. Dong Tam was getting mortared at night on a regular basis. Our C.O. figured having us out there in the paddies around the base would keep the V.C. from setting up the mortars. We were to set up in a tree line outside Dong Tam and send out L.P's at night. But plans changed at the last minute, so we were to patrol at night, sleep during the day. Sounded like dull, miserable work to me. We had done this job before and it was not fun.

By noon we were on our way, making our way through the mines, claymores and concertina wire of the perimeter. Two platoons struck out for a map coordinate that we were to wait at until dark. Then the patrols were to begin. We had arty and gunship support if necessary, so we felt better about hanging our asses out like this. We arrived at the small tree line that matched our coordinate. We settled down to wait till dark, placing security out and I checked in, letting our Battalion RTO know we had arrived.

We kicked back until nightfall, then each platoon went in opposite directions. We spent the next 48 hours walking through flooded rice paddies that reeked of buffalo shit. Our feet stayed wet the whole time, even when we stopped for a couple hours rest, our boots stayed on.

The good news was that Dong Tam didn't get mortared those two days. The bad news was that our bodies were ravaged by the time we got back. I took my boots off when we got to the barracks and they looked like fresh hamburger. Some of the guys peeled off their socks and the first layer of skin came off with them. I never found out if the patrols were continued, but our part had been done to keep all of Dong Tam in dreamland for a couple nights. I didn't know why the perimeter couldn't have been patrolled by gunships.

It took our two platoons a week of med visits and walking around in flip-flop sandals to get our feet back to normal. We didn't have any duty for awhile, a fact that made us all happy. I heard that the foot patrols were discontinued because it knocked out too many vital infantrymen for other duties.

I wrote Roxy's name on my helmet when we got back, and a lot of the guys had never heard of it before. They wanted to know what it meant. Our arty forward observer, Lt. Johnson kidded me about it. I had to explain to everyone that "Roxy" was short for Roxanne. Lt. Johnson was an excellent officer and knew his business. We kidded each other a lot, something you wouldn't see an officer and enlisted doing back in the States.

### MURPHY'S LAW OF COMBAT
### #33
### "If your attack is going really well, it's an ambush."

It was April 3 when we got word that we were heading for Indian Country, specifically a place called the Crossroads, an intersection of two major canals that harbored bad vibes by the vets who had been there before. The battalion C.O. had told the 3 C.O.'s of Bravo, Charlie and Echo that the chance of being ambushed was extremely high.

After the officer's briefing, the C.O.'s of the companies passed the word down to the platoon leader and RTO's. Their words were not very reassuring. This Crossroads area sounded really bad. We got our maps and overlays, arty frequencies and other info. I was wondering about air support frequencies, which we hadn't been given. The one thing that really was depressing was Lt. Croll wasn't our platoon leader anymore. He had heard about the Crossroads area weeks before and had told the battalion C.O. he wasn't going on April 4. Apparently the discussion turned ugly and Croll was taken from our platoon to one in Echo Company. I was shocked when he told me he was leaving. He said it would be either the change or a court martial for disobeying orders. He also told me he had a real bad feeling about this operation and that I should be careful. He was depressed and I knew he was mad about the whole incident. But a 2nd Looey couldn't buck the big boys. I wished him luck and watched him walk away. His gear bag looked like it weighed 200 pounds. I felt like shit — it was a bad omen.

When April 4, 1968 came, we boarded the Tangos at 4 a.m. and sped down the river until we entered the Crossroads area at 8:30 a.m. The rest of the day was a blur of death, confusion and madness.

About 8 a.m. we received word that we were about to enter the Crossroads area and to get our gear ready. I was in the same boat as our headquarters group, our C.O. our top Sergeant, our F.O., four RTO's, a film crew from a U.S. TV station, and our platoon. About 39 infantrymen in all.

*Tattletale*

    I was sitting on a pile of flak jackets checking the radio when we heard the Tango behind us had just taken a B-40 rocket and the race was on. Everybody hunkered down, grabbed weapons and started firing at the shore. I started putting my radio on when a blast above our heads caught my attention. I was looking into the boat's interior when a B-40 rocket hit the top port side of the overhead cover of the Tango. I saw the men directly under the blast blown outward against the steel sides of the boat. The concussion was deafening. I found myself still sitting on the pile of flax jackets, but my ears were ringing badly. I looked down at one of our new guys, Alvarez, and saw blood on his face, head and back. He looked at me and yelled something but I couldn't hear him. It took 300 stitches to sew up his back later, but he survived. I jumped up and grabbed an M-79 and started returning fire on the left bank. I glanced over to the center of the boat and to my horror, just about everybody was flopping around on the deck, or lying still. I got back to the business of throwing our 40mm grenades with the Thumper when I noticed the Tango was turning toward the right bank. We were landing! I was a little uncertain at this point if I wanted to get off the boat by myself. A one-man perimeter has been proven to be ineffective in heavy combat. I didn't have much time to think about it. The boat lurched to a halt and the ramp dropped like a headstone in a cemetery. I looked back at the HQ group and saw they were all on the deck hurt and disabled. Our Company commander had his bell rung and couldn't even stand up. He couldn't command, was incoherent and had no memory. Our top Sergeant was in the same condition. They were directly under the blast and the concussion messed them up. Most everybody else had shrapnel wounds and broken bones. Our Company RTO's were down — badly cut, broken collarbones. Wiste had both arms broken, one in three places. The arty RTO's were not moving.

    I ran for the ramp, grabbing a bandoleer of 40mm grenades off the floor. Out of 39 men on the boat, 6 disembarked and one of them went back to the boat and was evacuated. I was the only one of the five RTO's that managed to get off. I had just become the Battalion, Company and artillery RTO, plus what was left of our platoon. Our group of five ran ashore and formed a nice, tight little 5-man perimeter. I lay down next to a dike and started changing the frequency to battalion when I noticed my leg bleeding. I wasn't hurting, so I started giving battalion a situation report of the shit storm we were in. Our other three platoons had landed next to our tango and hauled ass onto shore. Their Tango had been hit first, but casualties were lighter. They joined us and we reorganized and found out what we had to fight with.

## MURPHY'S LAW OF COMBAT
### #14
### "Incoming fire has the right of way."

Enemy fire in our sector was sporadic, but further down river, Charlie & Echo Company were getting hammered. We could hear the unmistakable thumping of several .50 calibers, but they didn't all sound like ours. One of our other platoon leaders took charge of our force and had me organize our radios. I stayed on the Battalion net. Blue oscar became company RTO, and Green oscar became the arty RTO. Confusion reigned supreme. We eventually realized we had landed on the flank of the ambush force's bunker complex. We had contact with the artillery, but we were not sure enough about everybody's position to call in arty support.

One of the medics came up to me and said I was bleeding from the legs and shoulder. He cut off my right sleeve and I got my first glimpse of a real wound. There was a hole in my shoulder and the muscle was sticking out of it. He also cut holes in both my pant legs and several more holes were uncovered in my knees and thighs. I had 20 separate punctures in my body, but I hadn't even realized it until now. That adrenaline was something else.

The medic started patching me up. As he worked I watched him poke the muscle hanging out of the hole in my thigh with his grungy finger and I got a little woozy at that point. My ears were still ringing and a wave of nausea swept over me, but I snapped back to reality when my radio got busy again. I felt o.k. So I stayed with the force.

Charlie Co. had landed 150 meters down the canal from us and was in a full-blown firefight. Our illustrious Battalion C.O., flying around in his chopper above the firefight, told us, or rather screamed at us, to link up with Charlie Co.

Everybody was overloaded with ammo, grenades and anything else we could use, twice what we normally carried. I traded the M-79 I had for an M-16. We were in a tangle of ass-deep mud, nipa palm and small canals. We paralleled the river, moving towards the firing.

One of our guys stepped into the fire lane of a bunker and was killed by machine-gun fire. A couple V.C. guns became active and we hunkered down to fight. Our green platoon pulled their recoilless rifle into position and cleaned out a couple bunkers with their beehive rounds. They had several machine guns in the bunkers. We found lots of spent AK brass, B-40 rocket packs and lots of blood trails, but very few V.C. bodies.

## MURPHY'S LAW OF COMBAT
### #21
*"Professionals are predictable, but the world is full of dangerous amateurs."*

We inched our way through mud up to our waist. We ran into several more bunkers and the guys took them out with grenades and M-79 fire. It took us seven hours to link up with Charlie Co., our Battalion C.O. screaming at us the whole time. I got to the point where I hoped the V.C. would shoot his ass down. He was sounding like he was becoming more hysterical as the day wore on. I think about midday he realized what a cluster fuck he'd shipped us to and started seeing his career going down the toilet.

About 3:30 we finally linked up with Charlie Co. It took us seven hours to move 150 meters, and we were all exhausted. My knees had started to fill with fluid and they were very stiff. Walking became a problem. I stayed in a canal and helped organize a 3-company perimeter. Echo on Charlie's left flank had very few men to contribute, we found out later. They had literally been slaughtered. Some before they ever left the Tango. I wondered how Lt. Croll had made out. We were standing in canal water up to our knees, but as afternoon turned to evening, the tide came in and we were up to our chest in river water. It wasn't doing my legs any good to do this and by 6:30, I couldn't bend my legs at all. Lt. Hinton, who had taken over our company, told me there was a Tango leaving ASAP with wounded. If I wanted to be on it I'd better haul ass back to the canal. I didn't argue with him, I wouldn't be able to keep up with them anyway. So I literally crawled out of the canal and made my way back to the river. I felt like I was wearing full leg braces. The mud was up to my ass and walking through this morass without the ability to bend my legs was impossible. I finally, out of sheer frustration and the idea that I'd miss the boat, dropped on my belly and crawled to the canal. I probably looked like a catfish on a mud flat.

I finally got to the Tango and the sailors hauled me aboard. I sat down hard with my back against the side, and thanked Lady Luck that I had been spared. Hard to believe, but I was one of the lucky ones. Exhaustion gripped me like a bear trap. The Tango backed into the canal and headed for the *Colleton*. I don't know how long we were on the water; I slept a little and was pretty much out of it.

Once we got to the *Colleton*, I had to have help getting up, out of the Tango and up the steps into the ship. My legs were as stiff as a couple of 2x4's. I probably walked like Frankenstein's monster to the medics. My knees were swelled up like grapefruits. They simply would not bend.

The medics got me into the ship's hospital, laid me out like a huge submarine sandwich and started going over my body. My clothes were caked with mud, so they cut them off and threw them in a wastebasket. They stripped me down to my birthday suit and started probing and cleaning. I felt like a cadaver on an autopsy table. But the doctor, Doc Slaughter (YOW!), kept talking to me, asking me questions and keeping me awake so they had some input from me.

They found all kinds of small shrapnel wounds in my legs, knees, face, shoulder and wrist. The Doc got hit in the eye from a bleeder in my shoulder. He laughed it off, although I did not find it funny. It took about an hour to clean and sew me up. They gave me a fast sponge bath and gave me a ticket back to the *Benewah*. They told me the swelling in my knees would eventually go down, but it would take a few days.

I was taken back to the *Benewah* on a stretcher, and the medics looked me over one more time, then gave me a bunk into which I collapsed. I still felt dirty, especially my hair. It felt weird to be sleeping on clean sheets with such a grimy body. It took about 15 seconds to get over that. I had been pumped up with antibiotics and painkillers, so I dozed off fast. A couple hours later, the Battalion C.O. came by, shaking hands and telling everyone they had done a good job. His aides actually woke me up to congratulate me on my performance. I was in a haze and wasn't even sure who was shaking my hand until one of his aides told me. I would have given him a piece of my mind if I could have found it. His shitty planning had caused a lot of casualties. But I was too doped up to care.

I awoke on the 5th about midday. I was starving, in bad need of a shower and as stiff as a double shot of whiskey. The swelling had gone down a little so I waited for the medics to come by. They told me I could take a shower, then they'd change my dressings. After that, they'd see that I got some chow.

The Navy, bless their hearts, always had lots of hot water. I hobbled to the shower and soaked in the warm water, washed my hair and felt like a new cripple when I finally got out. Soap and water was almost as good as adrenaline to get a person up and running!

I slowly made my way down to the platoon berthing area to see if any of the guys were there. Still had some shrapnel in his leg, so we went down to the dock alongside the ship. I grabbed a couple of sandwiches on the way down.

We started talking to some of the Navy guys who had been at the Crossroads the day before, and learned just how badly we had been waxed. I found my M-16 in the company conex. It had a huge dent in the plastic stock where it was lying across my lap. I could have been rendered a full-blown soprano if that rifle hadn't been there. My helmet also had a multitude of dents in it. I had been very, very lucky.

Our company took the fewest hits, suffering 1 K.I.A. and 30 W.I.A.'s. The Navy had put us ashore on the left flank of the ambush force. Lucky for us! Charlie Co. had landed into the left side of the kill zone. They suffered 8 K.I.A.'s and 6 W.I.A.'s. Echo Company really got beat up. One of their landed Tangos told another boat to land on their smoke. Apparently the V.C. had one of our radios on our frequency and popped a smoke also, which the Tango landed on. They dropped the ramp and discovered a 51. position 30 feet from the ramp. It swept the inside of the boat until nothing moved. Lt. Croll had been on that boat and had been hit in the upper arm and head by a couple of .51-caliber rounds.

8 men had been killed right away in that luckless Tango. I talked to one of the few sailors that was on that boat and made it out unscathed. He said that the .51-cal was merciless in its firing into the boat. He had taken cover in the back of the boat as it took on water. The water and blood accumulated in his hole, and soon bodies and body parts and pieces of flesh started washing his way. He could hardly talk about it, and I certainly understood.

One of Echo's platoons was wiped out except for one of the medics. He played dead with two bullet holes in his chest while the V.C. stripped him of his boots, weapons and aid bag. He remembered them laughing as they kicked him before they pulled out.

I also found out that when I saw the explosion above the troop bay cover, I thought the hostile fire was coming from the port side. It all came from the starboard side and I took crap from what was left of my buds for shooting at the wrong bank.

I wrote to Roxy and my parents to let them know what had happened. I had been dinged a little, but was o.k. I knew this was going to freak out my family, so I had Still take some pictures of me smiling with my bandages on to show them it wasn't as bad as it sounded.

Our Battalion C.O. was relieved of command a couple days after the battle. The fact he knew we'd run into an ambush, but had no air cover for us was never explained. I heard he had been sent to the Pentagon. I think he should have been busted to 2nd Looey and burned shit for a year.

I got the word a couple days later that I may be leaving 2nd platoon and joining the H.Q. as their RTO. Most of my buddies were gone, them majority of them were in the hospital. I heard Lt. Croll was in bad shape and on his way back to the States. I never got to see him before he left. The door gunner job was looking better all the time.

We got 11 new replacements from Bearcat a few days after the battle and they were all wide-eyed, green and scared. It was a little unsettling to be tromping off in the field with mostly new guys. They didn't know how to set up trip flares or claymores and I felt sorry for them, 'cause I could remember being in the same boat a few months ago. A couple of days after that, 2 new E-5's arrived fresh out of NCO school — and they knew no more than the E-M's that had arrived! It was scary shit. What were they teaching these guys back in the States?

Before the end of April, our very own 9th Division newspaper printed an account of the Crossroads fight. I read it a couple times and couldn't believe what they had printed. They had us storming ashore like the Marines at Iwo Jima. They didn't mention the casualties we took, they never mentioned how screwed up the operation was, or that our Battalion C.O. was relieved of his command. They had inflated the V.C. body count. They made it sound like we had won this one!

I was flabbergasted. This was "cover your ass" journalism at it's best. I couldn't believe our own division paper was trying to pass this crap off on the men who were actually there. Did they think we hadn't been paying attention that day?

This incident did more to turn my head than anything I had experienced until now. I wondered, "If they are trying to pass this bilge off on us, what are they telling the people back in the States about how things are going?" It didn't look good. I began to see this as a giant black hole sucking down lives, money and time. It was a serious attitude adjustment. I still planned on doing my job, but the cynicism I started feeling for our governing body and the military higher-ups was growing like a cancer. They could not be trusted.

My bunkmates were all new, so instead of ignoring them, I tried helping them as much as possible. They had heard about the Crossroads and had lots of questions. I filled them in on what they needed to carry in the field, weapon care, foot care, anything that could make their life easier. Since these guys were going to be covering my ass out there, it behooved me to instruct them on the finer points of jungle combat. I was going to be out of the field for a couple weeks, so I also had to train a new RTO. We were going to be fielding a force short on experience and long on questions, so I worked to get them up to snuff, as did the remainder of the platoon.

I was being checked daily by the medics, and two weeks later I was back in the field as company RTO and with a new C.O. The one thing that hadn't changed was our mission. We were still wasting a lot of time searching areas that had been full of V.C. a couple days ago. We found nothing.

## MURPHY'S LAW OF COMBAT
### #36
"When you are forward of your position, the artillery will always be short."

Our artillery was still making me nervous. We had a couple of incidents recently where the marking shell fell between the main body and the point, again. This scared the shit out of me, especially since I knew how many factors were involved in placing an artillery shell at an exact spot on the map. Although we had a highly competent F.O., I always hated the idea of artillery.

Back in the field in late April, my wounds had healed and I was suffering no ill effects. The medics decided to leave the metal pieces in because digging them out would cause more damage. All of the shrapnel in my shoulder, wrist and knees was too small to surgically remove. The medics explained to me that they would be doing more damage to the injured areas by trying to remove the metal, so they left it in. Eventually some of the pieces might work themselves out, but it was likely that I'd be carrying them around forever.

Our company found itself on another sweep in some nondescript area of the Mekong. We were sweeping through a banana grove when I got a call from a B-66 bomber, call sign Batman, in our A.O. He told us he was going to drop a 2,000 pound bomb on a bunker complex ahead of us. He would let us know five minutes before the drop so we could take cover. He told us the complex was about a klick, or 1 kilometer, from our location, so I figured we'd be warned in time. That was close for a 2,000 pound bomb.

About ten minutes passed and I hadn't heard from the plane. Our new C.O. called a halt and told me to give him another call. I had just put the handset up to my ear when an explosion rocked the ground where we were standing. It was like somebody pulled a carpet out from under the whole company. Helmets and weapons flew in all directions. All I remember seeing was asses and elbows tumbling like dice out of a cup.

It was over before we knew it. We picked ourselves up; bruised, but nothing serious. Cursing and walking around trying to find our helmets and weapons, I got on the horn and thanked the pilot for his warning. He gave me a "roger" back, and I don't think he knew I was being sarcastic. The stupid bomber puke didn't even realize what he did. Jesus, it was tough surviving this war when both sides are shooting at us.

Life in the field always seemed to hold some surprises — some good, some bad. We tried to have a good relationship with the Vietnamese people we came in contact with. They took it on the chin daily and they couldn't do a thing about it.

HQ set up around a cluster of hooches one night. The people were dirt poor but Mamasan invited our group into her hooch and cooked us dinner. This little woman had nothing but a small hut, a dirt floor hooch, cooking utensils and a sleeping mat. She invited us four grimy strangers with hand grenades hanging all over us to have supper. I found this remarkable, but I wasn't going to turn down a free meal.

She started a small charcoal fire, and started boiling some water in a black kettle that looked 100 years old. She also had a small griddle she heated up at the same time. While the fire was getting hot, she left for a few minutes. We wiled away the time talking about the usual bullshit —

girls, cars, and food. About 15 minutes later, Mamasan came back in with a freshly butchered duck, picked and gutted, with the head still on! She plopped it into the pot and put some rice in a container she had in her hand. I snuck a peek and realized it was full of blood! What kind of menu she was planning, I didn't know, but I realized killing one of her ducks was a major sacrifice in her life. I felt like an honored guest.

While our duck was cooking, she took the blood and rice mixture and fried it on the griddle. We each got a piece about the size of a pancake and it was delicious! I was surprised. I sprinkled a little C-Rat salt on it and chowed down. If someone had told me I'd be eating fried duck blood and rice 10 months ago, I'd have called him crazy.

We were discussing this culinary delight when Mamasan declared the duck was cooked, and flopped it out of the pot. It was steamy, hot and cooked to perfection. Betty Crocker herself couldn't have done a better job in a modern kitchen. We broke out our C-Rats, putting together a little canned buffet with all the fixins; fruit, cookies, hot sauce, and cheese and crackers. It was the best meal I'd had in months. Mamasan was a gracious hostess, laughing with us even though nobody spoke a common language. It was a touch of home, and I really enjoyed the time we spent there, sitting around the cooking fire, our legs crossed and the war completely forgotten for a while.

We split our radio watch and settled in for the night, sleeping inside and outside of the hooch. When morning came, we collected extra food, candy, and spoons and gave them all to Mamasan for her hospitality. It was the first time I really felt good in a long while.

That feeling was short-lived, however. We went into an area that had been napalmed earlier and a young boy about 11 or 12 came up to us, crying. He had been hit in the chest by a glob of napalm and it had scarred his chest horribly. He was crying and obviously in a lot of pain, so the medics bandaged the wound and sent him back to the ship. I got a first hand look at what napalm could do. I was happy we were the only ones with the capability.

We also had several Chaplains on the boat with us, but only one ever went out into the field with us. He was a Catholic Chaplain, very easy going and personable. He also carried a Smith & Wesson .38 on his hip, which I found interesting. I asked him one day while we took a break if he'd use it to protect his own life. He looked me straight in the eyes and told me he didn't want to die anymore than anybody else. I respected that a lot. Putting one's life at the fickle will of the Lord had always bothered me.

My parents had tried their best to instill a strong religious faith in me, but it really didn't take. I felt one could live a productive, good life without a belief in God. I learned from history that religion was responsible for more deaths than any cause in the world. Catholics were fighting Protestants, Muslims were fighting Buddhists, all in the name of their religion, and this was all supposed to be based on the same God. It made no sense to me.

So, like a dutiful son, I attended church on Sundays, sang in the choir and did my confirmation studies on Saturday morning. It killed me to go to confirmation on Saturday. I felt it was a terrible waste of a day off. Memorizing the Catechism and the books of the Bible just didn't flip my switch. By the time I was out of high school, I wasn't even sure there was a God.

We had a church service one Sunday on the *Benewah* by one of the other Chaplains. We had been seeing action on a regular basis, had friends killed and wounded and were all a bit traumatized. I thought the service would help me cope.

What we got from this REMF Chaplain was a zealous lecture on our use of the word "motherfucker". He ranted and raved about our filthy language, especially the MF word…I had never been fond of the word, but the military, being made up of trained killers, had developed it's own rough language, of which motherfucker was widely used. I knew guys who could converse using the word every 3rd or 4th word in a casual conversation. Foul language was something you got used to. It appeared to me he was pissing in the wind if he thought that he could change this habit, even under the guise of religion. I thought a sermon about anything but this would have been more appropriate. We were combat soldiers and we needed to hear about other things, like dealing with the death of friends, or how to cope with killing another human. He got positively fire and brimstone up there and I finally tired of his rantings and walked out. It was the last church service I ever attended.

Our MACV (Military Assisstance Command-Vietnam) command had issued a bombing halt for the month of April, but things hadn't slowed down in the Delta or anywhere else. It was a foregone conclusion that while we sat on our asses waiting for the Communists to come to our door, hat in hand, to surrender to us they were not playing fair. It didn't take a genius to know the V.C. and N.V.A. were using the halt to re-equip and replace lost troops and equipment. The Ho Chi Minh Trail was packed with trucks and bicycles hauling the materials of war. And who was going to have to root out the enemy FNG's? The grunts, the LRRP's, and Seals, the ground pounders in general, as usual.

The news back home wasn't good either. Riots were breaking out all over the U.S. because of Martin Luther King's assassination. The rioters and cops were beating each other up pretty good. I felt strangely disassociated with what was going on back in the States. The consensus was that we had our own problems here and what the hippies, blacks and protesters were doing back in the States didn't affect us except to undermine our jobs here. The talk around the campfire was bitter concerning the draft card burners and those that fled to Canada rather than serve. Most of us felt that doing our duty allowed us to enjoy the pleasures of living in the United States. If you run to Canada when the country calls, and you don't deserve to come back. They hid behind the guise of not believing that the war effort was legitimate and we were chumps for serving.

I felt the kids that fled the country were limp dicks that simply didn't want to get their asses shot off. The difference was we showed up when the call came, they didn't. We knew better than anybody that the war was a bloody morass from the word "go," but once we got here we fought for each other, not for Vietnam, our country, or to save the free world. Granted this commitment was a large gray area considering how our politicians back home were running this conflict.

I read enough military history to know that most of the infantry recruited for fighting in WWII were really not that excited about going head to head with Nazi Germany or the Japanese. But they went anyway and kicked ass. At least they were motivated, if by nothing else but Pearl Harbor.

Sure, there were people that felt they couldn't kill another human being, but there were plenty of other things they could have done. Only 1 in 10 men in Vietnam were combat troops, everybody else was there as support troops. Plenty of jobs available. Medics we never seemed to have enough of and they were technically non-combatants. I think the people that burned their draft cards and went to Canada just didn't want to serve. That was o.k. because we didn't need them, want them, or trust them, period. I hope they enjoy living in the U.S.A.

Back on board the ship, I found several tapes from Donna and Roxy of Bill Cosby. They were hilarious and provided us with a lot of evening's entertainment while we were on board.

## MURPHY'S LAW OF COMBAT
### #17
"No combat ready unit has ever passed an inspection."

## MURPHY'S LAW OF COMBAT
### #18
"No inspection ready unit has ever passed combat."

Back to Dong Tam for our landlubber cycle. We were pulling berm guard right away, and the timing was just right. The Inspector General was coming through and the guys in the barracks were cleaning things up, even dusting the top of the rafters. We were sending squads on perimeter sweeps in the A.O. We all would rather have been in the field than putting up with the bullshit that came with an Inspector General inspection. We didn't worry about the I.G. coming out to the perimeter- somebody might shoot at him and we wouldn't want that to happen. The M.P.'s were threatening to toss into the pokey anyone who they found in the amorous presence of the local Boom Boom girls. Some of the guys went hooker hunting when off their guard shift. There were plenty of opportunities, but the M.P.'s had been cracking down. It didn't keep them from enjoying the pleasures of the flesh. It's a known fact that they were using the girls while keeping everyone else out. One of the guys in our platoon got tired of the double standard and rigged a C.S. grenade in the door of one of the hooches. An M.P. went through the door a little later that evening and got a snootful of gas. Justice was served and another legend was born.

I was on berm duty one day when somebody in another company popped a smoke grenade in an ammo bunker and started a fire. Before it could be controlled, it started burning the cardboard and wooden boxes that the grenades and ammo came in. The explosives and ammo started cooking off and before it was over two barracks had been burned down. Four platoons lost all their weapons and personal effects.

I sat on top of the bunker watching the smoke rise in coal-black columns, sweeping over a large area of Dong Tam and making things pretty exciting for everyone downwind. A couple cases of tear gas cooked off and things really turned crazy. Mark Walker was in the shower when the gas cloud washed through. He ran 1½ miles back to the bunker, abandoning his clothes in the shower. The M.P.'s made him go back to the shower and get his clothes. They didn't even offer him a ride. M.P.'s were not his favorite people.

I ran into one of my AIT buds in the EM club and found out that 2 of my best AIT friends, Connie Little and Angel Vasquez, were killed on a sweep the 101st was pulling in III Corp. Ed Tollar, another bud of mine, was wounded. I couldn't believe these two guys had been killed. AIT was eight months ago. It didn't take much time to have friends killed in this godforsaken country. I wrote to my parents with the news and Donna was shocked. She had written letters to these guys when she heard they didn't get much mail. They had quite a correspondence going for a while. Just what my family needed- the war brought in to their own home, as if TV wasn't enough.

Got some news from home, this 14th of April. Still taking my responsibilities as the kid's big brother, I wrote and told the twins the Easter Bunny tried landing a chopper on the *Benewah*, but was denied because he didn't have the proper recognition signal. He had taken a .50-caliber wound in the paw and wouldn't be delivering eggs this Easter. The twins took this line of BS seriously and bugged Mom relentlessly about it.

I got a few pictures of Roxy in her Easter outfit. She's looking more sophisticated and speaking French like Claudine Longe! I like it!

Some friends of mine, Karen and Morris, are getting married. Morris was with the 82nd Airborne when they went into Santa Domingo. Said the street fight was pretty heavy for awhile. Thank God for recoilless rifles.

Terry apparently paced the kitchen for two and a half-hours waiting for Roxy to come over with the pictures I sent her. I sent him some patches of the units around here and Mom sewed one on his baseball cap. Mom says he's sleeping with it, the little Gung Ho RA!

Sherry always mentions me when the family is eating food I like. I think Sher is a little afraid of me. Her voice on the tape sounds like she's quaking. Hopefully I'll be able to fix that when I get home. I'll show her what a warm, friendly human being I am.

Donna has written asking dating advice — from me! It's been so long since I've seen a "round eye," I wasn't sure what to tell her. I told her not to date Vietnam vets after they get back home. They are still in the animal mode and could have bad behavior problems. This I know! Be kind to returning vets, but for Christ sake don't date them for awhile.

Roxy's brother Larry is serving in the Chicago National Guard and his unit is dealing with the riots that King's assassination is causing. The people there are burning their own homes, which makes no sense at all. I decided if I get out of here alive and get sent to a unit that is sent in for riot control, I will show no mercy. I'm going to be pissed if I have to fight Americans after the crap we went through in Vietnam. Some heads will get cracked. King's death doesn't warrant that kind of action.

The black soldiers in our unit don't complain more or less than the white guys, but they do tend to congregate together when we have some down time. I've been reading that the blacks at home are calling this a white man's war and that there are a disproportionate number of black combat troops in the field. I know there are very few black officers. Whether the ratio is unfair, I don't know. Very few of the enlisted grunts have a college education. Seems the layer of society sifted for grunts is concentrated on inner cities and the farms and small towns of the country. The guys flying the jets are the ones with an education.

I read an article in Ebony that blacks were not given enough opportunities to fight in the combat units of World War II, and that Korea was the same way. Now Vietnam comes along and there are too many blacks in combat units. It made me wonder what they wanted. All I knew was if a guy did his job for the unit he was in; I didn't care if his skin color was pink or blue. A good man was a reliable man, period!

## MURPHY'S LAW OF COMBAT
### #26
"Communications will fail as soon as you need fire support desperately."

On April 20th, we airlifted into an area of the Plain of Reeds, a vast expanse of mud and 15' grass with blades as sharp as knives. We jumped from the chopper into this hell, not able to see the man in front of you unless you were right on his ass. It was slow going and miserably hot, the skeeters highly active during the day as well as the night. After a morning of humping through the grasslands, we walked into an area where the grass was about half as high. We also found a very well built mud bunker with an anti-aircraft gun mount made of mud with a path running around it 360°. Somebody was serious about taking out some aircraft. The mud construction of this emplacement had dried as hard as concrete.

I reported our find to Battalion. I stood and looked at the emplacement and got a really bad feeling about the area. Just because the heavy weapons guys weren't here now didn't mean they were all gone either. We were dealing with well-trained and equipped N.V.A., and they always picked the time to attack that benefited them. I remained nervous as we continued our sweep. Nothing came up the rest of the day until about an hour before dusk. Our platoon leaders got together with our C.O. and were discussing our deployment for the night. We were standing in an area with a multitude of bomb craters. It was decided to set up here tonight, get our re-supply in and hunker down for the night. I was in the middle of transmitting our orders when the first 60-mm dropped right in the middle of our company. The guys scattered like ants, jumping and falling into the craters with an amazing lack of grace. I ran back to the last of the craters, and jumped into one with our C.O. What I saw next scared the crap out of me.

## MURPHY'S LAW OF COMBAT
### #25
"Don't look conspicuous, it draws fire."

We had five RTO's in our company, including myself. I stuck my head up over the crater rim and watched the mortar rounds take out four of the RTO's. Three of these guys were brand new, their first mission. I watched the rounds walk right into the holes where the RTO's were hiding. The N.V.A. were eliminating our command system with an incredible concentration of mortar fire. A couple of the RTO's left their foxhole protection and ran for other cover. Once the N.V.A. spotter had picked them up, the mortar rounds dropped right into their holes! The accuracy was uncanny! I was yelling at them to hide their antennas and keep moving- advice I wasn't taking myself. The C.O. jumped up and headed for another hole, trying to spot the area where the observer was hiding. I grabbed my radio antenna and bent it over my left shoulder and across my chest to hide it, but I was too late. We hopped- forget that- we fell into the next hole like garbage out of a chute. I peeked over the rim and saw three rounds walking right up to our hole. The fourth landed just outside our hole as my head went down. It made my ears ring, but the shrapnel blew over us. Now I knew what real fear was. This was something personal. The N.V.A. had picked the RTO's out specifically for destruction. This kind of personal assault seemed much scarier to me than your average firefight. This mortar crew was like snipers except they were using light artillery.

They must have thought they got me, because the firing ceased and we started collecting the wounded. The smell of cordite was still in the air as I checked in with Battalion.

Watching those rounds pick off the RTO's was the scariest thing I had ever seen. We had wounded to deal with and it was almost dark. As the sun set, I noticed a low tree line about 400 yards from our position and thought that was where the spotter probably was. It was the only high ground with trees in the area.

All the RTO's were wounded, two of the radios were out, and re-supply wasn't coming for awhile. I had used my spare battery the day before and the one I had in now was getting weak. There were more on the re-supply chopper, so we had to get it in.

By the time our dustoff got in, it was dark. Doc Hargrove brought the dustoff in by standing out in the middle of the LZ with a strobe light. It presented him as a perfect target for any snipers out there. We lifted out the 2 dead and the worst wounded, and watched the chopper lift off and head back to civilization. It would have been good to be on that chopper. It was damn spooky out here.

Doc came back to our makeshift C.P. and told me that he wasn't doing that again! I was in contact with the re-supply chopper and he told me he thought they were about 5 minutes out, but he couldn't see us. It was pitch dark and I was motivated about those fresh radio batteries, so I grabbed the strobe from Doc and headed to the LZ.

## MURPHY'S LAW OF COMBAT
#7
"If it is stupid and works, then it ain't stupid."

The choppers usually landed into the wind at an LZ. Since there was no wind, I figured it didn't matter which end I stood at. I kneeled in the grass until I heard the Huey in the distance, then stood up and turned on the strobe. I stood in the middle of the LZ with this intensely bright strobe going off every few seconds. I could almost feel the sniper's crosshairs on my back. Only the fact that I had to direct the chopper in kept me from running and screaming into the night. It was a "tad" uncomfortable.

The Huey came in low and fast, flaring right in front of me in a hover. He leveled off and started to settle down when all of a sudden he whirled around in a 180° turn. I saw the rear rotor blade coming right at me. Why he did this I didn't know, but I couldn't ponder the question at the moment. I was on all fours crawling like a cockroach to safety. I came within three feet of being clipped by that rotor blade. I found myself lying in the grass, face down, the strobe next to my face, lighting up my mug for every sniper for miles. The chopper gunners tossed out our supplies and the rest of the wounded were put on and the Huey left in a windstorm of debris and grass.

I dragged myself up, turned off the strobe and wandered rather meekly back to the C.P. Doc noticed I was a bit pale and pointed it out to me. I told him that once my heart started, I'd be O.K. The blood would return to my head. I did, however, receive new radio batteries so I guess it was all worth it, but it had been a very stressful day. This day was one I'd never forget, because it was the day I truly feared for my life. All the other battles I'd been through hadn't affected me this way. I tended to focus on my job when I was under fire and usually got a little shaky afterwards. But this was a whole different story. I actually thought I was going to be killed during the mortar attack. That had never happened before. The sooner we got out of this area, the better. There is bad Karma here.

We air-mobiled out to Dong Tam the next day. Not soon enough for me. I could live a happy life if I never saw the Plain of Reeds again.

I got a letter from Roxy saying she received her birthday roses. That gave me a few more points for my side. I was also given a shot at the in-country R & R center in Vung Tau and I leaped at that.

It was a relatively short flight to Vung Tau via C-123. I had 3 days to lie in the surf, sample the local cuisine, (still couldn't choke down the Nuoc mam sauce) and sleep in. It was a bit cool on the beach, but I still managed to sunburn my legs.

The three days at the R & R center went by really fast. There was one highly memorable event, though. While eating lunch in a little cafe, the most gorgeous woman I'd ever seen walked in and sat down at the table next to me. She was ½ French and ½ Vietnamese, and knockout beautiful. She was about 5'9" tall, long-legged and had a fuller figure than your average Vietnamese woman.

Having little self-confidence when it came to the fairer sex, all I could do was stare at her with my mouth hanging open. She got up and walked to the bar like a cool breeze. The slit in her dress showed off those long wheels to their best advantage. Her vision kept my fantasies going for years. I regretted not having the courage to take a shot, but I felt an obligation to be true to Roxy. It would have been tough to turn her down, as much as I love Rox. A clear case of the other head doing the thinking, again.

I was back in the field the day after I got back. Our new battalion C.O. was obsessed about his ground troops making the day's objectives on time. He was constantly calling us on the net and bitching at us about our unit moving too slowly. In order to do what he wanted, we left the paddies and walked the trails, certainly faster going and easier walking but it also made us more susceptible to booby traps.

## MURPHY'S LAW OF COMBAT
### #11
### "The easy way is always mined."

So off we go, down the path like fucking Peter Rabbit. I was walking behind our C.O. about 30 feet and Dombroski behind me about 20 feet, carrying the company radio. We were didi-boppin' down the trail for speed, not safety, and it wasn't long before our order bit us in the ass.

Nobody knew who tripped the trap. There was a loud "whump" explosion behind me. I was stepping forward with my left foot and suddenly my left leg went numb. I put weight on it as I stepped forward and the leg collapsed like it was full of pudding. I saw the C.O. hit the ground also. I turned around and checked on Ski. He had been right on the trap when it exploded, and he was in bad shape. His legs took most of the shrapnel and were shredded. He was cursing me out, blaming me for tripping the trap. I let his comments slide but I wondered what prompted his outrage at me.

I sat back and watched the medic go to work. I was feeling very little pain, just numbness. He told me a piece of shrapnel about the size of a .22 bullet had entered my left calf and exited the front, missing the bone and main arteries. The gash was bleeding a little but not much. Being a firm believer in photographing my experiences, I took a shot of my bloody leg before the medic wrapped it up. I called in the dustoff myself, got a 15-minute E.T.A. and sat back while the pain started to build.

Our C.O. had a piece in his leg, but it wasn't as serious as Ski's wounds. The guys took off my radio and other gear, making sure my rifle got on the dustoff. There was metal V.C. flags nailed to the trees in this area so it was obvious to everybody except Battalion that the place would be booby-trapped, and the trap had done exactly what the V.C. wanted. It had maimed three men. They were crafty little guys. And with the help of our Battalion C.O., their mission had been accomplished. Combat doesn't keep schedules, one would think a combat commander would know that.

The dustoff arrived, but it couldn't land because of stumps and fallen trees, so it had to hover 3 feet above the ground while we were thrown up into the cargo bay. Ski had air splints on his legs and got the posh seat on the chopper, if there was such a place. Our C.O. and I settled in for the short ride to Dong Tam, a mere 2 miles away. The bare canvas stretcher did little to absorb the vibrations of the Huey as the pilot pulled pitch and got the hell out of there.

We landed at the Dong Tam hospital, and not a minute too soon. I had told the medic on the chopper that I didn't want morphine for the pain. I still wasn't hurting that much, but I knew the pain would come like a vampire in the night. I no sooner rejected the shot than my left leg cramped up right at the wound. It gripped me like a vice and I couldn't get rid of it. It felt like someone had stuck needle-nosed pliers in the wound, grabbed some muscle and twisted. It hurt like a son-of-a-bitch! All I could do was lie there like a stiffened corpse and suck it up. So much for handling the pain!

We all were hustled into the hospital, stripped and cleaned up. I lost track of my two compadres as the medics started cleaning up my wound.

As the medics worked, my right foot started bothering me. I mentioned it to one of the doctors and he took a look. He got a surprised look on his face, then mentioned to me shrapnel wound in the bottom of my right foot. It was apparently the size of a half a BB, and there was no exit wound. The wild part about this little discovery was the piece of metal had gone through the sole of my boot, including the metal plate in the boot that protected us from punji stakes. This shrapnel was weird shit.

The doctors decided to pack my leg wound open and ship me back to the ships and let the Navy medics sew me up. So they packed my legs, strapped me in a stretcher and I was carried from an ambulance to the dock, loaded on a Tango and taken to the *Colleton* for sew up. I felt like a piece of plywood being transported to the build site.

Once we reached the *Colleton*, getting me up the exterior ladder, into the narrow stairwells, out of the hatches and into the hospital was a true experience in wild rides.

I finally got to the ship's hospital bay and was met by a smiling Puerto Rican male nurse that joked and kidded around with me to take my mind off my problem. Another nurse came in and gave me a penicillin shot. He aimed the needle at my arm with his tongue out and squinted his eyes shut. I thought for sure I was his first victim, he seemed like an amateur to me. I was in the presence of a true beginner right out of medical school.

The nurse in charge cleaned and trimmed up the hole before closing. He scoured it out with an antibiotic and what felt like steel wool. He noticed my mouth was open and my eyes watering and asked if it hurt. "Hell yes it hurts!" He grinned at me and said the worst was over. He gave me a local and while it took effect, opened up a drawer and pulled out a large butterfly knife. In one fluid movement he had the blade out for me to admire. I kind of jumped in the stretcher- wondering what he had planned for his pigsticker. He laughed again, opened a drawer and I caught a glimpse of about a dozen of the knives he kept just to scare us poor wounded chaps.

I relaxed a little, confident that his guy was just pulling my chain and trying to make me relax. My confidence plummeted when he pulled out a scalpel and promptly cut himself. Yow! Maybe I should go back to Dong Tam for this work!

He trimmed a little more skin off, took a picture of my leg laid open like a Christmas turkey, and sewed me up. It took 6 stitches inside and 12 outside. I popped a couple painkillers and racked out in the hospital bay.

I was trying to get comfortable a couple hours later when I got a visit from a pissed-off Rick Davis. My first day taking over his field job and I got wounded. He was just settling into a cushy job with Battalion HQ, living on the ship, no more fieldwork, and easy hours. Now that I was out for a few weeks, he had to go back to humping the boonies again! He was not happy and accused me of being a big pussy for not being capable of doing my job in the field on a set of crutches. I listened to his ravings, apologized for those pesky V.C. booby trapping the trail and sent him on his way. He wished me a speedy recovery as he left the bay, knowing my recovery would get him out of the field. It's great to have pals.

I spent three weeks getting back on my feet. Moving around the ship on crutches was a pain in the ass. The sailors, bless their hearts, were patient with me while I clogged up the stairwells and hatches trying to get through them in my clubby state. I spent a lot of time basking in the sun, getting rid of one crutch, then the other, and finally a bill of health to go back to the field. Rick Davis was giddy when I replaced him again. My parents couldn't believe I'd gotten two Purple Hearts in a month and I was going back into the field. But I was going to finish this tour.

A small controversy was brewing about who had tripped the mine that had wounded the three of us. It had been determined that a trip wire across our trail had been hit. Since I was walking in the middle of the three men hit, and walking on the same trail, I assumed our C.O. had tripped it. Communist fuses being unreliable, I figured it was a long fuse that allowed me to walk by or it was on a timed-release device that didn't blow right away. But our C.O. was undeniably blaming me for tripping a wire he had apparently walked over. Ski had also cursed me a few minutes after the blast, also thinking I had tripped it.

Ski's thinking had always bothered me because I began thinking maybe I had stepped off the trail and set off a pressure release trap that didn't blow until Ski had come up on it. But I couldn't accept our C.O. walking over a trip wire that I hit. We had words several times about this and things got close to ugly a couple times. I was still his RTO, but I didn't like carrying for him anymore.

Rick Blair, our only "Airborne" qualified sky trooper was bitching to me that he wasn't getting jump pay because he was in a "leg" unit. I told him the Airborne units weren't making combat jumps anyway since they discovered the chopper. That didn't calm him down though. Even if you weren't making combat jumps, if you were in an Airborne unit you got jump pay! He was having a hard time with all the "legs" in our unit, giving him crap about jumping out of perfectly good aircraft. He especially disliked the one going around about only two things fall from the sky, paratroopers and bird shit! I felt a little compassion for him because he was from Illinois, but I liked to watch him get riled up.

Bravo Co. was in Dong Tam during my recovery, pulling perimeter security and running *Roadrunner* on the APC's on Highway 22. I had ordered 20 reprints of the dead V.C. I took pictures of in My Tho and passed them out to the guys. The picture was a big hit, the sick bastards.

Having served over here for over 6 months now, I felt like a combat veteran. I felt I could tell the newbies how to prepare for the field and do what they had to do to survive. This country is full of things that can make life in the field miserable.

Leeches are one of those little beasties that nobody thinks about until their first confrontation. These skinny little creatures live everywhere in the country. They were in the mud below the canals and backwater swamps in the Delta. They were small enough to get into the lace holes of your boots or the size of a big black Cuban cigar. The first two or three guys crossing a stream will stir them up to the surface, causing mild panic to the guys following. Most of the time you don't feel them when they attach, and infection is highly possible in the wound. After crossing a body of water where we knew the leeches were in, you got up on dry ground, stripped and checked each other over. You found out who your real friends were when you had to bend over and spread you ass cheeks so someone could look for leeches hanging from your ass or scrotum.

It was quite unpleasant. If one were discovered, the tip of a lit cigarette or our mosquito repellent would make them release their grasp on your skin. Simply pulling them could result in their head separating from their bodies. Removing the head from your flesh would be tough.

One day, our platoon crossed a stream when we noticed the leeches floating on the surface, their mouths sucking in and out like a carp. The 1st Looey I loved to hate walked out of the water after me, and started walking down the trail behind me. We walked about 50 meters when the guys behind the Lt. noticed drops of blood on the trail in front of them. Our Lt. stopped, and I noticed his right pant leg was bloody. He stripped, pulled down his pants and to his horror saw a leech as big as a cigar hanging from the head of his dick. It was black, shiny and wiggling- the leech, not his dick. He let out a high pitched squeal like a schoolgirl having her pigtails pulled and hollered for the medic.

I saw this huge black, shiny leech hanging there and couldn't help but smile. Justice was being served. The Lieutenant was hopping around like a bunny, while our medic tried to figure out what to do. A cigarette was out of the question, to everybody but me! I was cheering for the leech! Our medic was an old field doctor and had seen all kinds of nasty, horrible combat wounds, but this was something new. He knew the repellent would burn but this was no time to speculate. He squirted a stream at the head of the leech and as our Lieutenant hollered, the leech dropped off and I discovered my day had been made. The look on the Lieutenant's face brought a smile to my face for years afterward.

There was also a cornucopia of species of mosquitoes out there. With all the water lying about, the skeeter population was booming all year round in the Delta. They were as big as hummingbirds or little tiny ones, black as coal and able to raise a welt on your neck as big as a pistachio nut. Since malaria was one of the big ones on the hit parade, most of us took a large orange malaria pill every Monday, then spent the afternoon running to the latrine. It gave most of us the wild trots the day we took them.

We carried repellent with us, but sometimes a new strain would crop up that actually considered the repellent as icing on the cake. It didn't matter how much you put on they'd bite you. We'd wake up with bites inside our ears, inside our nose, in our scalp, and even on the tough skin on the palm of the hand. These little guys have been feeding on the Vietnamese, the Japanese, the French, British and now us. They were merciless and they feared no one.

Every man had his own protection system for avoiding the little bastards at night. Wet towels around the neck and hooded over the head worked pretty well. Ponchos were like sleeping inside a greenhouse when it was really humid. The best method was to mummy-wrap yourself inside a poncho liner if you were lucky enough to have one. The material warmed you, but let moisture wick out of your clothes and the air. They worked without suffocating you. I even wrapped myself up in a piece of heavy clear plastic I scrounged from a 105 battery one night. I watched dozens of mosquitoes trying to get at my face through the 3 mil. plastic. I laughed at them that night.

## Charlie Palek

An Army marches on its stomach and from the beginning; soldiers bitched about their field rations. C-rats were the staple for us and almost everybody but me hated them. We tried going local when we were in town or a small village. We'd get a Mamasan to whip us up some local cuisine and try it out. I was not much of a fish eater, so seafood of any kind I passed on. The Vietnamese did make the best French bread that ever passed under my nose. It had a crunchy crust and inside was soft and chewy. The best part was the bread would stay relatively fresh for 2 or 3 days. I loved making subs out of the C-rats with this bread. Beefsteak or ham steak subs with A1 sauce, some veggies bought from a village we'd gone through, and anything else I could pile on. Piece of Heaven! It always amazed me how guys in the field would come up with great ideas to keep their food imaginative. We stole enough hot sauce and A1 to sink a Tango boat, all from our hosts, the U.S. Navy.

I knew before I joined the Army what walking point meant to a field unit. Small squad size units like the Seals, Marine recon, and Long Range Recon, knew how to do it right. Point was out there ahead of the main unit to keep the main body from walking into an ambush, minefield or booby traps. The small squad size units can move slowly, quietly on their own time, their point men setting the pace, smelling the air, checking the bush for trip wires, listening to every little sound. The operative words here being — SLOW & QUIET. Anybody that's been in a line unit like ours knows they couldn't be quiet on a bet. Heavy footsteps, sloshing canteens, rattling equipment, chatter, radio traffic, all contribute to a line unit moving with all the silence of a speed boat with the engine bearings going out.

Our point was out there to take the first volley of ambush fire, period. Walking out in an open paddy with a tree line to your front always made me nervous. Tree lines could hide all manner of bad people and things that spewed lead. We were always told not to walk the dikes and trails because of booby traps. But I always worried about getting hit crossing a paddy. We had no cover, just a couple feet of mud and water to hide in. Anybody that has ever been in that position knows that you can't put your head under water and hide for very long. It was a kind of lose/lose situation. There was no cover in the paddies, and there were mines in the dikes and jungle. Our Battalion level commanders seemed to have us busting trail faster than was safe to make our objective on time. So we sometimes took the more expedient and dangerous route. Schedules! Point men be damned. What a way to run a war!

Speaking of running a war. Some genius in the Pentagon decided to ticket punch as many junior grade officers as possible in the platoon and company command positions, as the Army in general would have a more well-rounded, combat experienced officer corp. It sounded like a good idea, but when the Army implemented the plan, things started fucking up.

Take a nice, fresh butter bar 2nd Looey right out of O.C.S. and give him a platoon to command. This new officer, if he has any good sense at all, will learn about his command, especially listen to the N.C.O.'s and platoon sergeant in particular. The older N.C.O.'s are probably wearing at least one star over their C.I.B, and they know what's going on.

But usually, as per their training, they are taught not to get too close to their men. Keep aloof; avoid mixing with the low-level grunt riff-raff. You can send these men to their deaths, but you can't drink with them. The average grunt could see these guys coming a mile away. Everybody had to prove their metal in the field, but new officers were put under the infantryman's microscope right away.

So we have this new FNG officer who thinks because he is an officer, he knows what's going on leading men in the jungle. He was one of West Point's top running backs after all.

If he survives his first 6 months, doesn't get killed or severely wounded, he is taken out of the field and given an administration job behind the lines, just about the time he's becoming jungle savvy and learning what his men can do and who is who in his platoon. So what suffers is unit integrity. The N.C.O.'s in the platoon get another new officer and the whole process starts again. Jerking the officers out of the field after half their tour was so incredibly stupid we often wondered if the N.V.A. sent it over to the Pentagon for approval.

The grunts also didn't appreciate the fact that their combat tour lasted 12 months instead of six like the officers. The Army lost a lot of valuable experience when they jerked the officers out of the field. The Army got a well-rounded, combat-experienced office corp. And the U.S.of A. got more body bags. Thanks a lot.

The V.C. are still active in Saigon, the 4/47th are still there clearing the streets. We kept hearing that we may go in and join them or even go back to My Tho. The ships have been on the move almost constantly, up and down the Mekong to Vinh Long, Ben Duc, Long Binh, My Tho and

Dong Tam. The V.C. fired a rocket at one of the ships the other day and missed the fantail by 10 feet. The peace talks are grinding along, but you wouldn't know it down here.

I got a letter from Lynn Schultz, one of my high school buds. A black and white picture was enclosed. He has a beard now and looked like Jesus Christ himself. The mail has been slowed down because of the action in Saigon, but it gets through eventually.

I wrote Mom and Pop today, letting them know I was O.K., and that my leg healed nicely. What I didn't tell them was I wasn't sure what I was going to do once my tour was over. I still had a year and a half, and I didn't want to pound the ground any more than I had to. I had come, seen the infantry, and I was going to leave. I could extend, maybe get that coveted door-gunner position I wanted, but I wasn't sure right now. I knew I didn't want to go to Germany. Sitting on our collective asses waiting for Russia to attack sounded boring.

Wiste, the company RTO that was hurt on April 4th came back to the company. He had scars on his arms, shrapnel in his butt and a thumb that lost about half its function. He was made an E-5, sent to Battalion as an RTO and had 20 days left in-country. He was cruisin'!

Needham was back after taking a sniper round in the leg. He walked in with about half a dozen FNG's fresh as daisies and ready to pick!

Mark Walker's wife is pregnant and he is proud as can be. He shows his wife's picture to anyone who will look at it, with a big goofy grin on his face. She is only 5'2" but she is huge! Maybe having twins! He doesn't have long to go — he had the doctor write a letter to the C.O. that he needed to be available for his wife when she delivered.

So he got all the paperwork together. His brother was at Cam Ranh Bay with a Hawk missile crew and agreed to finish what's left of Mark's tour plus his own, but he could only get as far as Korea where he was reassigned. His father even got Ted Kennedy in on trying to get him to the States but it didn't happen. I hoped all went well. I lost track after he left.

Our company was still in Dong Tam in late June, but we kept hearing we'd be moving back to the ships. Our platoon spent its days resting up, guarding the perimeter and drinking beer at the air-conditioned clubs.

Dong Tam was full of brass and admin REMF's from Bearcat. The rumor mill was grinding out that the 2nd Brigade was possibly getting 3 more barracks ships. The Delta was a big place and we couldn't cover it adequately with the troops and ships now in place. We were seeing a lot of new replacements and Choi Hois, but I knew three more ships would take months/years to get here.

I got some cookies from home, still fresh and highly coveted. Aunt Marie sent me some apple butter, but the glass jar didn't make the trip. I cried for an hour. I wrote to my parents and told them rice krispie treats were great to mail, they were practically indestructible. They were great either dry or moist. Keep them coming guys!

Word started going around that we'd get a new company C.O. in a couple weeks. Our C.O. was still with us, but I felt we were drifting apart. He was becoming forgetful, losing his maps 3 times in one day. When we sat up at night, he didn't worry about anything but his hot meal, and getting to bed. Boice used to pitch in and help set the HQ. Our C.O. forgets about everything but his own comfort.

Burke and I set up an extraction of the company one morning. We organized everything, got our water cans out on the LZ, lined people in chalks and our C.O. slept through the whole thing. He broke camp 15 minutes before extraction. I know officers have privileges but let's get serious.

We were back on the ships for a brief stint then were told we'd be back in Dong Tam soon. The Navy and their hot showers always feel great after being in the field. Every time we come back from the field we put medicine on all the spots of crud we accumulated on the last mission. Good friends applied it to your back, ass, and back of your thighs.

Battalion seems to be a little confused these days. During Tet, our company was inserted and extracted 4 times in one day. Things were definitely crazy then, but recently we were airmobiled 5 times in 5 days. We'd insert, sweep, extract and do it again. We seldom found anything and once in awhile we'd take a little fire in the LZ. Hot LZ's by the way, was one of the events in my mind that had the highest pucker-factor ever. Hanging in the sky dependent on 2 thin rotor blades holding you up and you hear the sounds of bullets hitting and penetrating the thin skin of the chopper is a real nail-biter. Nobody liked it. It sounded like BB's hitting a tin roof. It was a totally helpless feeling, punctuated by the door gunner opening up, sweeping the landscape with 7.62. I think it was usually done to make us all feel better. At least somebody was doing something.

Our latest op included something new in the battle of the bunker. We had 6 engineers with us to show us how to use a new dirty trick the geeks back in the States figured out. They took a stick of C-4 and taped a stick of crystallized CS or tear gas to the C-4. When the bunker is blown, the CS crystals imbed themselves into the interior walls and ceiling of the bunker, preventing it from being re-used. Apparently the CS crystals will last forever. Great stuff if it works. Many times we've blown bunkers and go back a week later and find them rebuilt. Nobody carries their gas mask with them in the field, we're all hoping we didn't foul up leaving them at home on this op.

Bravo went back into the area I got hit for the 2nd time. That made me nervous. A sniper killed one of our guys, but he was found in a spider hole and killed. Two more snipers were killed within the next week; one of them was in a tree close to our LZ before we were lifted out. We walked up and down small canals for two weeks. We were looking forward to getting back to the air-conditioned comfort of the ships. When we finally pulled out and got back to the ship, we were told the air-conditioning was out and couldn't be repaired for a couple days. So we hauled our asses down to bunks and sweated like a bunch of slaves heading for the New World. The crap we had to put up with was never-ending!

We watched a *Star Trek* episode and *The Naked Prey*. The Navy gets all the good films. *The Naked Prey* was a story set in Africa. It left a lasting impression on me, especially the torture and death of several of the white men. And I thought it was bad here!

Recently, the 9th Division has been giving the short-timers "drops" or early Deros dates. Typically, you could get a drop of 1-7 days. Going home even 1 day early was highly favored, so everybody was anxious to see if they'd be going home early. One of our guys named Ziggy got a 6-hour drop and really got pissed. We all roared listening to him curse everybody but his mother over this one.

## MURPHY'S LAW OF COMBAT
### #40
### "B-52's are the ultimate in close air support."

Back to Can Tho on June 22. I didn't like going back after losing so many of my buds last time, but here we were again. We were supposed to be out 2 days, but ended up staying 5. We found lots of V.C. and after checking the area of a B-52 arc light strike, policed up a lot of dead, weapons and gear. The area was particularly nasty — the water and mud very smelly. The B-52 strike had turned the earth over and negotiating the land was grueling. Mountains of mud, fallen trees and holes full of septic water all blocked our path and had to be negotiated. The bodies we were finding were torn up, dismembered and tossed around the landscape like stuffed animals. Getting caught in a B-52 strike zone looked to be a bit dicey. The planes apparently had hit a bunker complex, so it was worth the time and the bombs. However, the silver lining turned black by the time we got back to the ship. Everybody has ringworm on some part of his body. My ankles and right knee is infected. Some of the guys have solid ringworm up and down their lower bodies. One of our guys ankles were so swelled up from immersion foot he couldn't walk.

The skeeters in this area were man-eaters. They were tiny but very aggressive. Their humming kept us up all night, along with the wet and miserable cold. Lt. Tomcik woke up the last morning and his lips were so swelled up with bites he could see his lips with his eyes. Big time protrusion! He looked like he'd gone a couple rounds with Joe Louis and took all his punches on the mouth.

Lt. Tomcik was a really fine officer. Ranger qualified, he came to us fresh from the States, but he had a handle on how to fight in the jungle right away. He was always cracking jokes and mingled with us low-life grunts easily. He was a ball of fire when things started popping.

We found quite a stash on the next op. One of our platoons uncovered a cache. 9 shaped charges, 10 pounds of documents, 5 Chicom claymores with tripods, and about 10,000 rounds of .30 caliber ammo. After slugging it out day after day it felt good to come across a cache now and then. Made it feel like we were actually accomplishing something.

Bravo Co. yo-yoed back to Dong Tam again. While here, I bought some gifts for the family — got a couple sport jackets made, some stuff for Roxy and the twins. Word from home stated Karen and Morris finally got married and Battalion told us Ski is in Japan recovering. He'll probably be home soon.

I had radio watch the second night back in Dong Tam. I was trying to get some letters written, but was assaulted by a stream of drunks stopping in the como bunker, regaling me about the Philipino band we had on base. Apparently the band had 4 girls in bikinis that were causing quite a bit of excitement. I got off radio watch and hurried over to the club to catch the last part of the show.

## Charlie Palek

Arriving at the stage found most of the guys standing and cheering the dancers on. Things were rowdy, noisy, and the air reeked with beer. Rick Davis was sitting at a table, staring at the women with his jaw hanging slack like he hadn't seen a woman before. One of the 1st platoon guys was duck walking back and forth below the stage taking photos under the girl's dresses. He had a good collection of interesting Polaroids by the time the show was over.

Entertainment for our boys came from everywhere, the Philippines, Australia, New Zealand, Hong Kong, Thailand, and the U.S.A. Most of the oriental bands try hard but their renditions of the popular songs of the day usually suck really bad. What keeps the audience riveted to the stage are the women they bring along. I think the women that appear in front of a crowd of sex-starved, drunken combat troops have more courage than anybody in-country. They are certainly appreciated! The U.S. bands are the best — the music is usually good and round-eyed women accompany the band. Caucasian women are few and far between here in the Delta.

It's July 19th and our C.O. left and was replaced by a big Airborne Ranger, which is good for me because it gives me more to hide behind. He had one tour under his belt in a cushy MACV admin job. Now he's commanding a company. He seems competent enough, but I'll hold evaluations until we hit the paddies!

About mid-July, I got a letter from mom telling me one of my childhood buddies had been killed. John Javorchik was a friend way back in the 50's. He lived across the street and we fought Indians, Germans, Japanese, and monsters of all types, up and down the block. We were at the age where everything was new and exciting. We made our own bows and arrows, experimented with water rockets, talked endlessly about guns, war and girls.

He was with the 1st Air Cav. and stepped on a mine after being inserted for a sweep. His passing was a hard one to take. This war was really starting to hit close to home. I wrote a letter to his mother, but felt the words were inadequate for the loss of a son. Hopefully it meant more because I was in Vietnam too.

Washington County, Illinois had a bad 3 years. We lost John, David Jones, and a Kellerman boy all in that one summer. Merrill Suedmeyer got killed while I was in basic, and that started the whole chain of deaths. Washington Co. was a small parcel, everybody knew everybody there, and when four young men are killed it left a huge gap in everybody's lives.

One of our officer's showed me his 9mm Browning he carries instead of his .38, It's a beautiful handgun, well-balanced and easy to hold. It fit my hand better than the .45. I figured I'd bring one back with me when I come back as a door gunner.

Bravo was sent to Tan Anh, an old French fort. HQ set up in the fort while a couple of platoons swept the compass around the fort. Not much happened, but the 2nd and 3rd platoons captured 4 V.C. alive and one conscript that carried rockets for those guys. It was a typical V.C. work ploy for this poor guy — carry our ordinance or be killed. He was absolutely positively thrilled at being captured. They also uncovered 4 AK's and a carbine. Never fired a shot.

About mid-afternoon, the 2nd platoon saw a V.C. dive into the river and try hiding close to the bank. An Arvin Lt. was with them and they fired close to the V.C., the Arvin hollering at him to surrender, which he did. Upon further questioning, 2nd platoon found out there were 3 more V.C. in a clump of grass. 2nd flushed them out, again no shots were fired. Turned out these 4 were local conscripts that didn't like fighting. Surrender was their only safe way out.

The 2nd platoon had entered the grassy area a bit haphazardly. They were lucky the V.C. weren't hard core or there could have been casualties.

Seabray got stuck in the mud crossing a canal. The tide was out and the canal was one big mud flat. He sunk to his navel and couldn't get his feet out to walk. They had to pull him out with an Alpha boat. Lt. Tomcik later got an Army Commendation Medal for catching 2 of the V.C.

Back in Dong Tam the 27th of July. I listened to tapes of Bill Cosby and Johnny Carson that the family had sent me. Bill Cosby is a real hoot; I'd love to see him when I get back.

I wrote to Ron Going, a local boy from Illinois who made it to a 4th Division mortar squad. I'd heard him and his squad spent over 30 days in their hole without clean uniforms. If re-supply includes mortar rounds and food they could stick a few uniforms in there for them. Another classic case of the REMF's not doing their job.

Bob Konkel, one of the High School basketball stars was on the *U.S.S. Okinawa*, a helicopter carrier. He was on one of the assault teams. What they planned on assaulting in the Pacific I couldn't guess.

Our mortar team has gotten much better now that they have a new N.C.O. in charge. He was an older guy that knew his way around a mortar pit. They fired some H & I into a tree line outside the perimeter and apparently scared up a bunch of V.C. The observer said the paddy was filled with black pajamas. 4th Platoon pumped out a couple illumination rounds, then, helped by the observer, nailed 4 V.C. into the paddy mud. That's what a good mortar squad does.

We're supposed to be back on the ships by early August. A lot of the old guys are leaving. Rick Davis has 12 days left; Tangel and Erdman are heading to the "land of the big PX" soon too. Takahara extended for six months. I'll be sorry to see them go. We'd been through a lot of shit together, and they taught me a lot about surviving the Delta. Now the FNG's are looking to me for the same help. At 19 years old, I'm considered an "old timer" around here.

Our company was on ready reaction one night when we got the call to "saddle up." This only happens when some other unit has run into more than they can handle and need help. Good for them they know we're coming, bad for us, because we don't know what the situation is we're being thrown into. 10 minutes later the alert was called off. Everybody was relieved, but I swear these things are going to give me a heart attack.

Our new C.O. for the company has turned out to have a few bad habits. One is he spends way too much time on the radio. I guess he likes to hear himself talk. He won't let me do much talking. He does it all. Over the past year I've learned to keep the traffic short and sweet. Our Captain rants on and on about stuff nobody wants to hear about. The other problem is his screaming. It happened the first time that we airmobiled into an LZ. Everybody unassed the Hueys and he started screaming, and I mean full-blown, pissed off, in your face screaming for us to watch our spacing, and keep up on line. It certainly wasn't very professional and it certainly was annoying. It never stopped and I could tell the guys in the company didn't like it. Combat vets don't take kindly to being treated like children.

A new program was announced for everybody in the Army that had six months or less in their service time. If you extend for 30 days in-country, you can get out 5 months early. A good deal, but it doesn't apply to me with 16 months to go. I chose to stay in the field until my DEROS came around.

There is still talk of us going into Saigon to help the units already there. Between the jungle and the streets, I think I prefer street fighting to the jungle. Why? Even though it's still dirty, hazardous, and a bitch to go through, I felt house to house was easier than dike to paddy to jungle.

*Tattletale*

More than anything, I guess, was the fact that we stayed dry, usually. That counted for an awful lot with me. You didn't sink up to your ass in an alley or street either.

Our next sweep ended up at Vinh Kim, a familiar little village outside Dong Tam. HQ set up in the middle of town, dispersed the platoons and pulled security. I pulled first radio watch in early afternoon, then me and Rick Davis, who needed to get out of Battalion for awhile, came with me into town. We walked around town, decided to get a shave by an old Papasan using a razor that looked at least 100 years old. He did a great job and it felt wonderful to be slightly pampered. He applied banana oil to our faces once he was done. We both smelled like $20.00 whores when we walked out of his shop.

We walked by a school and noticed recess was in progress. We peeked into the classroom and noticed a few kids hanging around inside. We stuck our heads inside and as usual the kids surrounded us and started chattering in Vietnamese and the Pidgin English they learned from us. We got caught up in their enthusiasm, moved to the blackboard and started making stuff up. We wrote on the board: Girls #1, Boys #10. The girls cheered, the boys looked at us like fools. One of the boys raced up to the board and put Boys #1, Girls #100. This brought squeals from the girls and things started getting fun and rowdy. The kids outside heard the racket and joined the rest of us. We had a real HooHa going and we were all having a good time.

The teacher suddenly appeared, the kids scrambling back to their desks while we stood there with goofy grins on our faces. The school marm berated us for screwing with her students and invited us out of the classroom with several "YOU GO, YOU GO!" We hauled ass out, waved goodbye to the kids and headed out to the street laughing like idiots.

We sobered up when we ran across an orphanage and stopped in. I was shocked at the number of orphaned children there, from a couple months old to 16 or 17. The facility was crowded with big-eyed kids that probably had experiences we could only imagine. About all they had was a roof over their heads and a couple meals a day. Some people might consider them lucky, but their life looked pretty barren to me. We walked around the place, laughing with the kids and marveling at their resilience. We left there with a better perspective about what war does to families of the people just trying to get by. No politics, just survival.

We decided that school made us hungry, so we hit the strip looking for a meal. We cruised the stands, checking out what was available. The meat all looked the same, and I couldn't tell what was chicken, water buffalo, fish, or dog. I finally settled on a frog's egg soup. The dark little eggs were floating in a veggie broth, a few vegetables floating amongst the eggs. It was pretty good. Add a loaf of their great bread and we got lunch!

The people in town eat awfully greasy food. Fatty ham, joints and jowls. I watched an old Papasan sit down to a meal of 2 pieces of meat, 3 pieces of fat, some stringy onions smothered in Nuoc mam sauce! Still couldn't stomach that sauce.

One of the kids on the street called me "Beaucoup Kilo," which is the polite term for fatso. I thought he was crazy. I weighed myself when I got back and found out I had actually gained 13 pounds humping the paddies in this high heat and humidity. Unbelievable!

We got back to the HQ we set up in an empty building and prepared for the night. While I was gone a message had been passed along that about 100 – 300 V.C. were heading our way. We beefed up security that night, but nothing happened.

The next day 2nd platoon saw 8 V.C. crossing a paddy and took chase. One of the guys tripped a trap and screwed up his legs. While they were airmobiling him out, an Arvin called to a farmer in a field and the guy took off running. The Arvin killed the farmer with one short burst.

About two hours later the family of the farmer brought his body in to the HQ and our C.O. had to deal with a pissed-off, crying family wanting to know why he was killed. Our Arvin told them he should not have run when called. It was an unwritten rule in the country that anybody stupid enough to run from the Americans or their allies was V.C. and would be shot. Even the lowly farmer/peasant in the boonies knew that. Doesn't seem quite fair, but that was the way this war was waged.

Back in Dong Tam, our Hawaiian sergeant, Kalei bought a whole pig carcass and proceeded to bake it Hawaiian-style. He dug a pit between a couple of the barracks, filled it with wood, and burned it down until he had a good bed of coals. Then he put the carcass on the spit and slowly roasted it for about a day. He watched it, tended the coals and by the following day it was a tender pink color, the skin brown and crispy. This was suppose to be a Bravo Co. party but the fucking officers from Battalion, Brigade and other companies descended on our porker like vultures on a kill. Nevertheless, you talk about "hog heaven!" It was absolutely sweet, juicy and tender. If you could get through the REMF officers for seconds you had it made. Our Luau lasted well into the morning. Everybody went to bed that morning sated from beer, good pork, veggies and chips. It was the best! The only prayer on our lips was "please don't call us out tonight!"

I sent a letter to Ann and the twins telling them about the orphanage, and ask them to send me some toys and hard candy for the kids. Mom wrote back when I got my first shipment that the kids went crazy, robbing cereal boxes for little toys, begging Mom to buy hard candy for them and putting toys in the box they weren't playing with anymore.

When I received the first shipment, I wrangled a ride to the village on a day off and took the stuff to the kids. I took pictures of the orphans getting their meager prizes with bright eyes and toothy smiles. I sent the pictures back and mom showed them to the gang. Apparently they reveled in the pictures, feeling good about what they did. They told stories about this for a long time.

Felt good to bring a little sunshine into their lives, and it certainly didn't hurt me either. I had a bad case of cynicism about how this war was being run. We did our duty in the field, but things were looking grim. Reports of poor performance by the Arvins were coming in from all 4 Corp areas. Things were looking bad from our low-life, mud in the face level.

Speaking of sunshine, or in my case, lack of, our new C.O. was turning out to be a real pain in the ass in the field. He's always screaming at us about one thing or another, even over the radio. The last time we were in the field, we received some sniper fire and I could have sworn we took a couple rounds from our perimeter. I couldn't prove it, but I started being real careful about getting too close. I was getting a sneaky suspicion that somebody was trying to take him out of the game, and it wasn't the V.C.!

During that same op, one of our officers was attacked by a water buffalo. They didn't like Americans very much, and officers in particular. This was the second time this happened. The first time a buff attacked one of our platoon leaders, but the owner pulled the buff off before any damage could be done.

This time however, the buff was serious. Our whole company walked by and I guess he got tired of looking at us. He charged one of our officers, nailed him to the ground, dropped on his front knees and started to do serious work! The buff had his face pressed against the Lt.'s chest, flopping his head from side to side to hook him with his horns. The owner wasn't around to help so we had to kill the buffalo to save the officer (a trade at best!) The farmer showed up while we were trying to get the Lt. out from under the animal. He screamed bloody murder, cussing us out in Vietnamese and demanding compensation. Ba tried calming him down, but he wanted money right now. I knew how he felt. It would be like a farmer in the Corn Belt of the U.S. losing his only tractor. It was his livelihood. Ba took down his name and the C.O. would have to talk to Battalion. Whether he got his dough, I never found out. We were very careful around them after this incident, though. Those buffs always seemed to look at us like we owed them money. It was unsettling. A 2,000-pound buff could be on you in a heartbeat, and the light loads of an M-16 were hardly effective. We all steered clear.

The race card was being played heavy by this time. The press had its agenda and we had ours. We were reading about the race riots that were occurring because the administration seemed to be emptying the ghettos of military-age black males and sending them to the 'Nam. Black activists were complaining about the proportion of blacks to whites in combat outfits; it was too high.

Our unit never had racial problems that I was aware of. When we had down time the blacks and whites tended to congregate separately at times, but our company mixed easily. When we were in the field, color lines became invisible. Everybody pulled for the unit and his buddy.

I had noticed a lot of brothers filling the ranks of the infantry and armor units, but very few serving in the aviation units even as door-gunners or crew chiefs. Black chopper pilots were rare. Frankly, this type of problem had little effect on me. There were other more pressing things on my mind than racial balances in my unit. Everybody was just trying to get home alive.

Rumors are flying again about Delta reinforcements. Two new ships and another Battalion to cover more area down here. We haven't seen much movement this last month, the higher ups think Saigon is in for another attack and the lack of activity is a sign of a buildup.

We continued pulling Vinh Kim security and taking it easy. Our H.Q. group set up inside a courtyard, several stucco huts surrounding a central courtyard with a small pool in the middle. A ramp runs from the edge of the pool to the center, where a small cubicle about 4' square stood elevated 5' above the water. It looked like a little latrine, but the concept escaped me until I saw it in action one morning.

I was just getting back on radio watch one sultry morning in July, when I watched a little old papasan walk the ramp up to the cubicle. His body disappeared behind the short wall, his head the only thing visible. He squatted there and took a dump. The instant his shit hit the water, the surface boiled like a school of piranha on a carcass. I jumped up to get a closer look and realized there were fish in there eating the waste. They looked like catfish and they were really going at it.

This was a startling revelation for an Illinois country boy, but I realized that for a complex with no plumbing, it probably worked pretty well. The fish broke down the waste even more and allowed it to eventually float out.

O.K., so another question about this culture had been answered. I thought the story was over until I saw another old papasan approach the pool with a fishing pole. What he did next was appalling!

He tossed the line in the water with some kind of bait on the hook and caught 3 fish in short order. He took them to the back door of his hooch, chopped off their heads and took them inside. I didn't want to believe that he was eating those fish, but that's what he did. Questions shot through my head, the first being — "Christ, what does that guy's breath smell like?" I was speechless. How could they eat those fish knowing where their food sources came from! This was the ultimate in recycling and that concept hadn't even been realized in 1968. All I could do was shake my head. I told the guys about this and some of them called me a liar! I guess you had to see this one to believe it. It certainly made the C's look more appetizing!

As the dredgers increase the square footage of Dong Tam, so does the increase in arty batteries. Our barracks are pretty much surrounded by 8" self-propelled 155's, 105's, 4.2 mortars and 81's. The 8" guns fire a shell and it sounds like an express train running down the center aisle of the barracks. The Air Force also laid in an arc light strike about 5 miles south of Dong Tam and rattled us right out of our bunks. Our cots were walking around by themselves; dust fell from our rafters, and the shelves holding our personals crashed to the floor! Felt like an earthquake!

Between the arc light strikes, endless artillery fire, patrols and dredge duty we're all getting about 5 hours of sleep a day. Just about everybody has become efficient at grabbing a combat nap whenever the chance arrives. Hard to believe, but I'm actually getting used to it.

I received a letter from Madelyn House, Roxy's cousin in Springfield, Illinois. She's marrying a prominent attorney and the whole wedding sounds very much 1st class all the way. The upper crust of Springfield society will be there. I wonder how they'd like me showing up in camos. It still sounds like more fun than I'm having here!

We're hearing from the locals that the V.C. are spreading propaganda about Bobby Kennedy's assassination. They claim their fighting spirit has climbed since Kennedy was killed because the U.S. is deteriorating internally as well as politically. Considering the news we're getting from home it's hard to argue with that. I wish I could say it was bullshit, but I can't. There's a pipeline running from M.A.C.V. to Washington that's spewing more crap about this war than even I can believe.

Right now we're enjoying a bit of relaxation, since the higher ups cut back on patrolling. Things are pretty good in Dong Tam now. We have a swimming pool, had another pig roast, cold drinks every day, movies every night, and live shows regularly. We're living the life of Riley and nobody wants to go back to the ships.

I got a letter today from our high school history teacher, John Dudley. He's in the Air Force, based in Thailand and looked like one of Terry's Pirates. (He was one of the guys counting the number of elephants being killed on Uncle Ho's Trail.) Never thought I'd see the day he'd be wearing a military uniform because he always gave me a hard time about my interest in the military.

We've been getting a lot of instruction on foot care now, especially the grunts. Immersion foot, ringworm, and all other manner of crud that attack the skin have to be dealt with quickly. We put ointment on our skin and walk around in flip-flop sandals and shorts to get as much air and sunshine on our legs as we can. Apparently skin problems are so bad it's keeping the grunt units from putting a force in the field that is up to full-strength.

I ran into Greg Ruffin today, one of my basic and AIT buds. He was with the 4/47th. He was a handsome Indian kid — jump school, 22 weeks at N.C.O. School and up for E-6. While he was in school one of the admin pukes found a knife in his desk and they busted him to E-2. Typical Army bullshit. They waste all this training over an infraction like this by busting him down to a skeeter wing. Apparently the U.S. admin guys don't realize how short we are of good N.C.O.'s! I hope they never find out we carry knives in the field, we could all be reprimanded, busted, and sent home early!

Our four companies were pulling the notorious Dong Tam Shuffle. One company guards berm, one guards the dredge, one on ready-reaction, and one on northern A.O. around Vinh Kim.

The paddies around Vinh Kim really reek. They smell like they've been fertilized with human shit for centuries. Trying to keep clean in this environment is impossible. A lot of us keep soap handy in case of a rainstorm. It provides us with clean water for bathing in the field. It's quite a picture watching a bunch of naked-ass grunts showering in a rice paddy. A couple guys told me they used to have trouble pissing in a public restroom. But now, thanks to Army training, they can strip down, let their johnson's swing in the wind while they run naked in the paddies showering! Gotta love it! Wait till the folks back home get a load of us!

We're back to patrolling again, 4 days on one of the four Dong Tam duty stations, then change over. The Vinh Kim A.O. is full of booby traps and to make it more of a challenge, for us, the powers that be have us patrolling at night. Echo tripped a couple traps recently. One 8" shell in an open paddy hurt 3; another 60-mm mortar round shredded another trooper's legs. Our Choi Hois said they know who's laying some of the traps. They claim it's an old Mamasan and her kids. We let our Kit Carson Scout take care of this problem. I didn't ask how.

A couple nights ago a REMF threw a mini-smoke grenade into one end of the barracks. The hissing noise caused a major panic and I found myself in the middle of a twelve-man stampede heading for the other end of the barracks. Most of these guys were short-timers with 20 days or less to go. They all hit the door at once and actually got through together, or so it seemed. The culprit never got caught, but everybody was highly pissed.

The next night, a drunk ran through our barracks yelling "mortar attack!" Everybody headed for the bunker, half asleep, disoriented, dinging their shins on footlockers and stubbing their toes on cot legs and field gear. It was a false alarm and we never caught this guy either. Everybody vowed if we caught a dickhead doing this again, he'd wish his mom never met his dad. This kind of crap is not funny to grunts. As if we don't have enough stress.

By early August, we were scheduled to head back to the ships, so we had to pack our gear and get ready to roll. The night before, we had spent the night in a village called Sin Kim. We camped out in a hooch with a family of 12 people, 2 adults and 10 kids ranging from 11 months to 10 years old. Their house had shrapnel holes in the walls and roof; it looked like a shrapnel magnet. The little girls didn't quite trust the big guys with weapons.

Papasan fired up a grill behind the hooch and we had a 1st class B-B-Q. Other neighbors came by and it looked like a block party. Everybody chipped in on food so we had a real variety. Squid, lobster, bread and lots of rice wine. The rice wine tasted like lighter fluid — I suspected it was homemade hooch. It did mellow everybody out though. Reminded me of my first taste of Ouzo. After dessert of bananas, tangerines and sweetened coconut, we retired wishing we could come back tomorrow, but the Navy was expecting us back on the ships.

I got notice once we were aboard ship that my R & R to Australia had been approved and I better get ready to go in 2 days. Were they kidding, I was ready in 10 minutes. Two days later I'm on a jet heading south to the "Land Down Under!" The guys on the plane were pretty rowdy and noisy, but I slept like I had been drugged.

Australia was a great place. I loved the people and they loved having us...GIs had a habit of spending lots of cash when on R & R, and the Aussie's were happy to accommodate us. I got to my hotel, put on some civvies and hit the hotel restaurant for some good food. I ate till I thought I would bust. Lamb kabobs, potatoes, fresh veggies, a salad and real whole milk that tasted like cream. Dessert was a heady combo of pastries, ice cream and liquors. I decided as I tried to haul my stomach back to the room that I can't do this every night or they'd have to get a chopper just for me on insertions. But oh was it grand!

I spent a couple days at the Coogee beach, hitting Kings Cross at night. That's where the action was, lots of bars and women everywhere. Since drinking was not my favorite pastime and the girls were off-limits (was I noble or stupid? The court's still out on that one.) I decided to see more of the country. I jumped a twin-engine passenger plane and went into the interior, spent some time on a sheep ranch (don't even think about it!) and enjoyed the ranch owner's hospitality immensely. They were the McDonald's and could she cook. Everybody that owns a ranch out the boonies has to be pretty self-sufficient so these two knew how to do about everything.

Mr. McDonald showed us how his sheepdogs work a herd with him guiding the dogs with whistles and hand signals. Those dogs were just amazing. The dogs looked like working sheep was about the greatest thing they could be doing. They were so intense and focused. I had a great time.

Two days later I was back in Sydney wondering where the time went. I thought R & R's should have been about 30 days long, not a week. A couple more nights of living high and I was back on a plane and the land of the N.V.A.

I was welcomed back to the ship after a three-aircraft flight back to Dong Tam. The ships were ready to move out for their next op and they had waited for me to come back! Are the Navy guys' true friends or what?

## MURPHY'S LAW OF COMBAT
### #19
"Make it too tough for the enemy to get in, and you can't get out."

We headed out at 0 dark hundred for another nondescript area to sweep. We hit the beach just at sun up and the temp was already over 100 and no wind blowing. We found a lot of bunkers, but no one was home except for one V.C. we trapped in a bunker. Two frags were tossed in but he survived both blasts. He was taken out with an M-16. His job was probably to set booby traps while we moved forward. We must have caught him napping.

## MURPHY'S LAW OF COMBAT
### #28
"Never share a foxhole with anyone braver than you."

We reached our objective about late afternoon, and it turned out to be an abandoned outpost. One building and three strands of concertina wire around. A canal secured the rear of the building. We got word that re-supply wasn't coming in that night, so we had to secure our perimeter with what we had, which wasn't enough. I like to have lots of claymores around cause the V.C. don't like them.

## MURPHY'S LAW OF COMBAT
### #8

## Charlie Palek

"When you have secured an area, don't forget to tell the enemy."

Everybody seemed jumpy that night. Our platoon kept seeing things in the dark, but they maintained fire discipline unless they knew for sure. One of our 60 guys saw a V.C. materialize from a grove of trees. He put the starlight scope on him and watched him creep through 2 strands of wire. The trooper popped up, yelled "halt," then proceeded to shoot the guy. Why he yelled "halt" no one knew. He only wounded him and the V.C. laid out there for an hour moaning. Listening to him was freaky and finally one of our M-79 guys got permission to put the V.C. out of his misery. It only took one round. The rest of the night was peaceful but very little sleep was had by all.

The next day our Red point walked into a hooch and surprised 4 V.C. eating at a table. They shot one but they all got away. Seems both sides got caught flat-footed. The V.C. scrambling to get out of the hooch must have been comical. They apparently jumped out of the windows and one went right through the wall! Motivated!

Later in the morning we walked through a cluster of hooches and were told to search all of them. I kicked open the flimsy door of a hooch and stared straight into the eyes of a Papasan screwing his wife. He was on top and when I busted in he looked up, smiled, nodded his head, and never missed a stroke! I made a quick sweep of the interior and backed out, Papasan still going for it. I had to admire his concentration. If somebody had crashed into my house holding an automatic weapon in the middle of a love session I don't think I could have been that cool! The platoon laughed about this one for weeks and I got all kinds of crap from small-minded troopers for not inviting them in for a look.

We were all issued flak jackets when we first got in-country, and the rule was we had to wear them in the field. They weigh about 12 pounds and they literally sucked the moisture right out of your body. They will protect you from small shrapnel, but not bullets unless you're really lucky. Carrying 60 – 70 pounds of gear is plenty. Add a 12-pound flak jacket and it makes things worse. We all cheered when the word came down it was our choice whether to wear one or not. We usually carried 2 canteens of water and on really hot days, they may last for a half-a-day — add the jacket and it's even a shorter time. About the only time anybody wore them was if they were short or on berm watch.

I trudged out into the jungle this morning to take my daily constitutional. I walked along a nondescript trail, stepped off the path about 6 feet and squatted in the bushes. I was enjoying the cool morning air, looking around nonchalantly when a Mamasan came short stepping down the trail. I was in an awkward position with no place to go, so I gave her a wave, and a smile and she did the same; covering her mouth with her hand and giggling as she went by. How quickly we lose our inhibitions over here! I had to laugh — just a passing moment, but something that my parents wouldn't believe, if I ever told them about it. Too weird!

We trudged back to the ships again and settled in. We all got our shots updated; some guys got 4 or 5 of them. The male nurses loved punching your arm. I thought they needed to spend some time in the boonies with us, they were starved for violence.

I had a stack of letters waiting for me, plus a couple from 2 of my grade school teachers, Mrs. Frank and Mrs. Prusz. A couple of the guys claimed I must have been a 1st class suck-up to get letters from my grade school teachers. I told them it was the only way I could pass my math classes!

A day of rest then back on the Tangos for an A.O. just down the river from where we were a couple days ago. It was about a three-hour float and as usual, I leveled my ass on the deck of the Tango boat and went to sleep. About 2 hours into the trip we received some sporadic fire from the shore and the boats turned in while the Monitors did their things; putting out a firestorm to cover our landing. Everybody was up, locked & loaded and ready to rumble except me. During my slumber, my feet had tilted to the left following the cant of the deck towards the stern. Apparently it had also twisted my legs at the knees and cut the blood flow to my lower legs, because I could not stand up. The Tango nosed in, dropped the ramp and the guys ran past me, feet ringing off the deck and gunfire on the shore. Fortunately, I had been sleeping with my radio on, so I was ready to roll I just couldn't stand up. My legs were without any feeling at all, and while I sprawled out on the deck trying to pound them back to life, my C.O. was screaming for the radio. He was standing on shore trying to find his RTO, who was back on the Tango trying to join the living.

I sat on the deck, massaging my legs until they started tingling. I knew the feeling was coming back, but couldn't do anything but drag my legs behind me as I crawled to the ramp. I'm sure I was a pathetic sight, crawling up to the ramp and trying to get on shore. My 6 was yelling for his Oscar and I couldn't do a thing but keep going.

I finally thumped off the ramp onto shore and my 6 came running up wondering what had happened. I think he thought I was hit. I felt like an idiot — everybody was doing their job and I was flopping around like a bluegill out of water. My 6 was running around like a madman, screaming for a radio, any radio while I was actually trying to stand. It took about five more minutes before I could walk again — 5 long minutes.

We eventually started our sweep and found out our V.C. shooter had left the area. We loaded back up and headed for our original A.O., about an hour away. I stayed on my feet for this trip.

We hit the beach, or mudflat, about an hour later and started our sweep. We were walking through a line of banana groves and paddies. Trying to keep everyone on line was tough; the banana grove tended to slow our advance up more than the paddies.

Two hours into the sweep, our Green platoon providing rear security, noticed a guy shadowing our rear. The green platoon would stop and our shadow would duck behind cover. His behavior was highly suspect. Green Oscar called in and asked permission to zap the guy. Bravo 6 gave them the go ahead and they made a plan.

## MURPHY'S LAW OF COMBAT
### #2
### "Recoilless rifles — aren't."

The whole platoon stopped for a short time giving the recoilless rifle team time to find a good camouflaged position. The shadow was observed hiding behind a coconut tree, waiting for the platoon to move out. The rifle team hunkered down in some thick vegetation and watched the rest of the platoon leave. It didn't take long and the shadow came bopping down the trail, walking like a stalker, low, deliberate steps. He stepped behind a cluster of bushes and dropped to his knees to check out the Green's movement. He was about 40 yards away from the rifle position when his head came up and they let him have it.

The bush he was hiding behind suddenly had no leaves as his head disappeared behind the twigs. We heard the shot and halted until we heard from the green platoon.

## Tattletale

The rifle team went back and found the shadow's body stretched out like a board about twenty feet from the bushes. He had flechettes from the beehive round from his ankles to his head. They apparently hit him dead center at the chest. Those beehive rounds were instant death, especially if all there is to hide behind is a bush. The body was searched, no weapons, papers or I.D. was found. The body was left where it fell. No dignity, no last words.

We continued our sweep, finding nothing or nobody until late afternoon, when a couple of light machine guns in a tree line in front of us started hammering away at us. My 6 and me were hunkered down behind a dike — him screaming like a chainsaw at the men on his left flank. He still was acting like a goddamned idiot when the bullets started to fly. Maybe it was his personal command style, but it was wearing heavy on our nerves. If this is what they were teaching these officers at Ranger School we could be in real trouble!

We were lying down behind the dike, listening to the round's crack over our heads like a crackling fire when we received a couple from our rear. They were damned close and my suspicions about our own guys trying to get him out of the field were pretty much confirmed. Somebody back there, maybe one of my own friends, was fixin' to take our 6 out, one way or the other. I was not in a comfortable position. I could end up with a hole in my radio, or one in my head if this shit kept up. I was going to have to report this to somebody.

The V.C. machine gun teams di-died after about 30 minutes and just minutes before some Charlie model gunships arrived to help us out. The choppers couldn't find 'em; they disappeared like a mist.

We stopped to set up camp in early evening, put out our guard dogs and had a quiet night. While on radio watch I noticed the twigs under the trees on the forest floor were glowing green like a fluorescent light. It was a spectacular sight. I had never seen anything like it. I picked up a handful, put them in plastic and sent them to Donna. Unfortunately, by the time they got to the States, they weren't glowing anymore. My sister must have thought I was daffy as a duck for sending her dead twigs.

The next day we swept back to the river, then hopped a Tango back to the ships for a rest. We heard during our bullshit session that night that one of Dong Tam's dredges was damaged by explosives. When it first happened, the H.Q. pukes tightened security on the dredges and freaked

## Charlie Palek

out about the possibility of another attack by V.C. frogmen. That was the official explanation for awhile. Then the real news broke.

Apparently the Navy had been dumping old, live ammo into the middle of the Mekong, where they thought it would lie undisturbed. It was another miscalculation by the U.S.N. The dredge sucked up a 4.2 mortar round and it exploded in the pipe system of the dredge. No V.C. swimmers, just another mistake by our own worst enemy — us. What a bringdown!

After we got back from our last sweep I talked to our company's top Sergeant about our C.O. He didn't seem surprised when I told him what was going on. I got the feeling I wasn't the first to discuss this problem with him. I hoped being his RTO threw a little more weight behind the observations.

It took a couple of weeks, but our Banshee captain was taken out of the field. Happy Days!

Sgt. Kalei had gotten a few newbies together and started one of his notorious poker games. He was famous for taking money from the E.M.'s. He'd regale them with war stories and intimidate them with his gruffness until they couldn't concentrate anymore. Experience will be their best teacher, just like the perils in the field.

The sarge was an E-7 and apparently had lost a few stripes over his Army career for one thing or another. He told Green 5 one day on the radio to "Kilo-Mike-Alpha," a way of saying, "Kiss My Ass!" It would be great to be able to say stuff like that; but I have no desire to go to jail. He is quite a character, and absolutely reliable in the field. He's been around!

I got a letter from Walker in Korea. It had taken almost four months to get to me, but it made it. He probably wasn't even in Korea by now. He said his brother was in Guam on the flight line one day when an SR-71 landed to refuel. I knew this was our top-secret, super-spy aircraft but that was it. Apparently it landed, was immediately surrounded by security and refueled like an Indy pit crew was handling the job. They juiced it up, and watched the engines wind up and head for the runway. It sat there for a final check, rolled down the runway and literally disappeared once the wheels were up. The pilots on the ground were in shock. It disappeared so fast nobody could believe it. The ultimate fast-mover! Wish I could have seen that.

I also got some pictures of the twins today. Sher is a real cutie — she put a beach towel down in the living room and laid on it to get a tan! Ter was standing there, arms crossed and a cocky grin on his face. Looks like trouble and he's only 4 years old!

We're supposed to be getting a new radio, 9 pounds lighter than the PRC-25 I'm carrying now. It will have better range also. It was exciting news for me; maybe I wouldn't have to carry a radio with an 8' antenna anymore. Walking with that long of an antenna in low brush was a pain. I knocked ants out of the trees on the guys behind me, and it points me out as a H.Q. R.T.O. as good as a neon light above my head. Naturally, the H.Q. group will get them first! Things are looking up!

We also got a look at the new Forward Air Controller aircraft that is replacing the old Piper 0-1 Bird Dog. The 0-1 has been doing a grand job of controlling areas the jets and artillery pound to dust. It finds targets, and directs the support right to the area. The problem was it was slow, unarmed, unarmored, with only a couple of rocket launchers to mark targets.

The 0-2 is new, fast, and armed so it can not only mark targets for the "fast movers," but it can pin the enemy down with it's own ordnance until the big boys arrive.

We're also getting some new modifications for the M-16's. The flash suppressor on the new ones has a ring on the outside to keep the barrel from grabbing brush and vines. They also have stronger buffer springs to slam the bolt home faster and harder. Some of them also have chrome bolts that don't foul so fast. We have been seeing one of these once in a while, but they weren't plentiful in our unit. A couple of the guys came back from My Tho the other day and noticed all the Arvins were carrying the new ones. That really got everybody's dander up. We felt that since we were doing the bulk of the fighting, we should be getting the new 16's. We were all pretty cynical about the fact that all the V.C. had to do was take a couple of shots at Marvin the Arvin so they would drop their weapons and run. Essentially, that meant the V.C. were becoming equipped with the new 16's before we were! It was a revolting development.

The South Koreans in Vietnam were mostly equipped with M-1 Garands and carbines, but it certainly didn't slow them down. These old weapons were used in WWII and Korea and served them and us well. Besides, the Koreans liked to close in close and do the hand-to-hand combat thing. Their soldiers are trained extensively in hand-to-hand techniques, and they like to put it to use. Needless to say, the V.C. usually try to avoid these guys.

## Charlie Palek

It was September 15. I was taken out of the field for a couple days to help with Battalion H.Q. I helped make the RTO maps, stood a radio watch and had the rest of the day to myself. I read, wrote some letters, grabbed some rays on the upper deck and just made lazy. It was a great way to end my tour but I didn't like being here. I missed the field, being in the action. I didn't like all the little admin pricks walking around measuring you up to see if your boots were shined, duds were clean and looking strack like a REMF trooper. These assholes just lived for something to bitch about and they loved sticking it to the grunts in particular.

I heard from the Battalion H.Q. RTO's that they were looking at Ben Tre, an area east of the Crossroads, as another Delta base camp. It was supposed to be filled with the hundreds of fresh, phantom troops who should be filling up a couple of phantom barracks ships that we were supposed to get. According to them, the province Ben Tre was in the last V.C. controlled province in the Delta, a statement I found extremely optimistic. Hadn't they heard of the Rung Sat or the U Minh forest? and a new 9th Division base was to be established there to clean the V.C. up and kick them out.

The next day Bravo went out without me and landed in a hot LZ right off the bat. While the Bravo troopers were trying to pry their puckered assholes off the chopper decks, their fire support base was being mortared and fending off a small ground attack! What was that again about the Delta being under our control?

I got another letter from Lt. Dudley. Seems his base commander was concerned about the base security, so he got together with the Army and they got 100 Green Berets to try and infiltrate the base. The good news was the Army was very cooperative. The bad news was that 90 of the 100 Green Beenies got into the base undetected, in one night! Dudley laughed about it and said the security forces are being beefed up and retrained within an inch of their lives.

Since I've got less than 90 days in-country, I'm trying to extend into the door gunner job. Dad would rather see me go to Germany, and Mom just wants me somewhere safe. But I want to be a chopper crewman. Door gunners are in short supply so it could happen.

We are reading a lot about the Nixon-Humphrey debates, but I see more "Alfred E. Newman For President" bumper stickers here than anything else. I'd vote for him!

I joined the company again the next day after they got back from their joy ride. They took light casualties and really lucked out.

The word came down a couple days later while we were resting and refitting that a new security tactic was going to be employed called Bushmaster Patrols. The idea was to insert troopers onto shore at last light with Tango boats, and have them set up ambush sights for the V.C. hoping to pop one of the ships with a B-40 rocket. I didn't think too much of the program. I didn't feel like we were really trained for this kind of op. The Seals were doing stuff like this, why weren't they called in? I wasn't in on the planning of this, but I had a bad feeling about it. But nobody asks an E-4's opinion, so the plan went forward.

The first night it was tried out, the Tango boat came in late and the 11-man patrol tried to disembark in the dark. The boat couldn't drop its ramp completely either due to the brush that grew right up to the bank. A few of the guys managed to get off the tango by climbing up and over the ramp, but several of the men fell into the water trying to get off. The boat skipper tried pulling back, realizing this was not the place to land. He was fighting the river current, as were the men in the water. The sides of the Tango were too high to reach from the water and the crew couldn't see the guys overboard. All in all, it was a real clusterfuck. The end result was that 6 of the 11 men on the patrol drowned.

The next day was very solemn. The higher-uppers were appalled at the losses and were looking for someone to blame. We spent the day plying up and down the river looking for the bodies of the 6 troopers. We checked the banks as well as the middle of the river. About 5 Monitors took part in the search and our boat was the only one who found a body. We pulled the black trooper out of the water and he felt like he weighed 400 pounds. His body was bloated, his skin purple, and his eyes milky. It was no way for an infantryman to die. An investigation ensued and I'm sure they found fault with somebody. If Army protocol followed it's usual path I'm sure nobody on the planning staff suffered.

It was the last Bushmaster Patrol we did. By the first of October, several companies left the ships and proceeded to a new land base for the 2nd Brigade called Tiger Lair. It was an engineering masterpiece that was marveled by all who lived there. The engineers, in their infinite wisdom, scooped a large crater out of a rice paddy and used the dirt to build a defensive berm around the camp. Unfortunately, being in the Delta, the hole immediately filled with water! When our company arrived, we found our tents with a foot of water on the floor, cots and supplies floating out of the tents into the grounds. There was a half-assed wooden walkway around the tents so you didn't have to walk knee-deep in the water, but sometimes the walkway was under water and nighttime trips to the latrine could be a wet walk. The conditions were shocking to us. There were no bunkers to hide in, no overhead cover; we were living on a terrarium.

The thing that really scared me was the skim of gasoline floating on the water over the entire camp! The smell was constantly in the air and I thought one flicked cigarette or mortar round and this whole wet mess would light up like a Roman candle. The whole concept was so incredibly stupid — even for the Army.

We tried to set up house as best we could. While some of the other companies set up around the berm, the H.Q. group chose a tent and moved in. We found some wood panels from ammo and shipping crates and made a floor above the water level. While we were working on our tent our Battalion C.O. came along to see our progress, stepped off the walkway, and disappeared under the water, his hat the only thing marking his presence. He came up spitting and splashing around, choking on the foul water. A couple guys helped him back onto the walkway, and he walked off trying to look dignified, in his clingy, limp, fatigues and muddy boots. I watched it all happen and all I could think of at the time was "maybe there is a God!" Morale skyrocketed when I told the guys what I saw. Just desserts! He put us here and nobody felt any sorrow for his accident. He wasn't going to be staying here, we were. And it wasn't going to be pretty.

The sandman punched us all in the face the first night we were at Tiger's Lair. We had worked our asses off trying to keep our heads above water in our tent and we were ready to hit the sack. There were no lights in our tent except flashlights, so nobody was interested in staying up. Four of the guys were on cots; the rest of us were on the floor, distributed around the tent, eight in all. Battalion H.Q. had way too many men packed into this shit hole, and I'll bet that if you saw it from the air we looked like a giant target sitting in the paddy. There were V.C. mortar crews all over the province rubbing their hands together, and breaking the mortar ammo out of their cases.

Right after midnight, the V.C. did their thing. I didn't hear any explosions before the mortar round dropped into our tent, but I think we took one of the first rounds. The 60mm mortar round tore through the tent roof and exploded right next to our company safe. The explosion was like the world was ending. It had landed about 5' from my head, but most of the shrapnel went over me since I was on the floor. My head was ringing like the bells of Notre Dame, and I couldn't hear shit. I got on my feet and swayed around like a punch-drunk fighter. We could hear more rounds exploding in the camp, men were screaming and yelling.

Our Top Sergeant had been sleeping next to the safe and he was really hurt bad. He was a skinny little guy anyway, but when we picked him up, he felt like a loose bag of bones. One of his legs was cocked at an odd angle, broken in several places. He kept asking if his balls were still intact, but nobody told him how badly his lower body had been shredded. While the guys tried to get Top comfortable, I went to the cot of Callahan and shined my light in his face. He was already dead, but he looked like his death was non-violent. Hardly been ruffled, still lying in his cot with a peaceful look on his face.

My head was pounding like a tom-tom and I started to get dizzy. I waddled over to Toomes' cot to see how he was. Toomes had the strange habit of sleeping with his eyes wide open. The first time I saw this phenom I couldn't believe it. He was snoring like a bear and his eyes were completely open! I wouldn't have believed it if I hadn't seen it myself. It was spooky.

He was lying on his cot; eyes wide open and dead like Callahan. No visible wounds, nor any signs of any violence. Peaceful in slumber is how he looked.

The guys who could walk started checking each other over. I had blood running down my face, but the dizziness still gripped me. Top had both legs broken and his testicles were gone, his crotch and stomach cut to ribbons. He was unconscious at the moment. Blair was the only one unscathed. Larrette had several small shrapnel wounds in his body (this was his 5th Purple Heart for Christ's sake!) The situation was desperate, but everything seemed to be going in slow motion. My head was swimming and standing up was getting tough for me.

A couple of the guys put Top on a cot and headed for the chopper pad. Everybody hoped that dustoffs had been called. The rounds were still dropping in and causing confusion. Me and one of the others, I don't know who, leaned together and limped and staggered to the chopper pad. I was having a dazzling fireworks display in my eyes, and my left ear started leaking fluid.

*Charlie Palek*

    We got to the pad in time to see the first dustoff come in. There already was a pile of wounded ready to go out and they were stacked into the chopper as quickly as they could. I sat down on an ammo case and tried to realign the gyro in my head. It felt like my eyes were spinning twice as fast as my head. I'd never felt so disoriented. The last thing I remember was starting to fall backwards among the ammo crates.

    I woke up the next morning on the *Colleton,* clean sheets on my bunk and a male nurse tending my head. He greeted me with a big grin and I told him I felt like shit. I had a headache bigger than all outdoors, but my head wasn't spinning. The nurse told me a doctor had examined me while I was out and they found my left eardrum had been blown open and I had small shrapnel wounds in my face. Otherwise I was O.K.

    The medics had a full house from Tiger's Lair, some slightly wounded and some real bad. I tried sitting up and I felt like my head would explode all over the infirmary. The dizziness had passed, as had the fireworks in my eyes, but Lordy, did my head hurt. I sat on the edge of the bunk; the smells of the infirmary washing over me like a wave. I asked the medic for something to kill my headache before it killed me. I took the pills, stood up, and hung on to the bunk. I felt really weak, but it felt good to be up.

    I took a shaky spin around the bunks, trying to stay out of the way of the medics. I found one of our platoon guys that had been hit in the back and the ass by another round in his tent. He had quarter-sized holes in his body, and was so drugged up I didn't try talking to him.

    The medics kept me on board for four days, then cut me loose. It took two days to get rid of the headache. I got what little gear I had together, got some new clothes, and hitched a chopper ride back to Tiger's Lair. The chopper arrived over the camp and circled while another chopper on the pad lifted off. I got a good look at the camp and it looked like a military ghetto. Charred wood and burned down tents scarred the inside of the hole. It was pathetic looking. Whoever brainstormed this piece of work had to have a two digit I.Q.

    I hopped out of the Huey and looked for Bravo's H.Q. I found them outside the hole in a hastily built bunker line in the tree line. The guys welcomed me back and I sat down and got the poop on what happened after I was lifted out.

    Top had died of his wounds. This had been his 6th Purple Heart, four in Korea and two here. The camp was about 250-300 yards square and had

400-450 men in it with little overhead cover. If the V.C. would have pressed a ground attack they could have taken the place!

The V.C. dropped 17 rounds into the camp, wounding 66 men and killing three, all from our tent. It was lucky for everybody that they were 60mm mortars and nothing bigger. I'd probably be dead if it had been a large tube. Bravo built a bunker the day after the attack, big enough to hold 40-50 guys. The boys said it went up super-fast. Nobody wanted another night like that one. The rounds also hit a fuel truck and an ambulance, adding more gas to the water. Why that didn't ignite, I don't know.

The round that hit our tent had landed next to the company safe and blew it open, destroying the records and money inside. We figured the reason Top got hit so badly was because his feet were pointing at the safe about three feet away. The safe tamped the explosion and threw the shrapnel right between his legs. Sleeping on the floor got me off easy.

The rumors were flying that the whole camp would be abandoned, but that would never happen because that would make the Battalion C.O. lose face and we couldn't have that. We'd stay here until the V.C. were cleaned out or we were all dead.

I tracked down my duffel bag. It was with the other wounded, under a half-ass roof, piled up in the mud. It was wet, the stuff inside was wet, and it was full of shrapnel holes. I sat down and dug out my personals. My toothbrush was broke in two by a piece of shrapnel that was still my ditty bag. The 126 camera had a shrapnel hole right through the back. The bag looked like a sieve, tiny holes in most of my clothes. Oh well, lets start fresh.

Our screaming C.O. had been replaced, but it didn't matter much to me. My job now was to stay in camp and monitor the radios. Four hour watches, then I'd be free to pursue the many activities awaiting us in the middle of a rice paddy; eating coconuts, putting medicine on our rotting skin, or maybe a quiet morning stroll past the perimeter claymores.

We lived in the field for the next month, strengthening our positions and sending out patrols. I missed the field but also felt I could use the rest. Three Purple Hearts and less than two months to go, then homeward bound. Being short was a good thing!

Life became pretty boring in camp, but things were popping around it. Our sweeps were running into small ambushes, snipers and plenty of booby traps.

Lt. Tomsic was leading White platoon on a sweep when a command detonated 4.2 round was triggered in a tree above the platoon. It killed and wounded several guys. Bai, the Kit Carson scout, traced the wire and found the V.C. still in his spider hole. He grabbed the guy by the scruff of the neck and hauled his ass back to White 6. Before Tomsic could do anything Bai drew his .45, put it to the V.C.'s head, and blew him away. Everybody was shocked for an instant. They were happier about Bai being with them. He was truly a jewel. He had no fear of retribution for an act like that, and frankly, nobody minded he did it. Payback is a bitch!

I managed to get out of the crud for three days with a couple guys and hit Saigon for awhile. We got us a cheap room downtown and vegged out. The first thing they did was look for some sex, I on the other hand spent two days walking around Tu Do street, sampling the food, talking and marveling at the madhouse that is Saigon. The traffic was absolutely the most chaotic I've ever seen. It seemed like there was a potential accident out there every 10 seconds, pedestrian or vehicular. There seemed to be no rules of the road, everybody weaving and yelling, honking their horns and gesturing wildly. All this was happening while pedestrians were weaving in and out of the street. Motorcycles were whizzing around a 2 ½ ton truck while it avoided a bus driving down the middle of the road to avoid a moped with about a dozen people stacked on it.

The White Mice, the Vietnamese police, were trying to keep things under control, to no avail. They might as well have been home sleeping. Hookers were everywhere, but they tended to stay inside during the day. I moved from bar to restaurant to bar for two days, soaking up the city. The hookers were always on the lookout for GIs sitting around indoors drinking or eating. Being alone was a dinner bell to these gals. I was asked every half-hour if I wanted to buy them a Saigon Tea, which was watered down whiskey at 5 times the normal price. I had to admit that some of them were beautiful, and it was hard resisting, but that mid-western upbringing kept getting in the way. I bought a couple of teas and spent some time talking, but they were all business, and when they found out I wasn't going to pay, they lost interest fast.

The second night I was there I introduced myself to a table of Australian infantrymen and told them I spent some time in their wonderful country on R&R. They thanked me and invited me to sit. I bought the first round and we regaled each other about our heroic exploits fighting the commies. These guys were already 3 sheets into the wind, but they continued to drink well into late afternoon. I was doing my sipping whiskey thing; trying to keep from drinking too much because I didn't want to get drunk and I did not enjoy hangovers. But these guys could drink like fish and I was way behind by sunset, a half dozen shots of whiskey sitting in front of me. I wasn't interested in trying to out-drink these guys; I was an amateur in their presence. They good-naturedly made jokes about my pussy drinking habits, but I let them fly right over me. I told them I was enjoying their company too much to pass out on them and I didn't want to be rude. They laughed and accepted my lame excuse. I had to get back to the hotel, but we had a great time and I was further convinced the Australians were some of the best folks in the world.

The food I tried those two days was a heady combo of a kind of onion-wonton soup, frog egg soup, a kind of chow mein with hard noodles, sweetened coconut, water buffalo steak, and God knows what else. I avoided the fish and Nuoc mam sauce, but things were very spicy to very hot. Dog was a big menu item and I tried hard to make sure I didn't eat puppy soup while I was out and about. I always had their excellent bread, tried rice wine, Vietnamese whiskey and 33 Beer. By the time I got back to Dong Tam, I felt I had done my duty as far as investigating the culture of Vietnam. The vendors were all friendly and eager to please and take your money. There was always someone around that could interpret, so it was fun to talk to the folks behind the counter. That and my country-humping fact-finding tour led me to believe these folks were basically hard working people just trying to live their lives without government interference. Made sense to me. I wished them luck.

The rest of my tour became antsy nights and days anticipating going home. The door gunner job never panned out, although the paperwork was put through. Lost in the shuffle probably. I stood some extra watches for guys that had to go into the field for a couple days, set up maps and helped train new RTO's.

All this extra time allowed for plenty of reflection time. I had asked to come here and perform the duties of an infantryman. That I had done. There were good times and a big share of bad ones, but I wouldn't have traded the experiences for anything. Despite the rioting in the States over this war, I felt the people over here had done their work and done it well. Policy for this war was originating from Washington, which typically knows very little about jungle warfare. Four star generals giving lawyers the low down on how the war was going. One's concerned about finishing retirement with a good record and a pension; the other worried about re-election. There was little confusion in my head why things were going the way they were. I just kept asking why?

Cambodia was a neutral country but the Ho Chi Mihn trail ran right through it. Supplies were also being shipped into the West Coast of Nam via Cambodia. The N.V.A. could find sanctuary there but our forces couldn't cross the border in pursuit.

It was a no-brainer that most of the supplies being used by the enemy was coming in at Haiphong Harbor. Since this was an undeclared war, dead bodies piling up on both sides not withstanding, why the U.S. chose to ignore this fact was a real source of discussion for us. It was bad policy as far as we were concerned.

The rules were don't fire unless you're fired upon; the Arvins are our Allies; don't cross the border or bomb "suspected" truck parks instead of Haiphong Harbor. When we accidentally kill civilians, it's murder, when the V.C. does it intentionally, it's guerrilla warfare. We're all baby killers and the dregs of society. There were too goddamned many rules. We discussed how good it would be back home but what if we weren't received well at the airport or bus terminal. This topic caused a lot of tough talk, but the truth was nobody knew how he would react.

I was still thinking I could pull another tour over here if I could get the door gunner's job. I figured I'd get to my next duty station and see how it went.

I received my E-5 stripes about a month before I left. It was a very proper ceremony. Our company clerk yelled at me one morning that I had been promoted to buck sergeant. He pulled a set of stripes out of his pocket and tossed them to me, one of which landed in the mud. On his way down the road, he congratulated me and said the paperwork was in my file already.

I was hoping to go back home as an E-5, so it was a happy day. I took some shit from the guys about being a potential lifer, the draftees being particularly brutal, but I let it all wash over me with a smile. They were just jealous I was so short.

My DEROS date finally came and I got a 3-day drop! It was like an extra three days of life. Three days before I was due to leave, I caught a Huey to Dong Tam, got my orders and spent the night, scheduled to fly out on a C-123 the next day.

# Tattletale

Dong Tam had changed a lot since I had last been here. The M.P.'s were being pains about bloused trousers in shined boots, head cover, no weapons in some areas; it was getting way too GI for me. I was glad I was leaving.

I went to the NCO club, had two beers (one more than usual), went back to the barracks and crashed early.

In-country flights being what they were, I arrived at the airport at least an hour ahead of time. The C-123 arrived on time and left on time, a good sign. The plane vibrated into the air and we headed for Long Binh. There were a couple of Green Berets on board, one looked like he had been in-country a while by his rough boots and washed-out fatigues. The other was new and about 50 pounds overweight. He couldn't have run an 8-minute mile if his life depended on it! I guess the replacement standards had dropped a little since all those A-Team bases had been hit or over-run. The veteran laughed and told the new guy this was the first time he had landed in an airplane, being a paratrooper and all. He looked my way and grinned. I grinned back and noticed he didn't have a Combat Infantry Badge on his uniform. "Christ," I thought, "this guy's in Special Forces and doesn't have a C.I.B.? Could the Special Forces have REMF's too? What a bring down job that would be."

Long Binh was the last stop before leaving the country. It was a tent city with new guys and short timers all waiting around for final orders or transport to their new unit. A lot of division patches were represented here, and the tents with the new guys differed greatly from the guys going home. I was in the reverse situation as I remembered when I first arrived. The guys in my tent had that 1,000-yard stare, cigarettes dangling from their mouths; posture stooped and tired, tanned faces. The tents with the new guys, well, I remember it well. I silently wished them luck. They were going to need it!

Our group was scheduled to fly out early the next afternoon, so we had our possessions checked to be sure we weren't carrying unauthorized explosives, unregistered weapons, contraband, drugs, Vietnamese hooch maids, claymores or the odd kitchen knife. We were then told that our hair had to be trimmed to regulation length before we boarded the plane home. I had heard about this shitty little reg before I got to Long Binh, so my hair was already cut properly. But the guys going home, to be discharged howled in protest. They considered it highly unfair that they had to cut their hair a couple of days before mustering out. These young fellows were promptly told if they didn't have their hair cut to reg the day they were scheduled to leave, they would lose their seat and may have to stay a few extra days for the next one. The bitching and moaning increased but nobody lost his seat the next day. A haircut wasn't worth staying in the Nam for one more day!

So we knuckled under the Army's bullshit rules. One more attempt by the Green Machine to let us know who's really in charge. You'd think they'd cut these guys some slack after a year of fighting an impossible war.

The next day we headed for Tan Sohn Nhut airport in a bus (I think it was the same one I came in on) and spent a couple hours waiting for our flight — the longest fucking two hours I ever spent.

When our commercial flight rolled up and stopped, everybody jumped up in anticipation, even though they were going to have to re-fuel, re-check and re-beer. That also took forever, but nobody grumbled. We wanted this plane to be in A-1, super-duper shape because we did not want to have to turn around and come back here! Land in Guam, land at Midway, land in the fucking ocean, but don't come back here!

We finally boarded, the air conditioning fighting a losing battle with the heat outside, but it still felt good. A lot of the guys were in hyper-speed, so happy to be on the plane they couldn't contain themselves. They were ya-hooing and rebel yelling their hearts out.

I was pretty quiet. Despite the fact that I was heading home, I felt an underlying bitterness in the way things were going here. I felt like I was running out on the guys. There was still a possibility I'd be coming back, so that helped the guilt a little, but not much. What I was looking forward to was getting a perspective on the war from the U.S. side. If our own division paper tried bullshitting us, I could hardly wait to read what the politicians had to say in that viper's pit called Washington, D.C.

Our plane taxied for takeoff and you could feel the exhilaration swell from every man there. The second the rubber separated itself from the tarmac, a cheer went up the likes I had never heard. The stewardesses had to unstrap from their seats and gather up several guys that were dancing in the aisle. Discipline was right out the window. Once everybody was re-buckled, we grabbed altitude and soon just the ocean was below. It was a beautiful sight. Once the seat belt light went off, the stews passed out cold beers for everyone. I took a long pull and rested my head on the seat, and took a big sigh. I don't remember another thing about the flight home.

*Tattletale*

Here is a close up of four of our Monitors docked alongside the Colleton. These are the boats that float down the canals and offer us fire support.

This is our Zippo, two flame throwers mounted on a Mike Boat. One of our better weapons.

*Charlie Palek*

Captured Viet Cong and Russian flags.

A Huey landing on one of our converted ATC's, a "baby flatop".

*Tattletale*

This is what the greater part of Dong Tam looks like. The ship in the canal at the top is the Korean dredge we used to guard.

The 2$^{nd}$ Platoon on its way to Vihn Kim. Quite a crew, huh? The dude in the middle with the weird look is from Illinois.

Here is my favorite. I wish they all came out this good.

A "Hook" taking part of our battalion from the Plain of Reeds while another load waits below.

*Tattletale*

This is how the Chinooks brought in our artillery Christmas Eve. See what I mean by dusty?

Here is Still crossing, one of the typically muddy canals we always encounter. The area in the background had been prepped with arty.

This is one of our dog handlers and his dog Princess.

Here is a close up of the Colonel's downed bird. Quite a mess, huh? The guy under the chopper is hacking the radio out of it.

*Tattletale*

These are the families of our male detainees that insisted on coming along.

Sergeant Kostecki (Pollock) striking a brilliant pose with a V.C. suspect.

Here is the Navy futilely trying to raise a sunken Alpha Boat.

Two V.C. POW's.

A kid we found at Can Tho that had been burned by napalm. The rag in his chest had been stuck in the open wound, and the wound was more or less healing and festering over the rag. We sent him to our aid Boat.

Tangel, Davis and Takahata doing the "Vietnam Hang-on". Very serious soldiers, they.

*Charlie Palek*

Kovach and the late Vernon Miller shaving in their homemade sandbag bikinis. Aren't they a stunning pair?

Good 'ol Barn about to begin eating.

*Tattletale*

This is Sergeant Tangel and Takahata (city boys) watching with utter fascination as a hog chews his supper. You really have to "stoop low" for entertainment over here.

Here is Walker crossing a typical muddy Delta canal.

These (three stooges) are Durand (Walker's assistant), Walker and Needham, our Georgia M-60 man.

Bai & Thai, our other two interpreters. Bai used to be a sergeant and Thai a captain with the V.C.

# Chapter 4
# HOME AND FT. HOOD, TEXAS

Our last stop before freedom was Oakland, CA. We got out of our khakis and into our dress greens and were inspected for unauthorized badges, patches and ribbons. One 19 year old E-5 had a ribbon from the Korean War on his uniform. He couldn't tell anybody where it came from! Him earning that medal was improbable since he was still crapping in his pants when the Korean War was raging.

I joined up with three other guys and got a cab to the airport. They headed for the airport bar when we arrived, while I got on a flight that was leaving in 15 minutes. I had time to call my parents and give them my arrival time in St. Looey. Since my flight out was so fast, my parents had to gather up the family quick to get to the airport on time. Zoo time in the old homestead.

Our reunion at the airport was an eye-opener. I could almost see Mom's face and body relax now that she knew I was O.K. Dad was beaming, Ann and Donna were smiling, Ter was in awe and Sher was scared to death of me. I had my work cut out for me while at home. I had to start harassing the smiles off Donna and Ann's faces, confirm Ter's look of awe, and work my magic on Sher so she didn't think I was some kind of psycho.

My leave was to carry over past Christmas, but I was to report to Ft. Hood, Texas on Dec. 30. I was miffed about spending New Years sitting on my ass in Texas, especially when nothing was going to be going on anyway. I'll never get used to the Army and their ever-present fuck-ups.

Leave was a little different this time. The home-towners were glad to see me back, and curious about how the war was going. I didn't pull any punches and tried doing it with my grunt language cleaned up, which wasn't easy. Days of sleeping late, mom's good cooking and getting reacquainted with family and friends, especially with Roxy. Her letters had kept my spirits up during my tour and I wanted to show her a good time while I was home.

As usual, the days went by way too fast. I didn't tell anybody I wanted to go back. I wasn't ready for a family confrontation about that. All the folks in and around my hometown were very supportive and I had no problems of the type we had all read about. No harsh words, no dog shit in

## Charlie Palek

the face, no hippies shouting "baby killer." I was in the bosom of good old Middle America, where folks still protected family and respect and integrity still reigned supreme. It was a good change.

Christmas was a blast, especially comparing it to 1967. The twins were old enough to freak out at all the gifts under the tree. I pulled my "I'm sleeping, don't bother me to open gifts" ploy I had developed over the years to frustrate my siblings. Everybody would gather around the tree to open gifts, except for me. I would fake a deep sleep, making the kids come upstairs several times to get me up. Mom actually helped in the conspiracy by telling the kids "we can't open presents until Charlie comes down." The twins must have been up and down those stairs five times trying to get me up. Each trip became more violent and loud, the final one with both of them bouncing on my bed and punching me to wake up. Life was good!

Real life snapped me back to reality after Christmas and my next duty station intruded on my leave. One of my high school friends, Betty Haake, was having a New Years Eve party and I wanted to go in the worse way, but my orders said Dec. 30, so I said goodbye to everybody, and flew down to Texas. When I arrived, one of the guys in the H.Q. asks me what I was doing there. I found out the other guys that were due on the 30th didn't bother showing up and didn't have a problem when they finally arrived. I spent 3 days sitting in a practically deserted barracks fuming about my naivete. What an idiot I was!

I was at my new duty station, assigned to an armored unit, on the crew of a 4.2 mortar tube mounted inside an armored personnel carrier. I was back in my original MOS.

About January 2, the new guys stumbled back to camp, many still nursing hangovers. A lot of Divisions were represented, 1st Air Cav., 1st Division, Americal, 4th, 101st, 82nd, 196th L.I.B.; and they were a bunch of characters. These guys were all combat vets and had stories that never ended. I could tell I would enjoy their company.

We started to settle in our barracks and were told that in a couple weeks we'd be moving into a brand new dorm complex that had just been built. Well, they finally figured out we deserved the best. 'Bout time!

Two weeks later, we moved into a brand new complex, two man rooms for E-5's and E-6's, 8 man squad bays for the EM's, It was a sweet setup. Easy to keep clean for the inevitable I.G. inspection we were sure to have, plus a brand new mess hall that I was sure would serve up at least acceptable cuisine. — Was I wrong!

Our first meal served in the new mess was a cornucopia of mediocrity. It was a bland, unexciting, and unimaginative. The topper came when I tasted the lime Jell-O I had picked up. What I thought were white grapes in the Jell-O turned out to be cocktail onions! Onions and lime Jell-O? I couldn't believe it. What lame brained idiot concocted this little surprise? So much for my highly trained cook fantasy.

The guys started discussing fragging the kitchen personnel for this outrage, but it never happened. But this first meal put off a lot of us eating at the mess hall. Pizza delivery and off-base fast food became our staples.

Besides the lime and onion taste treat, most of the lunches and dinners were short on food. Small portions, and running out of milk halfway through the meal — the guy in charge must have been a real low life. Trust the Army to screw up a perfectly good habitat.

Most of the Officers here are fresh out of O.C.S. with no experience at all, especially combat experience. All they know how to do is inspect, march, and inspect. We're treated like boots around here and had to learn to march again. We didn't do much of it in Nam and they are very big on parades around here. The officers like to see how fast they can get your stripes, too. There are an awful lot of E-5's and E-6's here so the pickin's are easy.

One of our E-5's was pulling C.Q. one night and an E-8 in civvies, recognized by the E-5, wanted to go through Top's desk. The E-5 wouldn't let him go into the office (which was doing his job). The E-8 article 15'ed the E-5 and he lost a stripe, for doing his duty. As much fun as the guys were here, it didn't take me long to start thinking about how to get out of this chicken outfit.

One of the fellows here is Sgt. Hampton, of the 1st Air Cav, and he is a riot. He claims that by driving down the streets of any U.S. city with his Air Cav. patch hanging out the window, he'd have more willing women heading his way than he could handle!

He received a serious shoulder wound while leading a patrol of FNG's. They were in the jungle and walked into an ambush. The second the firing started, all the FNG's hit the dirt. Hampton continued to stand in the open and shouted for everyone to get down. He realized just before a bullet tore into his shoulder that he was the only idiot standing out there under fire. He was what my Dad would have called a "corker" and I never tired of his stories.

Charlie Palek

One of the E-6's from the 199th (the patch was called the "Flaming Pussy") had never heard of the 9th Division and thus assumed we were pulling R & R duty in the Delta. I ask him how I might have gotten 3 Purple Hearts doing nothing and he said I probably tripped our own booby traps. Comments like that usually resulted in an extended middle finger and colorful language but it was all in good fun. Each unit had ghosts in their closets and everybody took shit.

As members of the 1st Armored Division we eventually got to go to the motor pool and start familiarizing ourselves with the tracks we had. My track had a 4.2 mortar in it and we started taking classes on firing the mortar, troop movements, how the track is set up, static defense, and all kinds of other shit.

We never drove the tracks, but we were out there every day pulling maintenance on them. Since you can only lube a track that doesn't move so many times, we started slapping a coat of paint on the things whenever we had a chance. In seven months we had probably put on another inch of "paint armor." I was starting to see that there were way too many E-5's and E-6's and the H.Q. staff didn't know what to do with us. When police call started, everybody out there was non-coms. And boy did these REMF's like to have inspections. They lived for them, and relished our hatred for them. Most of the guys considered the H.Q. boys as candy-assed, limp-dicks, who would have crumbled into a ball of trembling flesh the first time they got into combat. We had an underlying disrespect for them that was very apparent by the look on our faces when they gave us an order. We all became pretty good at the "you ain't shit" look when they were in our face about something.

Our C.O., a hot shot 1st Looey had wrecked his Vet in a drunk driving scene, and as a result wore a cast covering his right foot. There was a rubber bumper on the bottom and when he came to inspect our rooms every Saturday, he'd drag that damned foot across our floors and hallways and leave a white mark everywhere he went. The mark had to be cleaned off the floor with steel wool, which we considered extra work. What a putz he was.

Cliff Wulf was my roomy, a big Iowa farm boy that served with the 25th Division. He could drink whiskey, beer and everything else in one sitting and not even wake up with a hangover the next day. He had a big ol' smile all the time and had a few stories of his own. I enjoyed his company immensely.

We also had Sgt. Hill, a L.R.R.P. with the 1st Division, S.SGT. Green, a 2-tour Korea N.C.O. with a deep silky voice that could really belt out a tune in the shower, Sgt. Clark with recon in the Americal Division, Sgt. Besecke, another L.R.R.P., Sgt. Hunt, Sgt. Knight, Sgt. Fortune, who needed a lot of sleep, and an odd assortment of E-4's and P.F.C.'s to round out the company.

In January I discovered the Texas winters were brutal. Not much snow, but the wind could blow right through to your bare skin, despite the number of layers you'd have on. I guess my blood was still thin from the tropics 'cause I was cold all the time. I was miserable every time we had to go to the tracks and sit in them, and learn about the inner workings of the APC and 4.2. The Texas wind was crazed and I began to wonder if the tropical heat wasn't so bad after all.

So we put up with inspections, marched, paraded, police called, and didn't train one fucking minute through February. We worked in the classroom occasionally, and fiddled around in the motor pool, but nothing I would consider "intensive, work to save your life and kick the enemy's ass" type training. By the time March rolled around, the weather was getting better so to avoid spring boredom, I purchased a new Honda 350 motorcycle and a Remington model 660 222 with a 9x scope for those times when I felt like shooting something. I took the rifle to the range and zeroed it at 100 yards, and spent a lot of range time perfecting my shooting. The bike was my "wheels of freedom" for the weekends I had off, if we all passed those goddamned inspections.

In late March, we finally got to take our tracks out and drive them around the countryside, and we really wrung them out. We climbed steep hills, crossed streams, bulldozed trees and brush and raced them to maximum R.P.M. We were running rampant and roughshod over the terrain and had a ball. We brought the A.P.C.'s back covered in mud and smoking like chimneys. We cleaned them up and went home, content with a good day's work. It was the one and only time we actually got them into the country for a drive.

The first week of April, we hauled one of our platoons out to the range for a live fire demonstration for some of the bored officers and their wives. The weather was cold, rainy, and wet. I was put in charge of the snuffies for what was supposed to be a two day field exercise. So, like fools, we packed up for two days.

## Charlie Palek

We got on the site, pitched our tents, dug our latrines, and formed up to find out what we were supposed to do. We were to set-up 2 M-60's at the top of a ridge overlooking a draw with simulated enemy bunkers about 75 yards up the other side of the incline. 2 fire teams of 4 men each were to assault two of the bunkers using the basic cover fire and maneuver tactic; hopscotching up the hill by twos until a smoke grenade was tossed into bunker. The M-60's would be providing live ammo cover fire the whole time.

O.K., the first thing I did was pick the M-60 gunner. If we were going to have 7.62 lead flying over our heads, I wanted someone familiar with the gun. Since E-5's were plentiful, I picked a couple of Nam vets to handle the 60's. They thanked me profusely, not wanting to run up and down the hill a couple times. The gun was placed so it couldn't swivel right or left, and the elevation was locked down so no accidental killing could occur. A kill shot from one of our supporting guns could have been ugly, so all precautions were taken. I told them I wanted 3-5 round bursts, no rock and rolling here. We had no spare barrels so we had to have fire discipline.

The fire teams would be firing blanks, starting at the bottom of the draw and working our way up. We each got 3 magazines for our M-16's, and I picked our first 7 assaults, leading the teams myself for the first one. The rest of the platoon was to watch and learn, because everybody was going to get to act out this little piece of jerk-off playtime activity.

We worked out our maneuvers picking out our cover and fire control. We ran through it a couple times and once I was happy with how it looked, we took a break until the afternoon show.

It was muddy out on the range so the officer in charge made sure we were out of sight so the Generals couldn't see our muddy boots. This whole thing was getting too bizarre. It's a good thing these REMF's hadn't seen our company after a week in the field during Tet. They would have had a coronary! Dirty boots, indeed!

The show was to start at 1p.m., so we all got set up, test-fired the 60's, placed our fire teams, and waited till 2:30 for the arrival of the brass hats. They finally arrived, unassed their vehicles and trooped over to the bleachers set up behind the 60's. Most of the guys had been smoking for 2 ½ hours, so we kicked our way out of the butt piles and began the assault.

The 60's started their song, and we headed up the hill. The first performance went well, but we were really getting muddy. The rain was getting heavier and colder. Our audience lost interest fast once we finished, scurrying to their transport in a flurry of unfolding umbrellas and flying coattails. We had two more performances to do the next day, so we were off until morning.

There was some overhead cover by the bleachers so I got all the performers under the roof to clean up their weapons. The rest of the guys got our campsite ready for the night. We did get some hot chow that night, but they also kicked off several cases of C-rats just in case. I made sure everybody was tucked in and cozy before I hit the sleeping bag. It felt good not having to put out security, lay down claymores and keep radio watches. Our illustrious officer in charge had left his troops in the field for the comforts of the barracks, but that was typical and O.K. We didn't need him. A quiet night was had by all.

Our next program was for 10 a.m., so everybody was up early, cleaning up camp, and waiting for a hot breakfast. I organized our next 2 fire teams, kept the gunners the same, and ran through a quick rehearsal before chow. I put another E-5 in charge this time, planning to watch this from the M-60 pit.

Our two performances also went well that day. It was good to have experienced N.C.O.'s to do the show. We finished up about 4, and proceeded to break camp when our butter bar told us we were staying at least 3 more days to show other brass hats how it was done. There was some bitching and moaning, but I ask the troops if they would rather be here or suffering through another inspection. Most agreed they'd rather stay than do another inspection. There were other problems though.

After a couple days of wallowing in the mud and rain our uniforms were looking poorly. We had packed for two days and our spare uniforms had already been used. There was to be no re-supply of suits, undies, and other unmentionables. The hot chow would stop coming because the mess sergeant was told he'd only need to bring our hot chow for two days. He apparently wasn't prepared for another 3 days (like hell!). That meant cold C's for a few more days. That was a bring down. C's were bad enough to most troopers but facing a cold morning crawling out of the sleeping bag and having to look cold C-rats in the eye was too much. We'd done that already! I pointed out these little problems to our Lt., but he was so anxious to go home he off-handedly told me we'd have to deal with it as best we could; we were field troops after all. I watched his scrawny infantry ass jump into a jeep and speed off, probably to the O-Club. I figured he'd be fragged before he got his C.I.B., if he went to Nam. What a putz!

We put up with late brass, blustery weather and unwashed bodies for three more days. Our Lt. told me on the last day to keep the men out of sight of the officers that had come to view the show. He thought we looked very unmilitary. No clean clothes or showers for 4 days can make one look a bit mussed, so I made the guys relax in their tents until the brass had arrived.

When the day was over, everybody was ready for a hot shower and our beds in the barracks. Naturally we all went back in open trucks, the wind whistling past our ears like artillery fire. We were all pretty frozen by the time we got back to the barracks. We hopped off the trucks, our young bones protesting their abuse. We dropped the 16's and M-60's off at the armorer and he promptly stated that there was no way he was receiving our weapons until they were cleaned up. So amid a renewed round of grumbling, we all cleaned up our weapons and got that chore out of the way so we could go back to some uninterrupted down time. I was given a well done by the Sgt. Major, which I passed on to the troops. Our Lt. Prick never said as much as a "good job" to anybody. He was pretty typical of lots of officers coming out of O.C.S. They had a very high opinion of themselves, and very little for anyone under their rank. I was confident that fragging incidents were increasing because of so called leaders like him, the little wiener.

About three weeks later, we got a call for volunteers for a 10-day TDY (temporary duty station). No details were given, even about the location, but I signed up. It would be something different than this place.

I was accepted and was transported to Camp Pickett, Virginia, and old WWII camp full of empty space and ghetto-looking barracks. I reported to the proper authorities, was taken to a barracks a little more modern than the Vintage WWII ones I saw coming in, and met some of my bunkies for the next few days.

An SP/4 named Rogers and I hit it off right away. He had gone to the Dominican Republic with the 82nd Airborne, to the Detroit riots with the 101st, then a tour in Nam. He was a short little guy, kind of serious but easy going. I ask him what they were doing here and he told me I was the last to arrive and our new jobs would be laid out in the afternoon. So we all headed to the N.C.O. Club for some hangout time.

We played a little pool, had a couple beers, and shot the shit. Rogers, already known as "Airborne," had come to Virginia to camp "Ricketts" for the same reason as I had — out of boredom. I ask him about how things were in Detroit and he said it was weird going into the streets of America combat-ready. Things had gotten so bad there that Federal troops were called in and the "Screaming Eagles" got the job.

He said they were briefed on the flight to Detroit, issued live ammo once they landed, and had locked and loaded before leaving the tarmac. They got downtown and straight into a war zone, but they didn't dick around. If they took fire they wheeled up a 106 recoilless rile and took out the window. He told me Vietnam was less stressful because everybody was afraid of killing civilians in the city but there were very few around. The only people giving them shit deserved what they got. It must have been a real awkward position to be in.

We hustled back to the barracks at 4p.m., an officer meeting us and welcoming us to Camp "Ricketts". Our job for the next few days would be to walk, jog, and run over a 2-mile course to test some new boots for the Army. Not too exciting, but something to keep us in shape. We would have Saturdays and Sundays off, but with nowhere to go, that didn't mean much.

So we laced up the new boots, which looked like the standard issue jungle boots we all wore in Nam, and proceeded to walk a moderately rugged trail through the pine forest of Virginia. The mornings were cool and the smell of pine was quite relaxing. One little detail they failed to tell us about, our walks would be timed. No doubt to make sure we didn't walk into the woods and do the Rip Van Winkle thing. Bad new for several of the guys. They had planned to hit the woods and sleep away the hours, but this timing thing really screwed up their plans. I knew they would figure a way, though. They always do.

We walked and jogged the course 2 or 3 times a day, got off early, had a reasonably good supper at the mess and spent the off-hours in huge bullshit sessions.

We entertained each other one night telling about what the Division patches actually represented. For instance, the patch for the 101st Airborne was the "Puking Buzzard." The 4th Division — "Poison Ivy," the 25th Division "Captain Marvel," 9th Division — "Flower Power" or the "Crumbling Cookie," 1st Division — "The Big Red One," accent on the red! Sitting around talking to guys with similar experiences was very enlightening. Good stories, and good company. Things were fun for a while.

## MURPHY'S LAW OF COMBAT
### #43
"Killing for peace is like whoring for virginity."

When I got back to Ft. Hood, a new bug had flown up the asses of the Powers That Be. The guys told me we were going to begin riot control training soon. Apparently the H.Q. wienies decided they needed a contingent of highly trained, combat-experienced assholes that could be ready at a moments notice to put down campus rioting in Texas and the surrounding states.

Well this was going to be interesting. The Nam vets in my unit were taking things fairly casual, managing to come home alive from the Southeast Asian jungles. Discussion of this newest insanity was running hot through the barracks like a flow of lava. Nobody was anxious to stick a bayonet in another American's face. What they had planned we could only guess.

## MURPHY'S LAW OF COMBAT
### #15
"Teamwork is essential. It gives them other people to shoot at."

Two weeks later, we found ourselves sitting outdoors on our company bleachers, listening to a brand new "90 Day Wonder 2nd Looey" tell us about controlling hostile crowds in the streets of the U.S.A. This officer was so new he was still wrapped in plastic! 80% of the guys in the bleachers were Vietnam vets and frankly, we were not taking this guy too seriously. He was rambling on about wedge formations, drawn bayonets, intimidation by force, all kinds of stuff. He did get our attention when one of the troopers asked when we'd be issued ammo and he said we wouldn't be getting any live ammo. We all sat there in a stunned silence for a minute, wondering if this guy was for real. We were told by this stateside FNG that while we were marching in formation down the middle of the street, our bayonets flashing in the sun, any hostile fire we'd receive would be handled by an anti-sniper shooter, the only guy with live ammo! We were sitting in the bleachers looking like we'd all been gut-shot. We had all managed to survive Vietnam by luck or using our heads in some manner, one of which was to find cover when somebody shot at you. Now this numb-nuts was telling us we'd have to hold our formation, standing in the middle of the street while some dude with an M-14 would take out the sniper.

We were all starting to chuckle about this and the 2nd Lt. started getting a little miffed. He asked if there were any questions and we started firing volleys back. Would there be back-up shooters? What happened if more than one point of hostile fire was encountered? How long were we suppose to stand in the street with empty rifles in our hands? Would it be O.K. if we crapped in our pants while all this was going on? And most important, how do we get out of this chicken outfit?

He had answers for all our questions; unfortunately, they were all from the classroom and the textbooks. We were being trained by the book- the same book our cohorts told us to throw away or use for toilet paper when we got into Vietnam. The circle was coming around.

So we drilled the wedge formation till our feet bled. We had classes on ways to conduct ourselves in our own country. We foot-stomped our way back and forth across the compound, learning to respond to voice and hand commands about breaking into smaller units, recombining into bigger units, all the stuff we needed to know to look like a big slice of warmed pizza, heading down the road. It was almost laughable. The really ironic part was there never was an anti-sniper unit working with us, ever. That fact did very little to bolster our confidence. I kept thinking what Rogers had said when his unit went into Detroit. If we were ever called out for this kind of duty I was afraid "lock and load" would be one command we wouldn't get.

Right in the middle of our riot control training, we were informed, no doubt with much glee from H.Q., that there would be an I.G. inspection in two months and we had to start preparing for it ASAP. I.G. inspections were something the H.Q. pukes thought up to keep us busy while they ran rampant through the company area, counting the cigarette butts that had been missed, and making sure no oversized dust bunnies lived in the squad bays. Nobody like them, but it sure kept our days busy. We marked all of our clothes and equipment with our serial numbers- black numbers on a white field- waxed the floors till they glared like a mirror, dusted and cleaned all surfaces that could possibly catch a microbe of dust, cleaned and re-cleaned our weapons, painted our APC's again, and learned how to lay out our gear for a field inspection.

We worked for a couple of months for the I.G. inspection while I debated my next move. I didn't want to stay here another year and Europe sounded boring, so I started looking into another tour in Nam, only aviation this time. I had seen an Army magazine at the H.Q. and there was an article about a new helicopter being used in Vietnam called a Loach. They were used as scouts, patrolling ahead of the infantry looking for V.C. It held 2 crewmen, a pilot, and an observer. That sounded even better than a door gunner. I told myself I'd check into it further.

The day of the inspection came and we were out on the parade ground at 7a.m., so we'd be ready by 8. We got pre-inspected by our C.O. Our gear was laid out on our ponchos and we were ready exactly at 8a.m. At 9:30, a one star General arrived, hopped out of the jeep, walked around two of the displays, hopped back in his jeep and left! The whole inspection took less than a minute! Our whole company was dressed out for this and that was all he did, and I don't mind telling you I was pissed. If this was what they were going to do to keep us busy, I wasn't staying. I was getting out — and now!

The next day I trooped over and volunteered for another tour, as a door gunner. I figured it would be easier getting the door gunner job approved then maybe I could slide into the Scouts.

It only took about three weeks for my request to go through, and it had been approved. I was heading for the 1st Aviation Brigade, Vinh Long in the Delta. I was ecstatic. I had a 3-week leave then off for the next adventure.

I called my family the same day. I knew what they would say but it wouldn't change my mind. I got Mom on the phone first, and when I told her I was going back, I could sense her shoulders sagging in disappointment. She said "Oh no, Charlie, you're not." I tried laughing it off and told her I would be home in a couple days for 3 weeks of leave, but I knew I was in trouble. They probably thought at this point that they had raised a son that was crazier than a shit-house rat.

I bid my buds farewell, and rode my bike home on a two day trip. I got soaked the first day out, lost my socks in Little Rock, got lost in East St. Louis but managed to get home at dusk the second day. Nobody wanted to talk about a second tour. I tried to assure them that I would not be in the

*Tattletale*

infantry. Flying would be safer. Even Mom knew the choppers were falling out of the sky on a regular basis, but she didn't say anything. Dad was O.K. with going back, but he knew how things were going over there and his enthusiasm had waned a bit. Donna was not looking forward to another tour, knowing what it did to the family cohesion. Ann was still too young to understand, and the twins — well, Ter and I got along great, Sher was still afraid of me, not as much as before, but still afraid. The friends I talked to shook their heads when they heard I was going back. Why would I want to go back after 3 Purple Hearts the first time? I couldn't explain it to them. One of my high school buds wanted to know how I got so patriotic. I told them flatly that patriotism wasn't a factor here, getting out of Ft. Hood and flying was the motive. They still didn't understand, and I didn't try to explain. I had less than 3 weeks of real living to do before I flew back.

Dad was a whiz on the ol' BBQ grill, so we did that a lot while I was home. Mom fixed me my favorites again. She cooked all the foods I loved, especially her heavenly chocolate angel food cake made from scratch. Flour, cocoa, sugar and a dozen eggs and it's light as a feather. Real whipped cream to top it off. It was Heaven on a plate.

The day I left home, things were a little more tearful. The family was going to have to go through the whole tour again and I'm sure there was resentment about what I was doing. I didn't consider their feelings much. I was hot to fly and that's what I concentrated on. Young and dumb!

I flew out of Oakland this time. Some of the FNG's heading over for the first time asked me a lot of questions while we waited in the terminal. I didn't pull any punches. I told them to especially listen to what the experienced guys in their unit told them — then do it! Don't get creative until you've been there a while. One last thing- you are not invincible. That last one I had no right to tell them, but I felt Lady Luck and me were on pretty good terms, so I was qualified.

We boarded our plane and headed for Hawaii. I have no recollection of the flight, none at all.

# Chapter 5
# 2nd TOUR

When we came into Cam Rahn Bay, it was the first time I had seen this part of the country. The smell of salt air managed to creep into the flight line, seeping in among the odors of diesel fumes, JP-4, hot tar and the jungle. There were mountains in the distance- it all looked too tranquil. I checked in at the airport terminal, caught a Caribou to Saigon, then a chopper to Vinh Long. Flying in the Huey again brought back good memories and got my heart pumping like a train. It felt good to be up here, the vibration of the chopper making my teeth chatter. I was really looking forward to my new duty station. I hoped the Army wouldn't foul this up.

I reported to the 1st Aviation Brigade H.Q. and discussion of my new job started immediately. The Top Sergeant reviewed my file and asked me what I wanted to do. They had some openings with the Blues, which was the infantry contingent of the Air Cav outfit. I told him I volunteered for door gunner, not grunt. I'd done that already. He grinned, looked down at my file and said, "Yes, you have. Quite well apparently." He told me all the door gunner slots were filled, but Apache Troop needed a couple of new observers, and asked if I would be interested! I tried to keep from turning cartwheels in his office while trying to play it cool. I told him that observer was what I really wanted to do. He said, "You got it, Sergeant!" He took my paperwork and sent me out the door with directions to my new unit. It was about a 3-block hike when I found myself in front of Apache Troop, a Commie .51 caliber in front with a 122-mm rocket on display. H.Q. was on the left, Tactical Operations Center on the right, and the barracks behind a small troop area along the side. I had walked the three blocks about 6" above the ground. This time the goddamned Army had actually come through for me! I was flying without a chopper. I was in the tattletale business again.

Apache Troop wasn't far from the flight line, and it was busy. In and out-going choppers were everywhere. Chinooks, Cobras, Loaches, Hueys, Rangers, the whole corporate helicopter industrial complex was represented. It looked like a beehive out there. Oh yeah, this was going to be fun!

I checked in at the H.Q., and was welcomed with more enthusiasm than I expected. The scouts were a volunteer outfit so sometimes there was a shortage of observers. The H.Q. was thrilled with my prior experience and welcomed me with open arms. The staff got my paperwork squared away and one of the clerks took me to squad bay, found me a bunk, and told me I'd get a shot at the N.C.O two-man rooms as soon as one opened up, probably in a couple of days. The barracks were kind of empty. Most of the guys were out doing their duty. I halfway unpacked and went to the N.C.O. rooms looking for SP/5 Wells. He was leaving in a couple of days and I was to get his room. I found him packing his stuff, a big ol' smile on his face as he worked. I introduced myself and found out he was a crew chief on a Cobra. He gave me the low down on things around here, the kind of missions that were being run and all sorts of other stuff. Mike told me he'd be out of this room the day after tomorrow, early, and I could move in then. He was ready to go right then, but rules were rules. He had 36 more hours to go.

My roomie is a Sgt. Banlow, one of the top scout observers in the troop. He was on the daily mission, so I'd meet him tonight. Mike and I bullshitted the day away, until a half-witted E-5 Guinea stuck his head in the room and introduced himself as one of the infantry sergeants. His name was Tom Russell, and we became and would continue to be fast friends 30 years later.

Russ was one of the fast-talking draftees who absolutely despised the Army and all lifers thereof. He had no respect for Army tradition, ceremony, or leadership. He was a laugh a minute, kind of the Hawkeye Pierce of Apache Troop. I liked him immediately.

When Russ found out I had done an infantry tour already he seriously questioned my sanity. His thinking was that a safe haven stateside was better than anything over here. I explained how things were at Ft. Hood and he still didn't understand. I had 11 months to drill it into his head- so no sweat.

Just after dark the troops came in carrying a variety of firearms, helmets and assorted flight accessories including sidearms and body armor. They looked tired. Their hair was disheveled from the helmets and they had sweat stains where their body armor hugged their bodies. I went back into Well's room and met Banlow, my new roomie. He was a short, intense guy who had the highest kill count in the Apache Scouts- 29 up to that day.

Charlie Palek

## MURPHY'S LAW OF COMBAT
### #24
"In war, important things are very simple and all simple things are hard."

He carried a Car-15 that was obviously his baby. He told me, since he was leaving soon, that I'd inherit his beloved Car after he left. He was a bit put-off by my lack of enthusiasm about the rifle, but I explained that if it took good care of me I'd take good care of it. After that bridge had been crossed, we went to chow, which was a real disappointment. Back to c-rats, I guess.

That night, I met a bunch of the N.C.O.'s and E.M's, crew chiefs, Oscars, and infantry. SP/6 Roy and SP/5 McDonald were in the lift platoon, Sgt. Lemoyne, Sgt. Lyon, Sgt. Harrel, SP/4 Lineburger, Sgt. Stradley, a whole cornucopia of young and old aviation vets that were doing a tough job that was getting very little press.

I heard a lot of stories that night, and told a few of my own. All in all, this looked like a good bunch of guys. Morale seemed high and everybody seemed to be getting along. Sgt. Raabe, our scout platoon leader, came in and fit right in with the bunch. I met him and liked him right away. He welcomed me aboard and told Banlow, who wasn't flying the next day, to take me out to the flight line tomorrow and show me the ropes. I could hardly wait.

Sleep would not come that night. My mind was reeling with the possibilities of what I was in for. It all sounded pretty dam exciting. I was ready!

The next morning, I went down to the flight line with the crews to watch them leave. I met a few of the pilots, and, Jesus, some of them were young. Capt. Sprague was our C.O., and the rest of the pilots were Warrant Officers. Being a Warrant Officer was a good job. You had all the privileges of an officer but none of the responsibilities. I met some of the pilots, Mr. Sorenson, Mr. Willis, Mr. Dicresce, Mr. White, all confident and ready to go. Crews were going in and out of the flight line hooch, packing grenades and backup weapons into the Loaches, running belts of M-60 ammo into the mini-gun and doing preflight checks. Once the startup began, the Scouts hovered from their revetments, then the Cobras and the Command and Control Huey. The flight line smells were making me heady, and my ass was already itching to get into the seat of a Loach.

Once things quieted down, Banlow and I went over to one of the backup Loaches and started my education. I learned a lot about the Loach that day, and it was an incredible little machine, adapting to the Scouting roll perfectly.

Without the mini-gun, the aircraft weighed only about a ton. It had a small, whiney turbine engine, a four bladed rotor, 2 seats up front, a cargo area in the back, and a bubble for the crew to hide behind. A mini-gun capable of firing 6,000 rounds per minute was mounted on the left side of the ship, the barrels about two feet from the door of the observer. The cockpit looked a bit cramped, but livable. There were no hydraulics on this bird. All flight controls were the push-pull type, connected by cables just like the old B-17's of WWII. Controlling the chopper required muscle power. Both seats were armor plated underneath, on the back and partially on the sides. The skin was made of aircraft aluminum and would only deflect a BB it was so light. A .30-caliber shell would go through this thing like crap through a goose. The crew was strapped in their seats by a system of belts, across the lap and over the shoulders. The restraining system was loaded with a centrifugal lock that kept your body from being thrown forward on impact.

There were duel controls for both seats, and I found out that I would be required to learn to fly and land this thing in case the pilot got shot! Holy shit! That was a revelation I hadn't counted on. It made good sense, but my mind was having a mild anxiety attack just thinking about it!

The main function of the Scouts was to fly low and slow, looking for enemy soldiers, bunkers, tracks, trails, anything that would mark the ground of a human passing through the jungle. Operating altitude was less than 50 feet, sometimes much lower. Since they were slightly higher than the infantry, they carried a lot of grenades, frags, tear gas, incendiary, concussion, white phosphorus, and smokes- all packed into a console between the crew members and strung on wires over the Oscar's foot pedals. This was a lot of explosives to be sitting on. I was completely comfortable about handling grenades but this was a bit crazy. One well-placed bullet and they'd find a tail boom and nothing else! Oh well, one of the hazards of the job.

The chopper had three basic controls. The cyclic came up between the pilot's legs, controlling left and right banks, and forward and backward movement. The collective controlled the pitch of the main rotor and also had a power control like a motorcycle throttle. The pedals kept the ship pointed in the right direction via the tail rotor. I asked Banlow how you fired your weapon out the door without fouling the cyclic on the observer's side of the ship. He told me I would learn to fire an M-16 out the door by leaning outside, avoiding the stick and the pedals. I took his word for it.

There also was a radio console between the crew members below the instrument board. They had VHF, UHF, and FM; we could even pull in Armed Forces Radio for our tunes! I'd be in charge of the radios while the pilot flew.

The mini-gun had a 2,000 round ammo box in the cargo compartment of the ship. I was shown how to mount the gun, load it, and put it on safety. We spent the afternoon taking it apart and reassembling it. By the time the day ended my head was spinning from all the new info. We headed back, grabbed some chow and spent the evening talking about the mission procedure.

The Loach was made for the Scouting roll. It hovered and moved like a big ol' bumblebee, able to get in and out of tree lines fast, bobbing and weaving, making it harder on the enemy gunners to get a bead. It was a jewel, and if you had a good pilot strapped into this little beauty, you had yourself a hell of a weapon!

The nightly bull session included several of the pilots that night. I became the center of attention when the guys discovered this was my 2nd tour. Most of them couldn't figure out why I came back especially after an infantry tour. Most of the pilots just shook their heads until I pointed out that their jobs were strictly volunteer and what they were doing seemed to be like hanging your ass in the air, begging for Charlie to shoot it full of holes. They smiled and said "that's exactly what they did, but there were counter measures too. We were allowed to shoot back." I thought — "thank Christ for that!" They were a cool bunch, and I felt good about working with them.

The next morning, I moved in with Banlow and got squared away. I found out that there would be a hooch maid coming in once a week to do our laundry and clean up a bit. Was this plush or what! We had to pay them for our services but the cost was nothing to us. We also had, what sounded like to me, the only electric skillet in all of South East Asia. Cooking in our room was allowed and the skillet would be used a lot, instead of relying on the mess hall. We'd be cooking our own cuisine, getting our ingredients from downtown Vinh Long, home packages, or anything we could steal from someplace else. It was a highly coveted item, so we had to keep it under lock and key. We each had a wooden footlocker, a metal locker where our personal weapons would be kept, including ammo. Photos of naked women and posters hung everywhere. Seemed like the REMF rash hadn't reached this unit yet. Things were loose and that's probably why everybody was so happy.

Don't get me wrong. Our C.O. didn't take any shit and could come down hard, but he tolerated a little off-duty nonsense once in a while. He was known to drop into the flight line hooch once in a while to make sure explosives were stored properly and weapons kept clean. Doing this himself instead of sending a flunky said something about the guy that I liked.

Out platoon sergeant, Sgt. Raabe, had stolen a civilian jeep before I had arrived and was charged with larceny. He didn't seem too worried about it, and I don't think anything ever happened to him for his indiscretion.

I spent the next several days training to use the equipment I'd be using on the flight. I had noticed that there wasn't one M-60 in the flight line hooch that made me wonder if they were too big to use in the cramped cockpit. I decided I'd better hold off on big changes until I got some missions under my belt. I had been issued an M-16 that I used on my first several missions, but I kept my options open. There were a real variety of weapons used by the Oscars in this troop. Willis was using an old WWII grease gun. The rate of fire was a little slow, but it did the job. There were a couple of Thompson's out there, several 12 gauge shotguns and even a few AK's. The fact that the Oscar was using automatic weapons that fired the .45-caliber hand gun ammo meant their targets must have been pretty close because .45's are not known for their tremendous range.

The day of my first flight came and I was a little nervous. I didn't want to fuck up or do something wrong. I would be flying in the wing ship. Our job was primarily to cover the lead ship while it did its thing. The LOH's always worked in pairs with a pair of Cobras providing high cover in case things got real hot. The lead Oscar carried a smoke grenade in his left hand with the pin pulled during the mission. If the LOH's received fire — the grenade was tossed out the door, the scouts grabbed altitude and the Cobras rolled in and worked over the area with rockets, 40mm and their mini-gun. The Scouts then went back in to check the area again. This is what they did, everyday, all day.

## Charlie Palek

Our job as the wing ship was to provide low cover for the lead LOH. When the lead was checking out an area, we were pulling a left-hand orbit around them to put my gun on the area.

One of the crew chiefs helped me get settled in and made sure all was well as I crawled into the seat and strapped myself in. It was a cozy fit, with the armored plate over my chest, called a chicken plate, helmet, sidearm, weapon, ammo, and grenades — not much room to stretch. I was flying with Mr. Sewell, a laid back Alaskan that always had a shitty little grin on his face. He was an excellent pilot and he taught me the ropes about being a good Oscar.

I had been grilled the previous few days about the mini-gun, so I knew how to mount it for flight. The belt of ammo was fed into the gun but the safety plate was put on for the flight to our AO, then the safety was taken off.

So I settled in, prepared myself for my first mission. I checked the left side of the ship from tail rotor to the front to be sure there were no people or obstructions in the way, told the pilot clear on the internal intercom, and Mr. Sewell hovered our whining little bee out of the revetment.

Our four LOH's hovered out of the revetments and did a final hover check, before we moved down the runway into the clear blue. We formed up behind our 4 Cobras and our Command and Control Huey.

Flying over the countryside was exhilarating, especially early in the morning. The cool air was washing through the door refreshing our skin and cooling us off from the humid hell below. Maybe I was so happy because I'd spent a year walking in the mud below — I found this much more desirable. Most of the flight crews would never know the agony of walking around down there with 70 pounds on your back, up to your ass in mud and skin infections. This was the "clean war," and I like it!

We were heading for an A.O. called the Tram, and area of flooded thickets that had been a supply route for the V.C. since day one. We had a pleasant flight to our A.O. base, landed, refueled, and shutdown till our C&C gave us the call. We were the second team, so I started learning about down time. The first team would go out and patrol for about an hour and a half, then we'd replace them when fuel got low or they ran into trouble.

The call came in about 15 minutes and our first team left us at the A.O. fuel stop. While we were just sitting around, Mr. Sewell taught me how to use the radios, and what my job would be selecting the proper channels while he was busy flying. We talked about past missions he'd flown, events — good and bad, that happened to the Scouts. Mr. Sewell had the kind of personality that set you at ease right away. We got along famously and were enjoying our training session, when the call came for us to crank them up.

We lit the fires and headed for the A.O., our Cobras high and behind us. Twenty minutes later found us over the weirdest terrain I had ever seen. It was a thicket of thick bushes, brush, and small trees sticking out of about 3 feet of water. This was exactly like the kind of vegetation we used to hunt rabbits with our .22's back home, except without the water. It was a vast area, and it produced a smell of sweet, decomposing vegetation that made my head woozy. It was a peculiar odor and I came to hate this place.

We flew around for an hour and a half and found zip. About half way through the flight, I started getting sick. The motion of the wing ship flying back and forth behind the lead, circling the lead in a tight circle and the smell all contributed to a case of airsickness, I couldn't shake. I told Mr. Sewell I was feeling shitty, and he told me to following standard puking procedures.

They were:

1. Stick your head out the door and throw up, don't do it inside the aircraft. Nobody wanted to throw a frag with vomit on it!
2. Puke on the mini-gun had to be cleaned off by the pukee. Being a couple feet outside the door it was hard to miss unless...
3. The LOH was going fast and the slipstream blew the puke into the back wall of the cargo compartment. — My cleanup job also.

I made the mistake of having a big breakfast that morning and it ended up all over the side of the ship. After I had projected breakfast all over the port side, I was sweating, feeling bad and not concentrating on my job. I felt like an idiot, but Mr. Sewell said not to worry. I wasn't the first LOH crewman to puke on his first mission. He made me feel a little better, and fortunately we didn't see any action that day.

Between our first and second flight that day, I took a rag and some canal water and cleaned up the cargo compartment before things got dry and crusty. The second flight was the same except I had dry heaves for awhile because I hadn't eaten any lunch. This was a humiliating experience. I was going to have to get over this quick.

That night, the guys had a good time with my problem. I tried to explain that I never got sick flying in the Hueys in air assaults because we were flying straight and level, not erratic like the Scouts. It was all good-natured, and several Oscars admitted they had gotten sick too, so I wasn't alone. I decided that until I kicked this bad habit, I wouldn't eat a lot of breakfast just to keep my cleaning time to a minimum. This was a revolting development. I could take the crap from the other guys, a different story about getting over the airsickness.

My next six days of flying were repeats of the first. I got sick, barfed, and cleaned up. Mr. Sewell, tiring of the ship smelling like a hold in a tramp steamer told me to try and relax instead of being so tense. He told me I had to learn to ride with the movement of the ship, not fight against it. So I took his words to heart. My next flight I sat back in the seat chilled out and relaxed. To my surprise, I felt good. No airsickness! If just relaxing was all it took, the problem was solved.

My next several missions were puke-free. I learned to sit back and not fight the forces of flying. It was a relief to me, except for the Tram. The odor of that area always made me come close to being sick. Bad "ju ju," the Tram.

There was a shortage of Oscars so sometimes the crew chiefs filled in and ran the missions. After about 10 days of flying, I was told that I would start flying lead observers for the next mission with Captain Sprague. We would be going into the U Minh Forest, a haven for Charlie that was so secure they flew their flag right above their bunkers. That was pretty damned arrogant. Arrogant field troops mean they are probably willing to fight instead of running for cover. G-2 told us to expect lots of action, so we geared up.

I went out to the flight line early the next morning to run the mini-gun ammo into the box. I checked each round as I folded the 2,000 round continuous belt into the ammo box. As it was folded in, I ran my fingers along the back of the belt to make sure each round was seated properly in the links. One round pushed a little forward or backward in the link — a sure jam. Jams were bad, something we didn't need where we were going. I had also re-cleaned and checked the Car-15 Banlow had given me and I checked out a 12 gauge pump for a backup. I had scrubbed the chamber of the Car like my life depended on it. There were enough chamber brushes in this outfit to equip a battalion, too bad this surplus hadn't occurred 3 years ago.

Captain Sprague was a short, blond, officer that walked around with an air of authority and supremacy. He didn't laugh much, and I assumed from his demeanor that he was a career officer. No surprises there.

Our staging area was on the northern edge of the forest. We topped off our fuel and headed for the "Woods." This was my first flight with our C.O., and my first lead Oscar mission so I was a little nervous. He asked me if I was up to speed on radio procedure, which I was. We entered the U Minh right away and it didn't take long before bunker complexes started showing up — but no V.C. The further we flew, the more bunkers we past. Sure enough, we started seeing an occasional V.C. flag flying from a bamboo pole. Things were looking good for finding Charlie, but we saw nothing. We flew around for about an hour and finally saw some fresh tracks going into a bunker. Capt. Sprague put the bunker entrance outside my door and I tried tossing in a frag. — I missed. I tried with another one. — Missed again. We were hovering way too long and Sprague was getting pissed. I tried one more time and it finally rolled in. Nobody ran out so we packed up and left to re-fuel. I got read the riot act on the way back. He called me every name in the book. He couldn't figure out how somebody with my infantry experience could be so incompetent about throwing a grenade. I tried to explain to him that I carried a radio for a year; and during my first tour I hadn't thrown a grenade from a chopper at all. This was my first time, give me a little time. He wanted none of it and told me after today there would be some changes.

We flew a second mission that day but there were few words spoken in the cockpit. I felt foolish and partly deserved the verbal abuse I got, but I also felt he was being a bit premature of his assessment. So this day was a loss and the flight back to Vinh Long was very quiet.

That night, Sprague, Raabe and myself had a little meeting and the C.O. told Raabe he didn't want me as an Oscar anymore. I could fly lead with anybody else, just not with him. Just another humiliation from a gentleman officer. Raabe told me no to worry about it, the other pilots would fly with me, so there was no problem. The more I thought about it, the more pissed I became. I vowed to make him eat his words before he left country.

## Charlie Palek

The next day I flew with Mr. White. He was a CW-4, the oldest pilot in the outfit. His goal was to fly the brass around the country in their little twin engine Beeches. For now he was getting some stick time with the Scouts. I liked Mr. White because I felt he was going to be a little more understanding. He certainly had a better sense of humor.

Hey, I was well aware of the fact that I had to get my shit together. It wasn't like I didn't try. My mission in life at the present was to stop screwing up and dig myself out of the hole I was in.

Our first mission that day turned out to be my first look at the real action I'd be experiencing all year. We were checking out a series of bunkers that were so well camouflaged we almost missed them. They were burrowed into some small berms that were covered with a thick coat of grass. Suddenly Mr. White shouted over the intercom that he'd spotted a man with a weapon and he spun the ship around to put him outside my door. He was hiding in some high grass and Mr. White was yelling at me to take him out, but I didn't see him! I couldn't find the V.C. and Mr. White was going nuts. He couldn't point because his hands were busy with the controls, and I was becoming more frustrated by the second. He finally spun the ship around, zeroed the mini-gun on the target and fired a 100-round burst into the grass. I finally saw what he was yelling about, but it was too late now. The V.C. body was not going anywhere. His body and his weapon were chewed up like they'd both been through a meat grinder. The sound of the mini-gun going off two feet from my door scared the shit out of me. Christ, I was a nervous wreck!

Mr. White knew what was going through my head. He told me to be cool and don't worry about this little incident. My day would come. Another 30 minutes into the flight, I caught two guys with AK's diving into a couple of bunkers. I pulled a Willie Pete off our rack and Mr. White set me up. Instead of hovering over the bunker entrance, we swung around and took a run at it so when the grenade hit the entrance our forward momentum would carry it well into the interior. I leaned out the door on our run and noticed our wing ship was set up on the bunker entrance, covering our ass. Mr. White set the hole right outside my door and just before we flew over the target I tossed the W.P. It landed about two feet from the entrance and rolled right in. A split second later a V.C. flew out of the bunker before the grenade exploded. Our wing Oscar nailed him before he got 5 feet from the entrance. The grenade exploded inside the bunker and a puff of pure white smoke erupted from the bunker. Nobody else came out. We were pulling a hard right turn to come back around when the second guy ran out of his bunker, looked up at us, and lay down in the middle of the grass, rolling up into a fetal position. He closed his eyes, his weapon on the ground at his side. "What in the hell was he doing?" I thought. This was strange behavior for a guy about to get wacked. Mr. White put me right on top of him and I lined him up. The car fired 3 rounds and jammed! I grabbed the bolt handle and tried to eject the bad round but it wouldn't budge. It took all my discipline to not scream like a crazed idiot. Goddamn, was I ever going to get a break here?

Mr. White was yelling to finish him off. The three rounds had hit him in the lower torso, but he had only jerked when the bullets had impacted. He was still lying there like a well-disciplined soldier trying to remain hidden. It was spooky, but I didn't have time to think about that at the moment. I could pull out my .38 or toss a grenade. So I grabbed a frag, leaned out the door and let the grenade roll out of my hand like you'd drop a tomato into a salad. He was only about 8 feet away. I could see the pain on his face as the grenade landed right under his chin. We got out of the way quick, I heard the thump of the frag go off and we came around to check out a headless corpse smeared across the ground. We found his head 30 feet away, lying there like a busted melon.

We continued checking out the complex but found nothing more. I was using the shotgun; the Car tucked at the side of my seat. On the flight back, I reflected to Mr. White what a weird day it was. He laughed and told me not to worry. Seeing a human hiding from the air was different than seeing them from the ground. My eyes would adjust and soon I'd be picking out all the telltale signs. I had my first kill, but I felt a little unattached. Killing another human didn't bother me. I was out for payback for all my friends who were killed and wounded in the 9th Division. It was an "us or them" situation, and I wasn't going to give them a break. If this was how the game was played, so be it. If it seemed a little lopsided — us with all this firepower, and aerial superiority, them on the ground hiding like rats in a chicken house, you're right. But it only took a well-placed burst from an AK to blow us to cinders. So there certainly was a downside. Just about any caliber bullet would tear through this aircraft skin like a K-Bar knife through tin foil. The big question was what it struck on the way through.

On the way back to Vinh Long, I asked Mr. White about the guy that just lay there while we hovered around him. He told me he had never seen that before and was wondering the same thing. It was damned strange.

Our wing pilot told us that after I dropped the frag on this guy, the explosion catapulted his head 30 feet into the air, tumbling like a poorly thrown football. Sinew and muscle were hanging out of the neck as it fell. It was the wildest shit he had ever seen.

I also had one more mission. I wouldn't be flying tomorrow, as our schedule tried to give us one day off and one day on. Shortages usually prevented this fact, but we tried. I was going to trash this goddamned Car-15 and figure out how to get an M-60 in there as my main weapon. Even after the Car had cooled down, the bolt was locked as tight as a drum. I was going to give it to the armorer tomorrow and tell him to melt it down for a paperweight.

That weapon had been cleaned, lubed, and cared for like it should have been. I even wire brushed the carbon deposits off of the bolt head and chamber. There was no reason for it to jam like it did, so I refused to use it. The M-60 was the answer.

That night, the NCO's were sitting around talking and I told them what had happened that day. They enjoyed the story about the head and ask me how I like flying Scouts. I told them I had to keep the chaos down a little and things will get better. I just shook my head. They had better get better. Short of being killed, it couldn't get much worse.

The next morning, I hit the flight line early. A man with a mission. Our armorer, big Roger Hayes, listened to my requests in silence while I ranted and stomped around the hooch telling him I had to have a 60 in the cockpit, not an M-16. He pulled out a Huey door-gunner 60 and I told him I wanted the infantry version. He grabbed one from the rack and we talked about what we could take off to make it shorter and lighter. The first thing that went was the butt plate. The rear sights were taken off, and the barrel was cut off, along with the front sights until the barrel was even with the gas port. Once we were done, there wasn't much left, but a barrel, chamber and a trigger. It was light, short, and perfect. I gave the Car back to him, signed out the 60 and went back to one of the LOH's to see how it would mount.

I sat in the seat and fiddled about. Where did I want the gun hanging? There was a grab handle towards the top front of the door, but it was too far forward. There was a machined hole at the top of the doorframe that was in the right place, so I scrounged up a D-ring and mounted it in the hole. I put a knot in both ends of a shock cord, and then a carabiner was put into the D-ring. The bottom hole in the shock cord then went over the carrying handle of the gun. It was a little back heavy, but it was workable. I adjusted the cord so the gun floated about six inches above my lap. I could use it suspended or free hand just by slipping the handle out of the cord. I decided that the grab handle would work too, I'd just have to test them out.

The ammo could lay in a pile on the floor in one continuous belt. This would give me a lot more firepower than an M-16.

The one problem was the cyclic. It wasn't going to be possible to use the 60 with the cyclic in place. I asked one of the pilots that wasn't flying if taking my cyclic out would be a big deal? He told me it was flight procedure in the Scouts to keep a stick available to the observer, as far as he knew. We thought maybe we could take the cyclic out of the bracket and put it under the seat, but our C.O. put the BIG NO on that idea. Then one of the crew chiefs walked up to the loach with a 14-inch standard cast iron water pipe. He wondered if it would fit into the female end of the cyclic control. It fit perfectly! By golly, I think we got a system here! The pipe would still be useable as a control if I needed it, but it was short enough to not interfere with my gun or the ammo belt. I got approval from Capt. Sprague to try it out on the next mission. I felt good about my day's work and slept like a baby that night. Tomorrow was a fly day and I would get to check things out.

The next day, I flew with Mr. Fliss. He looked like the kind of guy that should have been wearing a pinstriped suit on Wall Street, instead of strapped to a Loach. Neither team saw anything that day, but I got to test the 60, and things worked great. I pulled the belt up and folded the rounds back and forth across my left knee to keep jams from occurring. We had to be sure the empty brass didn't collect in the lower chin bubble and foul the pedals. One of the expended pieces of brass also broke the glass on one of the instruments on the panel. We'd probably have to rig up some kind of deflector to aim the expended brass down rather than out. A couple of hot pieces of brass also landed in the pilot's lap, which we definitely had to resolve. Pilots get cranky when their balls get scorched during a mission.

I felt pretty good about the mission that day, even though we hadn't seen anyone. I felt I had a better system than the other Oscars were using, but I'd have to prove it's worth before everyone changed over. I didn't really care if anybody changed, I was happy. Out with the crappy 16 — in with the 60! It was show time.

Apache troop had a black mixed breed dog that lived in and around our flight line shack. Her name was Scumbag because she apparently knew every male dog in Vinh Long intimately. She looked like a black lab and was very friendly. It seemed like she had a litter of puppies every six weeks! She was a little puppy oven. The guys told me she had 75 hours of Scout missions under her collar. I wasn't sure if I believed that or not, but it made a good story. Scumbag would jump into my seat while I was refueling in Vinh Long so it was obvious she had no fear of flying and was used to the noises a helicopter makes when the blades are turning.

The Brigade H.Q. group had a big ol' hound named Gunner that rode in the C & C ship. The guys claimed Gunner had 5 KBA's, or killed-by-air. There seemed to be a lot of canine pets around the base but I think the animals knew the Vietnamese considered dog fine cuisine and if they stayed around the American bases their chances were better of not being sautéed or stewed.

In September we got a new Brigade C.O. and he freaked out about a rabid dog in Soc Trang. He ordered all dogs at the Vinh Long base exterminated. Word was he killed Gunner himself with his sidearm. The Oscars at A-Troop organized an angel flight for Scumbag out of the base. I thought they were kidding when they told me what they had planned.

The pilots got a flight authorized to Chi Lang — Scumbag's new home. Big John sat in the left seat, and hung on to Scumbag as they flew away. This was a wild thing to do for a dog, but you had to admire their loyalty. They dropped her off at Chi Lang and didn't worry about her. She had been a scrounger all her life and there were lots of opportunities there. Ever since then, Scumbag would greet us at the Chi Lang airstrip whenever we based out there. Somehow she knew it was us. She'd settle down with us and expected a c-rat meal for her loyalty, which she got. We always carried a couple extra meals when we based out of Chi Lang just for her. Americans and their dog — the Vietnamese never understood.

Roxy's letters arrived pretty much daily, and I was getting a lot of food packages from home. Licorice, cookies, popcorn, rice crispy squares, apple butter, canned food, candy, anything that would ship, I got. The guys were amazed at how much food I got from home. I just sat back and enjoyed everything. Being my roomie was a much-coveted assignment.

# Tattletale

When a box of goodies arrived, Tom Russell's head always appeared at my door, wondering what was going on. I think he had a spy in the mailroom that contacted him when a food box arrived. Tom had 200 hours as a Huey door gunner and was even pulling night sniper missions from a Huey. He also led patrols around the perimeter, checking the wire, claymores, and assorted other problems. His patrols usually ended up at Madame Nums, the local chicken house. His patrols usually came back smiling. He was a 1st class mooch.

All of our Loaches had an Apache head painted on both sides of the engine doors. Some of the heads were fading due to heat, age, weather, etc. I heard a couple of the pilots talking about it and I told them I could repaint them, no sweat. My Dad was a professional sign painter during his off-duty hours and he made extra money to keep his family of seven in food and clothes. I helped him paint quite a bit while in high school, so I knew about these things.

I told the crew chiefs what I needed and they got me some Vietnamese paint, which was of pretty poor quality, but it was all we had. While they were scrounging, I wrote home and told Dad to send me some good camel hair brushes of assorted sizes plus some model paint for a project later.

As soon as I got all my stuff assembled, I made a stencil from one of the heads and repainted all of our ships on the down days. The ships looked better, but the paint started to dull about 2 months later. Cheap stuff. The model paint I used on my helmet. I painted a pair of eyes on the visor, looking down. On the back went the Indian Chief from one of my favorite cartoons, *Tumbleweeds*. I painted "TATTLETALE" above the eyes on my visor. The helmet looked sharp and I ended up painting a few more for the Oscars and pilots.

Our three hooch maids took good care of our rooms, dusting, clean bed linens, emptying the trash, etc. Thuy, Bai and Saan were our 3 maids, all young, and they took a lot of teasing from everybody. Butterfly was the Vietnamese woman that sold us sodas from our cantina in the afternoon. I'm guessing she was in her early 30s, always had a big smile for everybody and took a lot of shit from the guys in the troop. She could handle the crap well, though she threw it back as well as she took it, and always with a smile. One of the guys may ask her for some boom-boom and she'll shoot back "no can do – too ti ti," meaning his dick was too small! She's a hoot!

# Charlie Palek

My next flight out proved to be uneventful, so instead of sitting idle, "Wild Bill," one of my favorite pilots, and me went out into a large open paddy and I practiced my hovering. I found out just how hard it was to keep this potential air crash flying. All the controls had to be balanced and stabilized with the others. If you forgot about the cyclic while you were fussing with the foot pedals, you were in trouble. Trying to keep the LOH pointing in the right direction, and forgetting about the collective for an instant, you fell to earth. It took me several intense sessions to get me confident enough to at least land and hover. It wasn't pretty, but I got it down.

Flying one of these things was similar to this: Get an 8' step ladder, put a bowling ball on the top, and sit on the ball. Hold a bowl of water in each hand, then have a couple friends push, pull and jostle the ladder around while you try to keep your balance and not spill any of the water. That's how I felt the first time. I had much more respect for these guys that fly these strange aircraft after my feeble first attempt. Still, choppers were the only way to go.

Wild Bill Sorenson was one of those boyish looking pilots that always had a shitty little grin on his face, like a precocious 6 year old. We were flying to our AO one morning when he had to take a piss, and he could not wait till we landed. I half jokingly told him he'd just have to go out the door.

To my surprise, he said that's exactly what he was going to do. He turned the LOH controls over to me, and proceeded to do his thing.

He unbuckled, turned his body around to the right in kind of a stiff-bodied hunch, his right shoulder into the seat back, and let it fly!

While he was literally pissing into the wind, I was rattling off a commentary about how I wasn't wiping the urine blowback out of the cargo compartment and since it was his side of the ship, all rules about barfing would also apply to pissing on the ship. He was shaking his head up and down while I prattled on, obviously agreeing to all my conditions.

When we finally got to our AO, I couldn't find a drop of urine anywhere on the ship! He gave me one of his smirky little smiles, but no explanation.

I figured he either had a huge dick and could get it out there past the slipstream (a fact I wasn't going to try to confirm, by the way) or we flew through a windshear outside his door that I wasn't aware of and his piss blew straight down! Another Vietnam legend was born.

Occasionally, while flying the Tram, we encountered a tree covered with bats. They have wingspans of 2 – 3 feet, hanging from a tree like giant, tattered pieces of black crepe. Once a tree was spotted we gave it a wide berth lest there be a collision. "Wild Bill" came a little too close to one of these trees and startled the bats into flight. When they fly they tend to radiate out in all directions. Sorenson had a head-on with one of the bats. It broke through his lower chin bubble and ended up flopping around on top of his pedals. He said things got real interesting in the cockpit, flying while trying to kick a flopping bat out through the hole it came through. We're talking real life comedy here! It served as a good lesson for the other pilots. Once everybody got a good look at one of the creatures, nobody was anxious to invite one aboard. They were ugly!

I'd been lead Oscar for a few weeks now, my kill number going up and every mission a new adventure. We caught a group of five coming out of a tree line into a paddy as we were dropping down to operational altitude. There were a couple tree lines and paddies between us and them and when we got to their location, they had disappeared. I found their tracks in the mud, but nothing else. We hovered over the trees to see if there were any bunkers around and found zip. On the other side of a narrow paddy were piles of vegetation like stacks of cornhusks. My eyes kept going back to them so I told the pilot to wander over and check them out. We came in low and slow and our rotor wash parted the stack of grass and my oh my, there lay a V.C. in black pajamas and an old bolt action rifle. I shot him with a short burst then did the same to his rifle. The pilot backed the LOH up to the next one and there lay another one, weapon at his side. Same procedure. We checked three more piles, three more black pajamas with weapons at their sides. It was truly shooting fish in a barrel. I couldn't understand why the last three just laid there. They had to hear us shooting their buds. They were in the fetal position again. Not one of them even had their weapon in their hand when we hovered over. Damned strange. Even if they knew they were dead, I'd think they would at least come out shooting. They were probably local conscripts, poorly trained, and unmotivated. They only carried old bolt action rifles, obviously unworthy to carry the better weapons.

One might ask why we didn't take prisoners, these being fairly docile and all. But the Scouts weren't prepared or inclined to take prisoners. We had an infantry platoon we could put on the ground to corral them and bring them back, but that took a lot of energy, planning and time. We'd have to hold them at bay until the infantry arrived, and we wouldn't be doing it from the ground. Killing them was much easier and certainly less hassle. Destroy them and their weapons and leave them in the paddies to bloat up and rot. Not much different from previous wars, but still a waste. The basic premise was the same as centuries before. Kill more of them than they kill of you. Don't leave them alive, they may be the ones that shoot you down tomorrow.

Getting past the killing was done individually by everyone. Some guys didn't mind killing. It was part of the job for them. Others enjoyed being in a unique unit like the Scouts and accepted the killing as part of the job. However you viewed it, you had to be able to pull that trigger or you couldn't fly Scouts. We never considered ourselves murderers. It was them or us and that's what we lived by. Cover you buddy's ass, cover the ship, and cover your ass, in that order. Period.

I was flying with Mr. Willis one day around Saigon when we landed our team for a little lunch break. We were fully armed and fueled for our next mission.

After chow, we were getting ready to fly when a light colonel came quick, stepping over to our LOH. He had tailored, creased, and finely laundered fatigues, a Ranger haircut, and a car-15 in his hands. No CIB, no jump wings, no aviation wings, and a MACV patch.

He claimed to be with Army Intel and was authorized to grab a mission flight with us. Mr Willis was going to put him into the wing ship where he could observe better, but he wanted to fly in the lead ship. Mr. Willis was not happy about this. I was getting bumped because some limp dick intel wienie wanted to get some Scout time so he could brag to his buds during Miller time. He didn't know our procedures, how our radios operated or anything else.

They were only gone for about an hour, but our newbie observer was a mess when they got back. His fine O Club lunch was, at the moment, crusting up on the mini-gun in the cargo compartment and on the side of the ship.

Our stalwart colonel wobbled out of the seat; his feet testing the earth as he got out to make sure the ground was solidly underneath him. Using the LOH to stabilize his stance, I had to stifle a laugh when I saw his condition.

The front of his shirt and both thighs were covered with vile colored brownish/green puke. It was also crusted on his chin. His face was the color of a cheap hookers sheets, kind of dull and gray. Talk about the living dead!

He staggered away from the LOH, his only mission in life to get back to his comfy surroundings, clean up and never fuck with Army aviation again. It was a thing of beauty!

Mr. Willis was smiling as he shut down and gave me a big thumbs up when I caught his eye. He told me later he started low leveling and pulling hard right and left turns right away, and it took less than 10 minutes for his holiness to get sick. Mr. Willis obviously had a rousing good time. I didn't even mind cleaning up the ship. The sight of that colonel walking from the LOH kept me smiling for months.

We'd been fighting this war for over five years now and most of the combat troops hadn't seen much in the way of progress. It was maddening, and nobody saw it getting any better. But we plugged along.

Our flight procedures had changed since I joined the unit. Most of the observers had gone to M-60s now that they knew how well they worked. Our armorer built an aluminum brass deflector that bounced the empty brass casings down onto the floor rather than out into the instrument panel. It also came in handy if the pilot gave me some shit about something. I'd just aim the 60 towards the front of the ship, rattle off about 10 fast rounds, twisting the gun to the left and the pilot got a lap full of hot brass. It gave me respect and a lot less complaints.

We always had a smoke grenade in our left hand when we were on patrol. If we received fire, the grenade was tossed out, we'd climb to altitude and the Cobras would work over the area. We'd go back in and check for bodies or damage. We always kept a large pin to stick back into the smoke if it wasn't used. Nobody lost his pin.

We were also carrying a new piece of ordinance called a superfrag. It was simple, really. We taped a 2 ¼ pound stick of C-4 to a frag grenade and used them for busting bunkers. They packed quite a wallop, blowing out the top or enlarging the door. The pilots I'd been flying with had learned how to set me up to chuck grenades into the bunker openings and I hadn't missed one in months. It was real easy now compared to my first flight with Sprague. The pilots were setting me up perfectly and it became easy to make that grenade roll right in, most of the time without even bouncing first. The rule was the Oscar couldn't claim a kill unless the body was in view for another crewmember to confirm. If a V.C. ran into the bunker and a grenade was tossed in, the kill wasn't good unless he could be seen at the door, dead or wounded. Otherwise, no kill.

My subsequent new skills at grenade tossing caught the attention of Capt. Sprague and he requested that I fly lead Oscar with him, now that I was properly trained. Raabe told me this one night after a long day of flying and I got pissed. He didn't want me around when I was fresh faced and untrained. He refused to take the time or had the patience to help me learn. Now I apparently was good enough to fly with him. I felt no allegiance to him. The other pilots took the time to teach me and I felt loyalty to them. This Captain was another typical lifer officer looking for points on the way up.

I told Raabe, our C.O. or not, the only way I'd fly with him was if he ordered me to. I felt like he was taking advantage of the whole situation and I wasn't happy. Raabe took me over to his quarters and we had another talk, this time I was refusing to fly with him. We hadn't talked much after his refusal to fly with me which was o.k. I didn't like him much anyway. He never fucked with my flying schedule or me so that I had appreciated. But he bristled up like a mother hen when I told him I didn't want to fly with him and told him my reasons. I think I caught him off guard, because he looked at me like I had just put a turd in his beer. Raabe was standing between us, but I wasn't planning on fighting the guy, I was just enjoying the minute. I had waited for this moment and I was going to revel in it. I knew if he ordered, I would fly with him, but I wasn't going to respect him like the other pilots, and he knew it.

His feathers thoroughly ruffled, he informed me I was ordered to fly as his Oscar on the next several missions. I gave him a "yes sir" and walked out. He knew the two of us as crewmembers was tenuous, but he had to assert his authority. So he was back to being a big shot and I had my little victory. The little ones counted too. Victories were scarce around here; you had to take them when they came around.

So we flew together for a week or so, doing our job together when we were down low. Flights to and from our A.O. were icy and it wasn't because we were flying high. He did let me leave the LOH on one mission when we discovered a V.C. graveyard with a bunch of painted grave markers. I hopped around on their graves like a well armored, helmeted Igor, breaking the stones off and putting them into the LOH. They'd make good decorations for our rooms.

# Tattletale

The flights were pretty much uneventful and unmemorable. Sprague was wounded shortly after and sent home. Several guys, including myself, went to see him before he shipped out. Everybody shook his hand and left. I was the last one to leave. We stared at each other, each waiting for the other to say something, but neither spoke. We were like two mongrel dogs standing over a chunk of meat neither one could eat anymore.

I finally nodded my head and left, silence following me out the door. I was glad to see him go, and I'm sure he was glad to be rid of me too. Now we could get back to the fun!

Flying out with Mr. White one day found us hovering over a brand new bunker complex, the dirt still fresh and new barefoot tracks in the sand. It was a large complex and as we hovered over the area, we wondered where all the people had gone.

My eyes were looking to the left front as Mr. White and I discussed using some of our willy pete's to see if the bunkers were occupied. Our answer came rather abruptly when some dude below us popped out of a hole and emptied about twenty rounds into the cargo and engine compartments of our ship. We were only about 10 feet above the ground, but it sounded like the AK was going off right behind our seats.

I immediately tossed the smoke out and we shot out of there like we were on fire, which at the time, we might have been.

While the Cobras rolled in and clobbered the complex, we grabbed some altitude and started watching our gauges, both of us pretty confident that something vital had been hit. Surprisingly, nothing seemed to be wrong. All the gauges were on normal and Mr. White claimed that there were no handling difficulties. We wisely decided to head back to our staging area and check the old girl out.

After we landed, we got out and started looking the ship over. There were holes all over both engine covers, but miraculously nothing vital had been hit. We also found several hits in the cargo compartment, the back of our seats and no doubt a few had gone through the back. We also found a couple of dings in the rotor blades.

We were genuinely amazed that the ship had taken all those hits but could still fly. Our euphoria ended rather abruptly when I lifted an ammo can full of frag grenades that I had strapped into the cargo area and found a bullet hole going into the can.

This was the first time that I had put extra frags in the back, but we were told we'd be checking a lot of bunkers and I didn't want to run out.

## Charlie Palek

I gingerly lifted the can out, put it on the ground and opened it up. The bullet had gone through three of the frags and stopped in the fourth, denting the blasting cap of the grenade about 1 millimeter! My knees got a little weak upon this discovery and I had to sit down. Mr. White's face was ashen, his mouth hanging open like he was thunderstruck. Jesus, one doesn't get that much closer to death and live to tell about it!

We looked at each other and we both had the same look in our eyes- "we are two lucky sonsabitches!" Our wing crew just shook their heads and claimed someone was watching over us today. I could hardly argue. I put the can in the field and destroyed the whole bunch with another frag and vowed never to pack grenades in the rear again.

Mr. White figured the ship was still flyable, so we went home early, our wing escorting us in case of trouble.

Back at Vinh Long, we shut down and sat in our seats, listening to the rotor blades slow down and smiling at each other. What a day!

While I was getting out and showing SP/4 Crummy, the crew chief, all of the new holes he had to patch, Mr. White filled out his log.

After each mission, the pilots were required to write a report in the ship's log book about any problems we had, hits we'd taken, etc. Mr. White reported the hits, then as the final entry he put "grommet excessively tight." I watched him fill out the final entry and laughed because I knew what he meant.

The next day I flew with Mr. White again in a different bird. We went back to the same bunker complex and checked it out, only this time we kept moving. The Cobras had torn it up good but we found no bodies.

At the end of the day, we hovered back into our revetment and before we had shut down, Crummy was at the pilot door with a wild look on his face.

He told Mr. White, quite incredulously, that he looked in every manual that existed on the LOH and he could not find a "grommet" in any of them. He went on and on about how he spent all day looking through the maintenance manuals and talking to the other crew chiefs but the mysterious "grommet" couldn't be found.

Crummy started suspecting something when Mr. White and I started laughing so hard we couldn't stop. It was one of the best jokes I'd ever heard. Mr. White meant that his asshole was excessively tight, not a control on the ship. We were sitting in our seats roaring about his, and Crummy got a little miffed about all the time he wasted that day, but he eventually came around and had to admit it was a first class joke. I loved flying with Mr. White!

Everybody was having huge success with the M-60s by now. Most of the Oscars were using them and loving it. Firing any weapon from a tight turning or jerking chopper while aiming at a moving target was to say the least, a real challenge. Fortunately we were usually flying so low that the need for tracers were not needed, even though all the belts had them. Our rounds were beating down around the target so fast we could make our corrections quickly. Keeping your brain, vision, arms and stomach all operating in sync when you're in a tight hauling left hand turn, practically looking straight down while your target's down there attempting the three minute mile through the jungle is a challenge, to say the least. By the time the action gets this hot, the adrenaline is literally washing over you. Your hair is standing up on the back of your neck and your asshole is tight enough to stand on it's own. There's no feeling like it on earth. Man hunting man. It was a rush!

We were supporting mostly Vietnamese troops now. We hardly saw any GIs unless one or two were serving with the South's units as advisors. The Vietnamese units that didn't have U.S. advisors usually didn't want to do anything. They took long breaks and simply wouldn't move or sweep. I was flying with Mr. Dicresce, trying to light a fire under an Arvin Company sweeping (I use the term loosely) around Chi Lang. We had found some bunkers in a tree line a rice paddy away from the Arvins. We hovered around, pointing in the direction they were to move, and they were ignoring us. We dicked around for a half-hour with these idiots until one of the grenadier's decided to fire a 40mm grenade into the trees, a half-assed recon by fire. So this guy steps forward, loads the Blooper and fires a grenade right into a tree limb about 50 feet away. The grenade explodes and peppers half a dozen guys with shrapnel! The wounds were light at that range, but they went through the whole gamut, being patched up by their medic and calling in a dustoff to take out some of the wounded. It was almost like they did it on purpose, so they could stall a little longer. We were pissed about it and told our C & C we were wasting time with these guys and we'd be better off working without them.

So our C & C had them line up in chalks for extraction. We were flying around grumbling about their lack of motivation. Vietnamization my ass. These guys were not going to beat the highly motivated troops of the North in 100 years. We were wasting time with these jokers and it made all our troops edgy.

We watched the Arvins eagerly line up to be pulled out, expending more energy than we had seen spent all day. They were ready to go home. I was so disgusted with the whole day. I wanted to do something to make the disappointment easier to take. My time came abruptly over the radio when our C & C told us to drop a smoke grenade at the north end of the chalks for the Hueys to come in on. We flew over the Arvins at about 100 M.P.H. and I leaned out and threw the smoker right at the first chalk on the north end. I was trying hard to hit one of the little bastards. I couldn't see what happened, but our wing pilot told us later that the grenade had hit a guy right in the back of the head and laid him out like a frozen fish. I felt my mission had been accomplished. My attitude was also changing even more. I felt at this point that this thing was not going to be won. It was sickening. We were being blind-sided by everybody, the military, the press, and our government. Trust was out the door! Never in 100 years.

We had a couple of down days so some of the guys took me into town for some R & R. We went to their favorite bar on Main St., a little place with about 8 tables and enough hookers hanging around to kill us all if we cared to overindulge.

We were the first in the bar and even though it was late morning, it was close enough to noon for some beers, so we all ordered a 33. The girls descended on our table like turkeys on a grasshopper, sitting on our laps, asking for a tea, rubbing our chests and running their fingers through our hair. My girl sat on my lap and the normal conversation began, exchanging names, she'd compliment me, I'd do the same to her then the sparring would begin. Teas were bought and everybody was rubbing against each other. My lady's thighs were smooth, soft and warm. Unfortunately, this was the end of the month and nobody had enough cash to buy their favors, so they eventually dropped out of our group and into another bunch that just arrived.

My tongue was as numb as an executioner's heart by the time I walked out of there. Half my body felt pickled from the goddamned beer we drank and the formaldehyde in it. It was a good thing we were off, because we all went back to the base and collapsed in our bunks. Some of the guys even missed supper, but most of us considered that a minor loss.

In Mid-September, our teams flew into Chi Lang. I'm with Mr. Fliss — Mr. Low key. The weather turned to crap while we were on our way to our A.O., so we turned back. We climbed to 10,000 feet and Mr. Fliss called to the tower at Chi Lang he would be making a 10,000 foot vertical corkscrew approach to the runway. The tower guy asked for a confirmation, apparently thinking he heard wrong. So, Mr. Fliss repeated his directions and began a slow vertical spiral to the ground. The controller wasn't thrilled with the new landing approach, and Mr. Fliss got an ass chewing when he got back to Vinh Long, but we sure had fun. Anything to break up the monotony.

We also discovered while dicking around Chi Lang airstrip, that the Car 15 with the large flash suppressor made a dandy emergency cyclic, the barrel fitting into the socket perfectly. I considered this use for the Car better than it's use as a weapon, but I still refused to carry one.

One of the kids that would hang around us when we were in Chi Lang attempted to lift a couple frag grenades out of one of the ships. I had lost a camera to the little scroungers a month earlier. We caught the kid this time and Mr. Sorenson and one of the other pilots threw him into the canal. Now one of us is always with the ships if the crews leave to eat.

Back to Chi Lang the next day with orders to try and capture some V.C. alive. The Blues were standing by with a couple of Hueys to extract our prisoners if we found any.

It was typical Chi Lang terrain — flood plains, vast fields of high grass and brush. We were flying around about 10 feet off the ground when we crossed a small canal about 5 feet deep. The water was murky and as we crossed, I noticed three reeds sticking out of the water that looked a bit out of place. All up and down the canal there were no reeds sticking out of the water, only in this one spot. I had the pilot pull a hard left and we went back to take a closer look. We hovered over the water and could see what looked like the faint outline of 3 people under the water. I had the pilot back off and I fired a fast burst into the water in front of them. The three V.C. came out of the water like rockets, their hands in the air. It was almost comical.

I was, however, impressed with their methods. I had only seen this type of evasion in the movies, but apparently it does work to breathe through a hollow reed. One of our lifts came in and picked them up and took them back to Vinh Long. I didn't find out if they had any info or not. No weapons, no I.D., but they were hiding. Not good for them.

## Charlie Palek

A couple days later near Cau Mau, we crossed a small banana grove and I saw three guys hiding behind the trees trying to become part of the vegetation. Their bicycles were lying in the grove of trees.

We did a hard left turn and came back up on them, spotted their weapons and I killed them all, then wrecked their bikes. While we were checking out the bodies, I noticed one of them had what looked like a courier pouch around his shoulder. I figured he had some intel that might be valuable, and I told the pilot to land and I'd get the pouch, but he'd have none of that. There was no way he was going to let me out. I begged, I pleaded, I threatened again. But it never happened. The pilots would not let their Oscars out of the Loach. It was frustrating.

The next day in the same area, we scared up a wild boar and thought we'd kill him and bring him back for a barbecue. Before we made our gun run on Porky, the lead Snake pilot ask if we'd step aside and let his new gunner take a shot. Since we had been having all the fun, my pilot gave them the go ahead. We climbed to about 2,000 feet and watched the show. The Cobra screamed into a dive and we watched the mini-gun tracers creep up on the frantically running pig. It was running a serpentine route, avoiding the 6,000 rounds per minute mini-gun like it was reading the gunner's mind.

The Cobra was in a left-hand turn, the pilot trying to keep the now frantic pig in a circle inside the gunner's sight. We watched the whole episode until the pig suddenly went stiff and hit the ground like it had been pole-axed. Its forward momentum dug a trench in the mud as it hit the ground. Our C & C chopper landed and the two gunners with a lot of grunting no doubt, tossed the carcass into the ship. This turned out to be the last mission of the day, so everybody headed back to fuel up and head home.

As it happened, the pig was too old and tough to provide us with our BBQ, but the best part was to come. The Snake gunner had only hit the pig one time! He'd fired 3,500 rounds at it, the one magic bullet entering the brain from the back of the head. The gunner starting taking shit about his gunnery skills the second this fact became known and I'm sure the joke followed him until his tour was completed. This incident provided the LOH crews with ammunition when the inevitable arguments came up about the skills of gun crews versus LOH crews! We laughed for months about this.

There were days that we had two teams out and never saw a thing, but they were rare. The completion for highest kills was raging between Doug Houston and me. I was running about four KBA behind him, and, as horrible as it sounds, when my team was out seeing action, the other team would be back at the A.O. pacing and bitching because we were seeing some V.C. We'd put the number of kills we got that day on the front of our windscreen in yellow grease pencil. That's the first thing our crew chiefs looked for when we got back to Vinh Long. Some of them kept track of the number of kills from their ship.

We didn't ponder too much about our lack of humanity. We considered the men we killed as dead enemies, not human beings. I kept that thought in mind because we were down close enough to see their faces, especially their eyes. I saw the look in their faces when they knew they were dead or going to be killed. I saw looks of desperation, anger, dumbfoundedness, and fear just before I pulled the trigger. I know I went through all these emotions while with the 9th.

Mr. Dicresce and I were low leveling around the Tram one day and we had found nothing. We rounded a clump of bushes and no more than 50 yards away was a V.C. in one of their sampans. The look on his face was pure surprise, apparently he hadn't heard us at all. He was right outside my door and as I watched him dive into the water, Dicresce sideslipped the LOH over to the boat. There were two items wrapped up in the boat, and one of them was a rifle, probably an SKS. I could see his body under the water and we hovered until he came back up, sputtering with a frightened look in his eyes. He knew that, as sure as water is wet, that he was a dead man. I obliged him from a range of about 8 feet, watching his body stiffen then sink into the murky water. Since there was no place to set down, I got out my trusty grappling hook and while Mr. Dicresce held a steady hover, I grabbed the rifle and the other package, hooking the green plastic wrapping easily. I riddled the boat with 7.62, and we left.

I waited to unwrap our prizes until we got back to our A.O. The SKS was old, with a dark, oiled stock and forearm and very well cared for. Not a spot of rust on it anywhere. It was a Chinese knock off, but we fired a few rounds through it and the iron sights were zeroed perfectly. A good trophy.

The other packet held some rice balls, three zip clips and some dried fish. Pretty sparse rations for a soldier but the V.C. seemed to be doing fine on it.

The one thing that amazed me about this little drama was how we managed to get the drop on this guy. He hadn't heard us until we were right on him. He was either daydreaming big time or that little LOH was a lot quieter than I thought. I think when we were low leveling and moving slowly at a low RPM; the LOH was fairly quiet. This incident seemed to bear me out. Another one for our side.

Our troop got in a new bunker buster mounted on the left side of a Cobra. It consisted of a 20mm gattling gun, similar to our mini-gun except with a lot more punch. It fired 2,000 RPM through its six barrels. It was a pee-bringer and the day they tested it was exciting. The Cobra lifted from the runway and proceeded to a rice paddy with some natural targets to shoot at.

It came back within the hour, the test over. Apparently on the first gun run the recoil of the cannon forced the Cobra so badly out of trim the pilot had to give a lot of right pedal to deep the chopper flying straight. A couple more runs and just about every rivet on the left side of the ship had popped. Apparently this bad boy was too much for a gun platform like the Cobra. Sounded like a good idea, but it didn't pay off. We never saw it again.

I guess something as big as a 20-mm gattling gun needed a bigger platform like the C-47 or C-130.

By mid-September, things were staying busy. Our fly 1 day on, 1 day off the next wasn't working out. We were short of observers and flying two days and off one became the new rule. Despite that there were times when I flew 7 – 10 days in a row. I preferred this to standing down. Things were getting down to the chicken shit level at Vinh Long. Ratty little REMF bastards were nailing guys for unshined boots, no naked women in the sleeping quarters, pictured or otherwise, locking up our ammo in the barracks, inspecting the flight line like it was located in the world, no pets, whatever kind of bullshit the little weasels could think up. I found myself volunteering to fly every day. Until one of our N.C.O.'s noticed I was never at reveille and forced me down a couple days. I couldn't stand those little REMF assholes.

One of our Cobras hit a paddy dike low leveling on the way home this week. It was pilot error. He got a little too close to the ground. The gunner was killed, pilot badly injured. There wasn't enough left of the gunner's cockpit to put into a trash can.

One of the Cobra gunners and I traded seats coming back from Chi Lang. He was curious about the LOH and having the opportunity to fly in a Cobra was one I wasn't going to blow off.

The flight home was smooth and interesting. It felt strange to be in a totally enclosed cockpit in a chopper. Every chopper I ever flew in had the door off, the wind blasting past the opening, making conversation hard without an internal radio. The narrow cockpit fit me like a glove, the instruments at the gunner's command all within reach. A 40mm grenade launcher and a mini-gun in the chin turret was a lot of firepower, I wish I could have tried the weapons, but I knew that would never happen. It sure was a lot quieter though. I just sat back and enjoyed the moment.

We have a new pilot named Mr. Landry and he is a wild Viking right down to his red hair and bushy, "don't fuck with me" moustache. Flying with him is combat entertainment in its purest form. He has incredible eyes and throws the LOH around like he was born in it.

During a recent lull at our staging area, he got bored and decided to ride a water buffalo. There was an old farmer plowing his paddy up the road and Red Dog went right up to the farmer, gave him a fistful of P's and hopped on board. He rode around on that big ol' buff for 15 minutes, hollering like a rodeo rider. The old man plodded behind his plow, looking up occasionally like he couldn't believe what he was seeing. I told Landry before he hopped on board that the water buffs didn't like Americans, but he blew me off — the ravings of an infantry guy that had one too many rounds exploded in his foxhole.

So he got his ride without incident and I decided that maybe the buffs only hated the infantry! Whatever, it was funny as hell and I always liked flying with Landry. He kept things interesting. Being a past Charlie model gunship pilot had given him the experience in target acquisition that comes with the job.

I flew with Landry staging out of Cau Mau in early October. We ran rampant through the U Minh Forest, blowing up or shooting anything that could be used by the enemy, including their laundry, flags, cooking fires, animals, anything that looked useful. We loved free-fire zones. It was like opening the door so the fox could enter the chicken house. We sunk several sampans, blew several bunkers, burned camouflaged hooches in the trees and had a great time. Didn't see any people — they were there, but knew better than to expose themselves. Our blood was up, and we were disappointed that we saw no V.C. that day. The U Minh was supposed to be a haven for V.C. training camps and rehab facilities. Going into the U Minh and not seeing any V.C. was like having a birthday party and not getting any presents — a real bring down.

Flying out of Cau Mau that night, we were supposed to form up with the lift guys who were cooling their skids in Toi Bin. A horrendous fog rolled in before we left and we couldn't see very well at the lower altitudes, so we climbed above the fog and attempted to hit Toi Bin by homing into the lift location with our FM radio, which promptly phased out on us just as we got our first signal. Landry was flying and kicking the console while I worked the pedals, calling the C&C ship and telling them his "thing-a-ma-jig" wasn't working! This brought a howl from one of the gun pilots, who offered to help his next trip into town with his "thing-a-ma-jig!" Landry let the comment slide, becoming more frustrated with the malfunctioning equipment.

I watched all of this going on in the seat next to me, laughing and having a good ol' time. I asked Red Dog if he was still interested in becoming a flight instructor when be called his instrument panel a "thing-a-ma-jig" He looked at me, laughed and said "if you tell fledgling pilots something with enough conviction, they'll believe anything. He was a master at shoveling manure, so I believed him.

We finally made it to Toi Bin through a compass heading, a partially working radio and the fact we outran the fog right at our airfield. The LOH wasn't equipped for night flying, and heavy fog was no better. We stumbled through the fog and got to where we were going by pure luck. What a way to fight a war.

Things at Vinh Long were getting worse. We had an I.G. inspection in December, and it was a goat fuck from the word go. Pant legs were being measured to make sure they weren't pegged too tight, we put new sandbags around our bunkers despite the fact we already had enough of them in place. — they just looked too old and weathered. New bunkers were built, uniforms were starched, compounds cleaned up, and rocks painted, roaches and rats lined up in formation, the whole works. I'm beginning to think the REMF's, the bureaucrats of the Army, think this war is over.

What I couldn't believe was that all the troops and their armorers in particular, had to give up all the spare parts they had scrounged or cannibalized. This was the most ridiculous thing I had ever heard of. Anybody, down to the lowest E-1 on the rank ladder, knew that there were always shortages and rat holing parts and equipment from one source or another was a necessity to keep the choppers flying and their weapons working. Apparently the geniuses in the High Command thought these weapon systems lasted forever, in a war zone! I couldn't fathom that kind of thinking. I know most of the guys spirited away their stash before the inspection rather than giving the equipment up. It was a brainless exercise and there was no need for it.

Leaving the I.G. inspection to the poor bastards on the ground, I stayed in the air as much as possible — in the Tram with Mr. Sorenson. We found 6 guys humping some heavy weapons in the grass so we swooped in, dropped a smoke and let the Cobras hammer them. Found 6 KBA, an air-cooled .30-caliber, some AK's and a Thompson submachine gun. I thought the Thompson would make a good backup weapon, but it disappeared fast once the lift ship that picked up the weapons got back to base. We were happy about the .30-caliber. That kind of weapon could rain up a shit storm on our little LOHs. Having it out of action made it a good day. Another one for us.

I had a couple down days in mid-December, so I went to the flight line hooch and re-cleaned and inspected my M-60. I also cleaned up a couple of the mini-guns, replaced some parts and generally enjoyed the time alone, letting the smell of the gun oil and the flight line lull me into a state of relaxation.

When I got back to the Troop area, our platoon sergeant cornered me in the compound and told me a slot opened up for assistant platoon sergeant and asked me if I was interested in taking it. It would mean a promotion to E-6 and no more flying. He was really selling this deal, wanting me to stay on the ground and help him with the administrative part of the Troop. I told him I appreciated the thought, but there was no way I was going to stop flying. The promotion meant little to me since I was getting out in six months. I had decided that as exciting as the Army was when a war was cooking, I didn't like the bullshit that went with it. There were too many idiots in charge and one could not walk away from the Army like you could in a civilian job. The Army considered that AWOL and sent you to jail for it.

So my plans for a military career were over. I told the platoon sarge that I wanted to keep flying and didn't care if I got promoted or not. He stopped the sales pitch, turned the conversation 180 degrees and asks me if I wanted to re-up for a burst of 6! This caught me by surprise and I was speechless for a second or two. Then my brain unlocked and I started my diatribe of why I would not be extending my service time. He threw out a hefty re-enlistment bonus of several thousand dollars, another cash bonus for pulling a 3rd tour in Nam, and E-6 stripes for my sleeves. No dice. He was pitching like Bob Gibson trying to close a no-hitter, but I wasn't even at the plate. He finally gave up and told me I could fly 'til I dropped. He was a career soldier and I knew he was doing his job, but I also felt he knew where I was coming from too. He'd have to find himself another REMF patsy. After all, I came back to Nam to get away from the REMF's at Ft. Hood.

We'd also heard that most of the Scouts would be going to Bien Tuiy to see Bob Hope's Christmas Show but I had doubts about that, and I was right. We never got there.

U.S. troops were pulling out of Vietnam as if the war was over. 50,000 more were leaving in December and the scuttlebutt was that Vietnamization was working and we were gradually going to turn all the fighting over to the Vietnamese. It didn't take a Ph.D. to see that wasn't going to happen. There were some good, aggressive Vietnamese units, but more often than not, they were lazy, unmotivated and perfectly willing for us to do the fighting for them. They didn't have any kind of Cav outfit like ours, which meant we would probably be the last to leave this hole. We would do all their air support for them. The idea of fighting this war without American units backing us up did not appeal to many of us. The American public was being sold a bill of goods and I felt we were being sold out. History was not going to be kind.

Boredom set in a week before Christmas and somebody tossed a smoke grenade at us while we were cooling our skids at Chi Lang. Retaliation followed by several others until the LOH's couldn't be seen through the fog of red and yellow smoke. It was all in fun — bored with inactivity and itching to fly again.

Somewhere along the line this episode was reported to our C.O., and he laid into the pilots that that kind of crap had better not happen again. Throwing any kind of grenade around choppers filled with ammo, fuel, and explosives were dangerous to the extreme. It's not like we were not aware of this fact. But we had been handling grenades, white phosphorus, and super frags on a daily basis and it was to the point where it had become casual. We piled frags on the console between the pilot and observer like apples at a fruit stand. It wasn't safe, but we weighed the danger to the fact that they would be immediately available, and the danger came in second. Dicking around with your weapons while under fire is not advisable.

## MURPHY'S LAW OF COMBAT
### #31
### "All five second grenade fuses are three seconds."

I did have an incident one-day over the Tram that almost made me give up frags for good. Mr. Dicresce and I had found a shallow bunker in the trees and decided to toss in a frag. I picked one from the tree, pulled the pin and waited for the pilot to line me up for a run. To do one of these drops I had to lean out of the door as far as I could. My right hand was holding the grab handle on the doorframe, my 60 resting in my lap. The grenade had to be thrown beyond the mini-gun, which was outside my door. Most of the pilots pulled a little sideslip with their right pedal putting the mini out of my way, just slightly. Once I'd gotten the hang of this routine, I never missed. I was hitting bunker openings as small as a Wheaties box. It took teamwork and skill to do that, and we had it down pat.

So I was leaning out the door, the slipstream slapping my face, making me squint. We scooted over the bunker and I tossed the frag. About the time it passed my fingertips it popped, sounding like a .22 going off right next to my face. I swear my heart stopped for at least 10 seconds. The grenade was defective and never exploded but I was seriously frazzled. I looked over at Mr. Dicresce and he was looking at me with eyes as big as 40-mm shells. He had that "What the hell was that?" look followed by "I need clean underwear!" I laid my head against the rest and took several deep breaths, trying to get my heart pumping again. Shit! That had scared the hell out of me. I had thrown hundreds of grenades and that was the one and only time that had happened. We pulled some altitude, took stock of the few nerves we had left and took a short break. Dicresce told the guys what had happened and since we were due to rotate soon, we headed back for our A.O. strip. It took the flight back to unclench my ass so I'd at least be able to get out of my seat to fuel up. That was one experience I didn't need to repeat.

## Charlie Palek

Back at Vinh Long, there was talk of a Christmas Truce but I had grave doubts. Spirits were always a little higher during the holidays, but it didn't take much to get your spirits crashing down fast around here. I tried to keep from getting too maudlin. I always enjoyed Christmas at home with the kids, aggravating them to no end. The food, the smells, the good cheer with family and friends. Christmas could have come and gone and I probably wouldn't have noticed if it weren't for the feeble attempt by some to celebrate.

Russ was stopping in often, posing for me for his submission to Goliath magazine. He claimed to have a beautiful body but he looked pathetic to me. I enjoyed having him around. His head was the first in our doorway when we got a package from home or was cooking in our room. He got a package from home once and brought me a can of Blue Point Oysters. I tried one and it tasted like a booger. I told him so and he puffed up like a guinea fowl and told me I was an ungrateful bastard. I told him he was a chincy bastard for bringing inedible food after all I've given him. The conversation might as well not even happened; his ugly mug was in my doorway the next day after I received a package. What a mooch!

Cosmo came into our room the other day with a Viet peasant hat on and put on an embarrassing little show that was enjoyed by all. Madam "Cosmo" Butterfly and his cracked sense of humor. Thank goodness for guys like them!

Our mess hall is serving the same old roast beef 3 – 4 times a week with stringy carrots and warm milk. Guys have actually been scrounging around for C-rats to keep from eating mess hall food! I find the C's easier to take than most of the guys, so I gave them some tips on making them edible. Some of my underlings looked at me like I was mad. What does an old infantry grunt know about making good food! The innocence of the young.

Christmas Eve found us staging out of Cau Mau and cruising the West Coast of Vietnam in the Gulf of Thailand. Our job was to check boats along the coast for weapons, ammo and other wartime goodies, especially replacement soldiers. Word was the supply line from Cambodia by boat was increasing, especially in the 3 & 4 Corp area. Flying over open water like this was new to us although picking out targets was considerably easier. I was a little apprehensive about being over the water. I wasn't much of a swimmer and mechanical failures being an ever-present danger,

I didn't like even thinking about a water crash. Oh well. Faith in our crew chiefs was what it was all about.

We spent our first flight checking the water off the beaches and small river inlets for boats that possibly could have already put in. Things were pretty slow until the guns told us a 20 footer was heading south to the north of our position. We buzzed off the beach and headed north, finding our target about a ½ mile off shore chugging away like he didn't have a care in the world.

We circled around him once, giving the once over. It was a diesel inboard, wooden keel supply boat with a compartment above and below. From what we could see there were wooden crates inside the upper compartment and it appeared to be a viable target. We motioned to him to head for shore and the only guy we saw on the deck turned the wheel and headed west like there was no tomorrow. A bit suspicious, yes? The old diesel was pumping out smoke, the engine pounding out max RPM's. The captain was watching us over his shoulder while we hovered in a circle, watching him head for the seven mile limit. The rules of engagement were a bit hazy on this one, but cutting and running seemed like a violation to us. The guns called the C&C and asked them what to do. The simple reply came back — "sink him."

Before we went back down, we talked to the snake drivers and decided unless we had real problems we'd take out El Capitan and let the Cobras take out the boat. But we were going to give him one more chance. We were fudging on our orders a little, but we were curious to find out what he was carrying. We dropped back down and I fired my 60 across his bow. No change. We sideslipped over to the guy on the wheel and I pointed back to shore. He hunched over the wheel and kept his heading.

That was enough of this shit. We came around with the boat outside my door and I fired a burst at the deck near his feet. I started to point to shore and he jumped right into the water and went under. We dropped down to about 10 feet, hovering over the spot he went under and waited.

A few seconds and he came to the surface, spitting water and staring right into the barrel of my 60. I had seen the look before, and I would never forget his face. He knew he was dead and was just waiting for the gun to start hammering.

Just before I pulled the trigger, I thought to myself that this whole scene could have been avoided if he just turned his boat east and headed for shore. This type of killing was so one-sided. He was going to die, by

## Charlie Palek

my hand or someone else's, that was a fact and we both knew it. Whether this was a combat death or murder is a gray area as large as all outdoors. I considered it combat despite the fact that I had shot a guy, treading water with no weapons as I hovered like the "Angel of Death" from a chopper. It was hard not to consider it murder.

As his body sank into the ocean, a pink cloud of diluted blood appeared on the surface, marking his grave. Just before we climbed to altitude, I screamed "Merry Christmas asshole" out the door, out of anger more than anything else did.

The lead Cobra made a run on the boat and hit it with dozens of 40mm grenades. It broke in two and sunk in less than a minute. No secondaries. Nothing to mark the spot except a bit of flotsam. Christmas in Vietnam — what a bitch. Bing Crosby was singing on AFVN while flying home that night, but it did little to put me in the spirit. It's too hard trying to maintain the "good will towards men" when you're flying in a machine built to blow them away. I wasn't going to let depression wrestle me to the ground. I knew this incident would be in my head forever, so why fight it. I filed it away and didn't let it affect my job.

The next day was Christmas, but we were still flying, out of Chi Lang this time. We patrolled the Tram and found nothing. The higher ups, taking the 68 Tet Offensive to heart, believed the truce would be used to bring in more men and materials over the supply routes. It wasn't happening in the Tram. We saw zilch all day.

When we got back, I got the good news that I was perimeter duty that night. I couldn't believe they were putting me in a bunker after flying three missions that day. Where in the hell were the troop grunts. Perimeter security was their job. As I said before, "Merry Christmas Asshole."

I got off perimeter duty at sunrise the next day, so I crashed till midafternoon. I found a package from home. All kinds of goodies to eat plus some toys to give to the orphans from Ter & Sher. I grabbed a pass and went to the orphanage before curfew. I took some cookies, and the toys, distributed them and took pictures of the kids' happy faces for the twins. Kids being kids, they enjoyed the toys and food immensely. Maybe I was looking for absolution after Christmas Eve, penance for my sins. Whatever, I left about 2 hours later, feeling better in general and ready to get back into the air. Self-absolution. Self-vindication. I wasn't even Catholic.

*Tattletale*

It was New Year's Eve, and the Archies song "Sugar, Sugar" was the #1 hit for 1969 according to AFVN. At the magic hour the perimeter was lit up with M-60 and M-16 tracers and flares popped everywhere. The town of Vinh Long joined in with some real fireworks. A feeble attempt at a joyous celebration. One suicide was recorded at the 214th. Another holiday truce, not much happening, yet. 1970 came in like a lamb, at least in our area.

New Years Day we flew the Tram again, and saw nothing. Nobody was moving that we could see, but our guts told us the Commies were busy building up for the year. They loved our truces. They could re-build and re-arm while we pulled back. Even though we were still hunting V.C. during the truce, the rules of engagement were a bit hazy. Possible targets had to be cleared through Cav higher ups, even if they were running with weapons. Rules — I love'em!

A few nights later, somebody procured a particularly disgusting porno film that's showing was eagerly anticipated by all. Half the troop gathered by the pilot's hooches, sitting on the concrete pad of the common area, the film projected on a white board put up for just such a cinematic treat. The main characters of the film was a young woman and a Great Dane, the plot...should be self-explanatory. It looked to be a 1930s vintage, and it was horribly debasing to women and pets and was met with hoots of approval, laughter and ribald comments of every sort. About two thirds of the way through the film, the crowd got quiet. My guess is that most of us were starting to envy the dog. No saltpeter for us.

All of a sudden there came a booming voice behind us, echoing across the compound. We all turned as one and heard "You dirty sons of bitches!" It was our new battalion C.O. and we weren't sure if he was kidding or looking for some M.P.'s to have us all impounded. But that's all he said, and then he walked off. Somebody mumbled an "Oh shit!" and all heads turned back to the screen. After all, the damage had been done.

As a group, we were one big walking hard-on heading back to the barracks that night. That was the first time I had seen anything like that, and I walked around with my mouth open for a couple days. Jesus, this was a bunch of sickos, and I was a paying member! It was a terrific evening!

The truce passed quickly and a week later we were out in a new area, free fire zone all the way. If they are armed or running, they belonged to us. All things living were fair game also. We started our mission checking out a cluster of large huts and saw a couple guys run into a large hooch with a bunker inside. Once we reported people down there, some Arvin troops were inserted and swept through the hooches. We circled the huts, directing the troops to the hooch with the bunker.

We watched the Arvins approach the bunker and toss in a CS grenade. Three black P.J.'s streaked out of the bunker and were captured by the Arvins. The three V.C. were slammed up against the hooch wall, their eyes tearing from the gas. The Arvins backed off about 10 feet and executed them all, their bodies' left where they fell while Marvin checked the other hooches. These boys meant business and obviously had their own agenda.

We hovered above this grisly scene like opera patrons watching a bad play from the balcony. Two of the Arvins was searching the bodies when one of the Arvins jumped up and fired an unnecessarily long burst into the head of one of the V.C. Blood and gore flew everywhere. Apparently the makeshift execution hadn't gone too well. Things were getting messy down there so we checked out several tree lines and headed back to our staging area for chow. The second team went out and saw nothing. Another day in the Republic.

A few days later Red Dog got shot down while doing a fast low level pass across a rice paddy. The paddy was muddy and he hit the ground at a slight angle, smearing the chopper across the mud. The bubble rolled forward, snapping off the tail boom and landed right side up. Red Dog and his Oscar walked out of the wreck through the missing plexiglass in the front of the chopper. Red Dog got a cut on his head and his Oscar, short of a nervous tic, never got a scratch. The lesson for the day — if you're going to crash, do it in a LOH. End of lesson.

## MURPHY'S LAW OF COMBAT
### #42
"Peace is our profession — mass murder's just a hobby."

One of our teams caught hell in the Plain of Reeds. The lead LOH was shot down, but not before they nailed a few V.C. Mr. White was hit several times, and Frenchie Lemoyne ended up with a bad leg wound (the leg had to be removed later). Nyberg, the other observer, was severely burned when the white phosphorus and incendiary grenades went off in the cockpit and he threw them out of the LOH with his bare hands. We weren't used to this kind of loss. I never saw any of them again and I was sorry about that. They were all good men.

A couple weeks later while flying to our A.O., we witnessed an arc light strike going in about 20 miles away. The light was just coming up, the western sky a deep purple velvet. We watched the dozens of 500 and 750 pounders exploding, the shock wave from each bomb making a dome shaped shell over the impact area. The explosions walked across the horizon lighting it up like hundreds of flash bulbs. It was an awe-inspiring sight and we were glad we weren't down in ground zero. Somebody was taking a terrible pounding.

We got to our staging area and found out we were to check out the bunker complex the B-52's had just mangled. We refueled and headed for the A.O., wondering what we might find. We had a free fire zone, so I got all my shit ready while still at altitude in case we saw somebody while flying in. Frags were close by, Willie Pete's hanging over my feet; a 900 round belt on the floor, up and folded over my left leg, the 60 locked and loaded for bear.

We hit the area and found the earth still smoking, destroyed bunkers and some still intact. The ones that had been destroyed weren't just blown up; the overturned earth had swallowed them up. The bomb craters were big enough to land the LOH in and cover it up. The line of craters stretched a couple of miles, smoking and smelling of cordite. This was Air Force devastation at it finest. These boys knew how to shake up the terrain.

We hovered around for an hour and a half, seeing zip. The smell of hot earth was heavy in the air. I had smelled it before in my first tour, but not to this extent. Few people living normal lives outside a war zone has the opportunity to smell the earth when it's been super heated from an explosion. It's a pungent odor, sharp enough to dull the senses if you're exposed to it long enough. We had several hundred acres of this smell and we were floating above it like a vulture. It made my head spin.

Just as we were ready to go back for fuel, the Arvins decided to insert some troops and scout out the bunkers that hadn't been destroyed. We climbed to altitude and headed back leaving our new team of LOH's and Snakes to cover the insertion.

After refueling and shutdown, we were sitting around listening to the radio chatter during the insertion. The Hueys found a paddy to put the troops in and just as they touched down, the N.V.A. came out of the bunkers and shot the shit out of the whole force.

I couldn't believe what I was hearing! The N.V.A. actually had the discipline to hold their fire while we were close enough to swat us out of the air with a 2 x 4. We hung our asses 10 feet from the ground for an hour and a half and saw nothing. Then the N.V.A. still have the guts to come out shooting when the Arvins come, especially when they've just weathered one of the worse military weapons on earth, the B-52 strike!

This was another one of those earth-shaking moments for me that changed my perception on how things were going for us. I figured we'd have to kill every swinging N.V.A. dick in North Vietnam before we won this war. They were highly motivated, much more than the Arvins. There was going to have to be some big changes in our thinking if there was going to be a victory parade in New York. I didn't see it happening.

So why was I still flying? Because the Army doesn't give a damn about what you think. I volunteered to do a job, we were short of observers, and I was not going to back off. Things were looking grim to my personal way of thinking, but I had a few months to go yet and I still wanted to fly. So I continued doing my job. Suppressing those feelings was tough though. I told the guys how I felt one night and was surprised how many felt like I did. They all had their own stories to tell about this, so I felt like I was not alone in my depressing thoughts. What a way to run a war!

We all continued to march.

Capt. Zitwick decided we were due for a troop party, so when we had a couple of down days, a couple of the pilots flew to Saigon to get us some steaks and other party fixins. Several hours later they came back with enough beef to feed the V.C. in the U Minh forest and a whole stack of dirty movies. When asked where they got the films — they remained silent. They had sources, apparently, that didn't need any publicity. It was going to be a great party.

We had a half of a 55-gallon oil drum cut the long way and a steel grill that made the perfect BBQ pit. Once the coals were hot, the meat was slapped on and the griller kept a can of beer handy in case of flare-ups. The food was exceptional.

The entertainment began later. We watched ten or more X-rated films and when we had seen them all, there was a hands up or down vote to watch the best ones over again. The positive and negative exchanges during the voting process were as much fun as watching the actual movies. We were all so tired of laughing after we made our choices we could hardly talk. We also learned a lot about sexual preferences that night which naturally was cause for personal jokes for months afterward. It was a rousing good time.

We broke up about midnight; everybody thoroughly sated with beer, liquor, food and our perverse, sexually explicit film fest. The scout line hooch looked like a Chinook had landed in the middle of it, a total wasteland except for our weapons room. We all kind of wobbled around, picking shit up. I was never much of a drinker, so I ended up pointing people in the right direction for the trash can, the pisser, keeping them from screwing around with our weapons. If our mothers could have seen us, their hearts would have broken beyond repair.

The party did us all a lot of good. Steam was released from our brain pans and it was something we all needed. The next morning hangovers be damned, most of us were up and running, at half speed, but we were running. Russell was pissed he hadn't been invited but I told him it was a scout party and grunts were not allowed. All low life forms were banned. He put some kind of Guinea curse on my pecker and left. I didn't know Italians could curse something. After our two days of down time, we were all ready to get back to the war. It's a rule of war that the worse the hangover, the meaner a soldier is when combat presents itself. We'd have been a force to reckon with the morning after the party!

I had heard from several reliable sources that the Ace of Spades was a bad luck sign for the Viet Cong. Several of our Army units were having cards printed up with the ace of spades and their unit patch on them. Leaving them on enemy bodies, blown bunkers, and destroyed hooches. Sounded like a sound psy-ups plan for my little corner of the war, so a plan was born.

I wrote to the U.S. Playing Card Company and asked them if they'd send me about a dozen decks of just ace of spades and a bill. 3 weeks later, I get a box from them with 50 decks of just aces of spades and no bill, just a letter saying it was their pleasure to fill my request!

2,600 cards, I'd be throwing these things for the next 10 years, if I lived so long. I had spades to burn, and when I have extras of anything, I do what my mom taught me; I'd share them!

Our next mission included our Blue platoon of grunts. We were to go in and scout out an LZ, cover the insertion and their sweep. Things went well, no hot LZ, no enemy fire, and no fuck-ups. I decided after watching all this that we needed some excitement. So I set the pilot up for a run over the grunts as they trudged through the paddies. We zipped past the main body and I dropped a whole deck of Ace of Spades on their skirmish line, laughing my ass off. The cards fluttered down like half-drunk butterflies, peppering the paddy the grunts were humping over. I was having a good time up in the LOH, knowing that my old bud Tom Russell was down there leading the platoon. Icing on the cake. He'd be riled up like a stick-poked gator and I loved listening to him rant and rave. This was a lot of fun!

We flew cover for about an hour, the grunts were extracted and we headed home, our exercise done for the day. It was a chance for the Blues to get out in the field and practice their movements and techniques. They needed to get their feet muddy.

Back at Vinh Long, Russ came into my room looking tired and beat up. I knew walking those paddies were hard on one's body, especially if it hadn't been done in awhile. I could sympathize. I was also laughing. He came in looking like Sad Sack himself, wondering out loud what I thought I was doing aceing his men in the field. He wasn't pissed; he was just putting on a show. I couldn't keep a straight face and the longer I grinned at him, the worst his name-calling got. He was a cupcake. He eventually started laughing too, but trying hard not to. He told me when he saw those cards fluttering down he knew the Pollock was flying in the LOH, cursing me long and hard for the benefit of his troops. I reveled in this kind of shit!

He couldn't stay pissed at me, his stomach would have missed my care packages and he knew it. I had him by the digestive tract, which, in this case, was better than having him by the scrotum. Power over other poor slobs is a wonderful thing! Now I know why officers love being officers.

A couple of days later, to show Russ how sorry I was that I had aced them in the field, I hit them again. The Apache grunt's perimeter bunkers were located at the end of the airstrip. How convenient!

On our flight out that morning, I leaned out the door as we passed over their bunkers and dumped a whole deck into their wire. Oh, the horror! Those poor bastards were going to have to go out there this morning and police up all those cards around the bunker, amongst the claymores and out of the concertina. They needed to get off their butts anyway.

Two days later, I did it again. I figured I was stretching my luck. If you piss off guys with automatic rifles, knives and grenades too many times you could end up with a krait in your p.j.'s.

After a long day of flying, I got back to my hooch to find my room had been violated by the grunts. There, taped on my locker, was one of my cards. Crudely written across the front were the words- "We'll get you, Pollock. – The Grunts"

I thought I'd better stop acing our own men. It was fun while it lasted, though. Making life miserable for Tom and the grunts was as much fun as harassing my siblings. I knew if I pressed them, they'd get revenge. I didn't need that from my side. Who knew what sinister plans those guys could hatch.

February 1970 rolled around and U.S. troops were pulling out, although enemy action was not declining. Seeing U.S. troops on the ground was becoming a real rarity in our A.O.'s. I was getting a real uneasy feeling about the U.S. pulling out before the job was finished. I was getting more concerned by the day about being the only U.S. Cav unit down here being supported by Arvins. I couldn't believe we might have to depend on Arvin troops, airstrikes or artillery in case we got shot down. Arvin artillery! Good God! I didn't trust U.S. artillery, what would Arvin arty be like?

Doug Houston got a chance to do what I had wanted to do since I started flying. His lead LOH hammered four V.C. in the tall grass in our A.O. one day and they were all carrying AK-47's. Doug suggested to the pilot that he set the LOH down to pick up the weapons and the pilot agreed!

The LOH set down. Dougie unstrapped and started gathering things up. One of the V.C. was lying next to his weapon and when Doug grabbed the AK, the V.C. pulled it back — he was still alive. Doug jerked it out of his hands and killed the man with his own weapon, and recovered some much sought after enemy weaponry.

I was hopping mad about this. I'd been trying for months to get the pilots to set me down and let me out to gather intel, or weapons and most of them refused. I pointed out to the pilots I flew with that Doug came back with something useful and didn't have any problems, except for the undead guy.

They used the fact that the guy not being dead could have provided them with a real big problem. What would have happened if this guy had shot Houston while he was on the ground and out of the LOH? What if the V.C. had the nuts to shoot Doug then the pilot? They had a whole shit load of "What ifs" until I mentioned the fact that the wingman would be there to cover that scenario. That's why they were there!

It was a great argument but I still didn't get through to them. They were afraid of losing their Oscar on the ground and that was that! End of story.

In mid-February, we were checking around Chi Lang when we came across a Viet farmer walking across the grassy plain with a sack over his shoulder and a curved sickle in his hand. He had been out in the plains cutting something for home.

Since this was not a free fire zone and he didn't have a weapon; he avoided a violent death from above. But we came back around and checked him out. He was your basic farmer/peasant judging by the way that he was dressed. But he had a look of pure hate in his eyes as we hovered several feet above his head.

He stopped walking, put the sickle in front of his chest as if challenging me to a knife fight. He didn't like us one bit and he was not cowtowing or backing down.

He was standing outside my door, and I had my 60-barrel pointed right at his chest. The pilot was checking in with H.Q. to find out what to do with this guy. While higher up mulled over this problem, I found myself wanting to grease this guy real bad. I wasn't sure why I felt this way besides the fact that it steamed me the way he was staring us down, not respecting the fact that I could end his life with the twitch of a trigger finger. I started asking the pilot for permission to fire, but he refused until we got the word from H.Q. The farmer and I were staring at each other, my finger on the 60 trigger with a couple pounds pulled, ready to rock and roll. My hate for this guy was growing fast.

The pilot suddenly reported our guns had seen people running in a tree line and they needed us down the road. Permission to waste the guy was denied. As we pulled away, our eyes were locked and never wavered until we were out of sight. I found myself breathing heavy, the desire to kill pushing down on my chest like 100 pounds of dead weight. The feeling passed shortly after, but I pondered about my feelings for weeks after.

I had read somewhere that everyone has a dark side that can, under stressful circumstances, gravitate to the surface, causing feelings and actions one normally wouldn't consider. Apparently my dark side was alive and well and just below the surface. Why this guy triggered such feelings I never figured out, but I was determined to reign it in until it was needed. Maybe I should have painted "Psycho Observer" on my helmet.

The end of February we got some intel about a bunker complex north of Vinh Long. A plan was hatched and preparations were made. We could stage out of Vinh Long because the complex wasn't too far outside our perimeter.

We put our team together and headed for our target. Flight time was about 20 minutes and our target turned out to be an island of trees surrounded on all sides by a huge rice paddy. We spotted the area until we got the word to go in. We dropped out of the sky like an anvil, Mr. Dicresce keeping my gun on the target with a fast left-hand turn. I saw one guy dive into a bunker just as we hit our scouting altitude. There were a multitude of bunkers in this spot, and they looked hard as concrete. We told our wing to keep his eyes open and we set up a CS run on the bunker.

The bunker was in the northwest corner of the complex, so we ran a fast pattern, I chucked in the CS and we came back around and sat above the bunker over the paddy so we wouldn't have to worry about our back.

It took about a minute for the tear gas to fill the bunker and start clouding outside the entrance. We had checked the wind direction so it wouldn't blow into our cockpit. We did, however, underestimate the rotor vortex potential. I noticed the cloud heading our way, and yelled at the pilot to back off, but it was too late. We both got a snootful of tear gas as it surrounded and penetrated our perimeter, the rotor blades continuing to feed the cockpit with the poisoned air.

Mr. Dicresce was trying to back us out of the cloud to keep my gun on the bunker, but the cloud was following us like a veil follows a bride. Both our eyes were tearing up badly and Dicresce was having trouble keeping the LOH stable. Shit — this was miserable, bad luck. Anybody who had gone through the tear gas exercise in basic knew that rubbing your eyes just makes the gas more irritating and could possibly scratch your corneas. Letting the wind dry it out of your eyes or washing your eyes with water was the only way to rid yourself of this airborne menace. Since there wasn't a water spigot within 30 miles, we had to rely on the air to do the job.

Our wing was watching this little drama and asked if we wanted to grab some altitude so that they could take our place when two black pajamas shot out of the bunker entrance, bent over and coughing. They had no weapons that I could see but my sight was a bit watery, like looking through a layer of shower glass. I was hanging my head out the door trying to get some wind in my face when the pair popped out of the bunker. Despite our problems, my gun was still on the door of the bunker and when they came out, I nailed both of them to the forest floor.

My eyes were starting to clear up but my nose was running like a faucet. We climbed out of the A.O. to wash some fresh air through the ship. Our C & C told us to head back to Vinh Long for refueling.

On the way back, one of the gun pilots suggested a new strategy that sounded exceptionally brilliant for a snake driver. He thought we should all go back, refuel, rearm, and come back to the same A.O. about an hour later. The guns would fly in first, high and hot, then dive on the A.O. with a salvo of "nails" rockets, hoping that anyone out of the protection of the bunkers would be literally "nailed" in the paddy. The 2.75-inch rockets they would fire contained thousands of tiny darts and could carpet the whole area.

It was pretty damned sneaky. Our C.O. loved the idea, so that's what we did. We kept the same teams since we already knew the area. After everyone had landed, the ground crews swarmed around the ships, making sure all was well.

I restocked my M-60 with enough ammo to sink the *Missouri*, loaded up on grenades, got more shotgun shells for the 12 gauge and even checked my .38. I had a feeling things were going to start popping. Our 6 called for Arvin ground support to sweep the bunkers after our attack—things were getting interesting.

We left Vinh Long and formed up behind the guns, letting them take the lead for the initial attack. Flying the Cobra death machines and trying to look unobtrusive was not easy but the plan actually worked.

The guns got set up and dove into the complex. The rockets fired from the pods left a white smoky trail behind them. The second stage of the rocket that released the fleshettes was marked by a pink puff of smoke about halfway to the ground. The two gunships saturated the area, climbed back to altitude to cover our part of the mission.

We got the word from the guns to move in and we low leveled back into the complex. The first thing we found was another male body by the two I had capped earlier. He was dead, riddled with fleshettes. He was wrapping the two bodies in plastic, for later removal. A good deed done at a bad time.

We checked the rest of the complex and found nothing else. We were hovering over the northwest corner when suddenly I saw four people in conical hats heading south with their backs to me. My 60 was already lined up on them. The grass along the trail was high on both sides so all I saw was the hats and their necks, and the tip of an M-1 carbine barrel in the hands of the 1st V.C. They were running one right behind the other. Since this was still a free fire zone I didn't have to ask permission to fire. I unloaded a single 30 round burst into the back of the last, as he dropped the bullets carried into the next, and the next, like dominoes dropping. The whole incident took a few seconds.

We overflew the pile of bodies and checked and covered the East Side of the complex to cover the Arvins being inserted at that moment. The choppers hit the ground and dumped the Arvins into the paddy. It was a short hike to the complex and as the Arvins slugged it out with the paddy mud, we held our covering position.

We directed Marvin over to the four bodies to check them for papers and weapons. As we were hovering, I got my first good look at the 4 V.C. I had killed. My gut twisted into a knot when I saw the bodies, because the first two in line had lost their hats and long, black hair was spilling out onto the ground and their shoulders. There was an old M-1 carbine under the one in the front. My blood was up and in the heat of the moment I didn't realize what I had just done. I had killed two women!

The Arvins got to the bodies, picked up the carbine and one of the Arvins rolled the V.C. that was in the back over, ripped off his shirt, and I found myself looking at a pair of breasts. "Jesus," I thought, "this keeps getting worse by the minute." I held my breath until the fourth body was also identified as a woman. The Arvins were roughly rolling the bodies around, checking for papers. They sent a couple of guys into the bunker the girls had run out of, but it was empty.

I had a small battle occurring in my head — would I have killed them if I knew they were women? — One of them was armed, did that make them all combatants? — Should I have held my fire and let the Arvins take them alive? — My gut was twisted like an anaconda as I pondered what I had just done. What in the hell were they doing down there? It was common knowledge that the V.C. were recruiting women for combat, but this was the first time I had seen it instead of just hearing about it.

Charlie Palek

The whole incident was playing over and over in my head and I knew as sure as God created napalm this would be another experience I'd have to tuck away in the old brain attic, but it was really getting crowded up there! I was pretty quiet after the mission on the way back to Vinh Long, despite our good fortune. The new attack strategy was considered highly usable in other situations.

When we got back to the barracks, one of our TOC guys told me the Arvins discovered our bunker complex was a sort of field hospital, the four women — nurses. It didn't make me feel any better. The only thing that kept me from retching my guts up was that the gal in the lead had an M-1 carbine and no doubt would have put a bullet in my head first if she had the chance. Small consolation.

I didn't fly for two days and all I did was mull this whole thing over. I forced myself to be busy, avoiding everybody and trying to decide how this was going to affect my job. Since we were short of observers, I couldn't quit. I was needed and I wasn't going to let the troops down. I was going to continue flying, add the four ladies to my kill count, and put this whole thing behind me, or at least off to the side.

## MURPHY'S LAW OF COMBAT
### #35
### "If it fly's it dies."

I started flying again. I think the best thing for me was to focus on something else. Mr. Dicresce and me were flying around at altitude on March 8, one day before my 21st birthday. We were waiting to get the word to drop into our A.O. at the Tram. We were doing lazy circles when all of a sudden there was a loud thud from the rear of the aircraft, and we started spinning and dropping like a stone.

Mr. Dicresce started screaming that he couldn't control the ship. This being a totally new experience for me, I kind of sat dumbfounded while grenades and anything loose in the cockpit started flying by my face and out my door. This spin was extremely fast and to the right, my ammo belt was unfolding and flopping out my door too. I hardly noticed the fact that we were falling at the same time.

The pilot couldn't control the spin, as it was obvious we had lost our tail rotor. While Mr. D. was fighting for control, I noticed my M-60 was flopping around outside my door and for some reason, my mission in life at that moment was to keep from losing that gun. This was the same 60 I had from the very beginning. I had babied and pampered it through countless maintenance sessions and it never jammed or failed me in any way.

So I was being a bit infantile while I was dying, but we're talking about my baby! The spin was twisting me in my seat and I was grabbing for the 60 and trying to dodge the grenades still flying by my head. What a week I was having!

I don't know how long we had been falling. I did know we were at 700 feet when the shit hit the fan. I never even considered impacting with the ground while we were falling, just getting that damned gun back into my loving arms. Mr. Dicresce was on the radio telling everybody that things were out of control. No shit!

Suddenly, the voice of an angel came over the intercom. It was an incredibly soothing voice, filled with strength, and confidence. All our angel said was "Use your autorotation to slow the fall." Mr. D. got it together and used the blade energy to slow us down. We still had engine power but I certainly didn't know it, and I'm not sure he did either. It was hard reading the gauges when your eyeballs were stuck in the left side of your eye sockets.

I could feel the power in the blades grabbing air; my ass came back down into the seat. I grabbed my 60, tucked it into my lap, and we hit the ground.

The ship landed in 3 feet of water, spun about a half turn and settled about 15 degrees to the port side, favoring a buckled skid. Our rotor blades hit the ground, but the water and soft mud kept them from shearing off.

When we hit, I was sitting on my left cheek, unable to sit straight in the seat. The impact sprained my back and my chin came down on my chicken plate, busting it open. Mr. D. never got a scratch! He apparently had hunkered down in his seat like he was supposed to. I, on the other hand, hadn't been paying attention to the ground coming up to grab us, so I wasn't braced for the impact.

We both sat in the ship for a minute, wondering why we were still alive and whether the ship would explode soon. To say we were both a little dazed was an understatement. Fortunately, we had crashed not far from a platoon of Arvins that we were supposed to support that day.

We both drug our asses out of the ship into the swamp. I broke my 60 belt off and grabbed the gun to take with me. My back was killing me, but I humped the gun away from the ship. The Arvins were heading our way to secure the ship while our wing checked out the nearby tree lines for Indians. I immediately complained to Mr. D. that as an aviator I wasn't supposed to be getting muddy feet and I held him personally responsible for my feet getting wet.

We were a couple of sorry looking troopers when we headed for some dry ground. I was walking like a crooked little man, and Mr. D. was having trouble in the mud. The area was secure, so that took a little pressure off our predicament. My sensations started piling on. I knew if my back hurt this bad today, tomorrow it was going to be a bastard. The sweet, pungent odor of the decomposing grass and mud brought back strong memories of the glory days with the 9th Division. Mud was squishing between my toes, our wing was buzzing around us, my chin was dripping blood and the shouts from the Arvins coming to secure the ship rang in the air.

We finally reached an area that was only a foot deep in water and wet grass, which in the Delta is considered higher ground. We took stock of our situation. My chin was still bleeding, but the Arvins had a medic with them and he taped a dressing on it to stop the bleeding. He pulled a syringe out of his med. pak and grabbed my pants at the waistband, pulling down at them. I finally realized he wanted me to drop my pants so he could give me a shot. I looked at the syringe and it said penicillin, so I figured that was a good call.

I noticed some of the Arvins were standing around, smiling and leering at me. I was starting to feel a little uncomfortable dropping my drawers amongst these guys. Who knew how long they had been in the field? If they got a glimpse of my fine, alabaster ass, there could be trouble! I may have been a bit over the top, here, but I still told Mr. D. to keep his .38 handy, thumb on the hammer in case Marvin decided to rush me in an uncontrollable burst of paddy lust.

Well, this was a fine mess. I was standing out in the middle of nowhere, holding my pants up with one hand and holding my chin bandage with the other while an Arvin stuck a needle in my ass and his platoon standing around with big grins on their faces. I took a look back at ol' 274 to realize just how lucky both of us were to be alive. The ship looked like a broken toy some kid left in a vacant lot. Hard to believe we were flying in the wild blue just 30 minutes ago in that piece of wreckage. It was sitting in a little nest of grass and mud, the engine still smoking. It looked lifeless, like a dead insect that has finally succumbed to the end of its short life. Ol' 274 had got us back from a lot of hairy missions, but I figured she'd flown her last flight. Impacts like ours tend to disrupt the integrity of the engineering. The cockpit will probably be a little out of kilter, not true anymore. Getting the ship's shape back to true, factory warranty was hard to do after a crash like ours. Kiss her goodbye.

I also realized that having my machine gun in my lap when we impacted had caused a couple of bruises across the tops of my thighs. I noticed them already turning purple as my pants hit the paddy water. If they were blue now, they were going to be beauties in a couple days.

Some of our grunts were called out to strip the ship and secure it for the crash crew to rig up. We found out our "angel" was the lead Cobra pilot that was with us and watched the whole thing happen. Our wingman flew in and picked us both up after I got my shot. I fired off a few quick photos of the ship as we lifted off. Unknown to me there was mud on the lens and the shots came out a little soft, but I told everybody it was a special effect.

We flew straight back to Vinh Long, and we were both taken from the flight line to the medics. My chin took four stitches and my back was x-rayed and the doc told me I had a severe sprain, nothing cracked or out of place. He gave me something for the pain, and Mr. D. and I walked back to A-Troop. We went into my room and talked about what happened. We both considered ourselves truly blessed that we were still sucking air. I tried getting comfortable by sitting, standing, lying down every way I could think of, but my back still killed me. I could hardly wait 'til tomorrow. I shook hands with Mr. D., he left, and I popped a couple more magic bullets and tried to get some sleep. A lost cause as it turned out.

I couldn't get comfortable and didn't sleep a wink. It took about 30 minutes to get out of bed the next morning, bending my stiff spine a little at a time until I could rise from a sitting position and walk upright. After I moved around a little, I loosened up so I went to the mess for breakfast, ate standing up, and decided if I kept moving, I felt better. So I went back to my room, got a 5 pack of Tampa Jewels and headed for the flight line to look at 274.

I hitched a ride to the flight line and wandered over to maintenance. Old 274 was sitting there, tail boom missing, tipped forward on its chin bubble. Sad looking. I went across the airstrip, found my M-60, and cleaned it up, then smoked my first cigar. 21 and still kicking. Lady Luck must have liked me a lot. Close calls were getting to be a habit with me.

After about three days, I was ready to fly again. I was still taking pain killers, but only twice a day and I felt I was ready to hit the unfriendly skies again.

## MURPHY'S LAW OF COMBAT
### #46
*"It's not the one with your name on it — it's the round addressed 'to whom it may concern' ya gotta think about."*

In late March, after flying for an hour and a half, and seeing nothing, we came back to our staging area and shut down. As usual, since we had at least an hour to kill, we kind of walked around the LOH, checking for problems and other nasty little surprises that could rise up and bite our ass in the middle of a mission.

So we kind of walked around it, running our hands across the smooth metal skin, the rivets and the rotor blade. I was checking the mini-gun when the pilot said "holy shit," and told me to come around to the right side of the ship. In the tail boom was a nice raggedy .50 cal. hole, the entrance wound underneath. The bullet had passed through the tail boom missing the tail rotor shaft by about one inch. Since the bullet path was within the radius of the rotor blade, we checked the four blades and sure enough, we had a nice big hole in one of our blades too.

Since it takes very little to knock a blade out of trim, the pilot was amazed that he felt no vibration in the blades while he was flying. We had no idea where or when we got hit. The fact that we spent an hour and a half out there without seeing anything, but still got shot by a high powered weapon was a bit sobering. The pilot decided to take the ship back to Vinh Long especially to have the shaft inspected.

We had missed the "Big D" again and hadn't even known it. The trip back to Vinh Long was uneventful. The ship was thoroughly checked, the holes patched and the rotor blades replaced. The LOH was ready to fly again.

Somewhere along the line the idea of putting a second gunner in the back compartment on the right side of the LOH was conceived and adopted by us with much enthusiasm. This would give a manned M-60 on the right side of the LOH, giving us a bit more security. Doug Houston and I volunteered immediately to be the first two to try to cover both sides of it out, so we went to the flight line one day to see if the concept could be worked out.

We first thought we could sit on the floor and do our duty, but it turned out the little jump seat made for a third passenger in the cargo compartment worked better, We put a piece of armor plating under the seat to protect our ass and "the boys." We'd be wearing two pieces of body armor, one on our chest (our chicken plate) and one on our back. There was a single strap that was connected to our back plate then to a bolt eye on the far side of the compartment to keep us from falling out. The strap was long enough to give us the freedom to step out on the skid and fire under the LOH if we had to.

For weapons, we both agreed the M-60 would be best. Attaching it to the top of the door would limit our movement, so we decided to try it hand-held on our first flight. We folded the ammo belt into a wooden ammo crate, and put another crate next door for our grenades. Our extra weapons were jammed between the jump seat and the inside of the door. The whole idea seemed solid. We even thought about having another man on the right side that would counter-balance the weight of the mini-gun on the left side. Might keep the ship in a little better trim. How cool was that?

We hopped in and out of the chopper with all our armor on to see how easy it would be to operate back there. The two pieces of body armor made me feel like a ham slice between two pieces of wheat bread. It was bulky, but necessary. The only thing I didn't like about it was our tenuous position if we crashed. We'd either be thrown out into the blades or mashed into a skin full of broken bones against the back of the bulkhead. Another little trade off as it were. As usual, we didn't think it would ever happen to us, so why worry.

This gun position gave us a 180-degree arc of coverage. We could fire straight to the front of the LOH or straight out the rear. Step out on the skid and we could fire under the LOH too. This was going to work great. We could hardly contain ourselves. We wanted to get into the air with this!

Two days later we got our chance. We staged out of Moc Hoa near the Cambodian border. We were flying with the regular 2 teams, but with an Oscar covering the right side of the lead LOH, Doug and me. Our second mission that day started when we got a call about a .51 cal position on the border. We scooted over to the border and watched two Seawolf gunships working the area.

## MURPHY'S LAW OF COMBAT
### #12
### "Tracers work both ways."

The Seawolves were an elite Navy unit that spent their time cruising the Delta and supporting the Seal Teams doing their thing out here. They normally flew Charlie Model gunships. They had seen one .51 caliber gun position down there and it was pounding away at them like the ammo was free. The only problem from our end was it was on the Cambodian side of the river. The Seawolves had been on station for awhile so they turned the mission over to us and headed back to refuel and rearm.

Our C&C was with us today and was carrying a high ranking South Vietnamese officer that was in charge of the mission. He ordered the LOH's to go down and take a look, on the other side of the border! Our C.O. was not crazy about the idea because the N.V.A. down there were ready and able to blow us out of the sky. Nevertheless, we got the word to drop down across the border and make a fly by as fast as we could, then grab for altitude.

We weren't crazy about the orders, either, but we went. We dropped out of the sky like a Stuka, pulling up about 100 feet from the ground and hauling ass across the gun position. We flew like a bat out of hell across the area. From my perspective, the trees were going by like a picket fence. I was leaning out the ship, watching ahead and saw 2 .51 caliber setups, the crews scurrying around to try to track us as we flew over. I was firing my 60 almost straight down but I don't know if I hit anything.

Suddenly our wingman got on the radio and said he was taking hits and going down. I looked behind us and saw him bank hard to the left and then I lost him. He definitely was going down because he wouldn't have left our formation otherwise.

The radio was chattering with all kinds of traffic. Somebody instructed our wing to come down on the East Side of the river, not the Cambodian side. Politics had reared its ugly head here and we couldn't attack them.

Fortunately for our wing ship, he did have enough control to crash the LOH on the Viet side of the river. The crash was semi-controlled; meaning the pilot did have a few options about how he landed. They hit hard, but they had no casualties. The .51's stopped firing and our C & C swooped in and picked up the two crewmen. Apparently the .51 crews were not going to bother us unless we overflew their positions. N.V.A. with a conscience? I doubt it.

We escorted our C & C back while the other team secured the down LOH until they could sling it out. Once we got back to Can Mau, we found out that there had been quite a drama on board the C & C when we were catching shit.

Denny Workman was the crew chief of the C & C and he told us the Arvin C.O. insisted our LOH's make a flyby to check out the .51's. Our C.O. didn't appreciate the flippant attitude the Arvin had for our lives. Our C.O. told the Arvin he would not give them the order. They went round and round, butting heads — the aircraft commander vs. the mission commander. In this case the Arvin had the final word, so our C.O. reluctantly sent us in, but he was steaming.

Our quick flyby and subsequent shoot down of our wing ship brought a flurry of activity in the cargo area of the C & C. When our C.O. saw the wing ship go down, he ordered Denny to get out of his gun position and put the Arvin officer just inside the door. He then told Denny if either of the crewmen were killed, he was to kick the Arvin out the door! Things had definitely gotten interesting up there. The Arvin's military bearing got a big shock when Denny grabbed the back of his shirt and stood him at the door.

This Arvin spoke English and was listening in on the intercom so he knew what was happening. He started chattering in a high pitched voice about his rank, being mission commander, and all the other stuff he hoped would make these mad Americans see the error of their ways. He was definitely worried about the outcome of the crash, now. All of a sudden he had a compelling reason to see the LOH crew walk away from the crash. Motivation! A little too late but...

The Arvin officer was no doubt relieved when the C & C landed and picked up the two crewmen. They were both a little shaken, but we understood. We'd been there too. I would have given a month's salary to have been on the C & C to see the Arvin's face when he got shoved into the door! We headed back to our staging area to check our ship too.

When we landed, I unstrapped and hopped out and "whoa" — my knees were a little weak. My heart had stopped racing but normalcy hadn't reached my legs yet. I braced my ass against the LOH and took a couple of deep breaths. I was fantasizing about flying a few protesters, congressmen and Jane Fonda over our A.O. and showing them N.V.A. gun positions in Cambodia, a neutral country and one the N.V.A. claimed they had no troops in. They'd get an eyeful if they lived! That would be sweet!

Mr. Willis, our intrepid pilot, called me around and showed me a couple of bullet holes in the bubble, one through the dash and one in the blades. Mr. Willis said he saw the one coming through his bubble, almost like a slow motion film. It was probably a tracer. They tend to look like glowing golf balls coming at your precious head. I looked at the path of the bullet and discovered it exited the LOH through the plexiglass above my head. The damned thing missed my head by about 3 inches! Damned ol' 379 had been a lucky ship today. I didn't even hear the .51-caliber bullet ramble through. Old Lady Luck was still with me. What a babe she was!

We slung out 379 that afternoon. Mr. Willis felt a little uncomfortable flying it home, which I applauded. Falling out of the sky once was enough for me.

Later that month, Denny Workman joined the observers and moved into my room. He came from the lift platoon, a crew chief of a Huey. He was a handsome son of a gun, with wavy black hair and olive skin that tanned easily. He had a tooth missing in the front, apparently lost when his first wife hit him with a frying pan. He was a good roomie and his company was always welcome. He could whip up some mean suppers with our skillet, so I let him cook when he wanted to. He was always getting tagged by the REMF's because he wore his fatigues pegged, just a little on the regulation side. It pissed them off that they couldn't bust him for his tight fatigues and he reveled in it. He was the crew chief on our C&C for awhile and our C.O. even questioned him about his pant legs. Things were going to start getting interesting.

Denny and I caught a flight to Can Tho one day to register a couple of rifles to take home as souvenirs. We were standing outside one of the admin buildings, waiting for our paperwork. Sitting on the steps of the building was an obviously exhausted field soldier. His boots had not seen polish for months, his fatigues were practically bleached white, hair uncut, unshaven, dead on his feet.

He was sitting with his head in his hands grabbing a combat nap. Coming around the corner of the building was a bird Colonel at full parade gallop, head high, a model of efficiency and grace. Right behind him a Captain a foot shorter with his head so far up his C.O.'s ass it was amazing he could breathe. The Bird stopped abruptly at the foot of the steps, and waited for his second to grovel around to the front. The Colonel looked down at the grunt and the Captain immediately made the grunt stand up and salute his holiness. Then the Captain chewed his ass up and down for failing to salute an officer. The Colonel returned a limp-wristed salute and stood by with an air of indifference while his lap dog spewed forth. It was such a totally fucked up scene we both decided we'd better get back into a combat zone to avoid this kind of shit. The closer we got to H.Q., the more of this kind of crap we ran into. Back to the shooting boys, we're being invaded by REMF's! I guess it's true, the closer one gets to the flagpole the more chickenshit it gets!

I asked Denny about the incident in the C & C and he said it certainly was a new experience for him. When I ask him if he would have pushed the Arvin out the door, he said "Fuckin' A. The gook was an idiot and would have deserved it." Denny was a man of action. I knew we'd get along great.

We started flying together, Denny up front, me in the back and Mr. Willis at the controls. We were a good team and we requested we fly together as much as possible. Mr. Willis was only 19 at the time. The other pilots called him "Chatty Randy" 'cause he was always talking. He took the crap and gave it back, just like most of us did. And he was a great pilot.

In early April, we went out on a security mission. Our job was to fly a perimeter around a village surrounded on all sides by a huge rice paddy. The paddy was fairly dry and we were not to allow anybody out of the town. We weren't to shoot them, just turn them back if they attempted to leave. The Arvins were going to insert some troopers to check I.D.'s on the villagers.

So we set up a nice lazy circle around the village, flying about 15 feet above the paddy. We hadn't made three trips around the track when we saw this dude walking out of the village into the paddy at a rather brisk pace. He was being so brazen about it. There was no place to hide so he just put himself in overdrive and defied us like we weren't there. Big balls, this guy, or he had a screw loose. Our wing set up on us while we hovered down to this guy to see what he was thinking. Mr. Willis and Denny started signaling to this guy to go back to the village. He ignored them. Mr. Willis put the LOH right in front of him, hovering about three feet off the ground, and this guy walked around the ship! His pace had picked up, the walk becoming as brisk as a winter walk in an Upper Peninsula of Michigan in the wintertime.

This was unbelievable! We had enough firepower to blow this guy into a fine powder; he had to know this. But he was determined to walk away from that village. So Mr. Willis gives Denny permission to fire a burst at his feet. Mr. Willis backs off, goes around and puts this dude right outside Denny's door. Denny put a short burst right at his feet, and the guy never missed a step. He hunched up his shoulders, closed his eyes, gritted his teeth and kept going.

I'm sitting in the back watching through the front bubble and to me it was getting funny. This guy had to be brain-dead. I was starting to laugh but I could tell Denny was getting pissed. We swung around ahead of him one more time and Denny let loose with another burst, longer, and closer this time. It never even slowed him down!

All of a sudden Denny's voice comes over the intercom "Set this son of a bitch down!" Mr. Willis looked at him and thought he missed something. He said "Say again." and Denny told him to put the LOH on the ground. He was going to turn this guy around.

Since nothing else had worked, Mr. Willis told our wing we were setting down to try a different tactic. The Vietnamese guy didn't look like he had a weapon, so Denny unstrapped, pulled his .38 and walked right up to the guy's face. He poked the barrel of his piece right up into the guy's forehead, pushed the guy's head back with it, and pointed to the village.

The guy turned around and walked right back to the village! Denny stood there watching him for a minute, his hands hanging to his side, his helmeted head shaking in disbelief. By the time Den got back to the LOH I was laughing so hard my stomach hurt. He settled back into his seat, strapped in, and got back on the intercom, calling our "dude" every name in the book. Denny was seething, bitching and moaning about the guy not having any respect for us.

We did mange to keep everyone in the village and the Arvins found a few military age males with no I.D., so it was a good day. Bizarre — but good. Hilarious in the extreme!

# Tattletale

There was some scuttlebutt going around in mid-April that something big was coming up soon. We started getting surpluses of 60 ammo, grenades and other lethal goodies, but we didn't know what they were for. Since we were combat troops and the lower end of the intel ladder, we just had to wait for the info to come our way.

We continued flying and maintaining. There were 1,000's of things to do to keep an aviation brigade flying. On our end, the crew chiefs were responsible to see that their ship was ready to fly on the day it was scheduled. They patched the holes, replaced parts, read the manuals until they knew every nut and bolt, every wire and control lever. It was their baby and they loved to see them go out and perform, and come back again. Sometimes they flew observer. They even learned to fly the ship if they had the time and a pilot was willing to teach them.

Our warrant officers were like the Mercury astronauts; they sat around waiting for the next mission. The astronauts trained between missions, our W.O.'s sat around mostly, waiting for the call up. I thought W.O.'s had it dicked. They hardly ever pulled O.D. Good rank to have!

We were reading about the rioting back home. "End the War" seemed to be the rallying cry. There was usually some *Time* or *Newsweek* magazines lying around, even though they were weeks old. We were usually several weeks behind main events unless somebody heard about it and passed it along the ancient military grapevine, which was as reliable as a politician's word.

I didn't even know we put a man on the moon for two days! One would think an event like that would cause some excitement around here, but I felt sadly detached with events happening back home, no matter how wondrous. It was discussed and analyzed over beers at night, but we were more interested in our own present situation. The rioting caused a lot of talk, mostly tough. Some of the guys itched to have some draft-dodging free love asshole stick a peace flag in his face and call him a baby killer. We thought up all kinds of brilliant ways to show them our anger: a block of C-4 up the ass with a very short fuse, CS powder in their joints, Willie Pete in their cigarette lighter, or maybe just drag their ass back to the Mekong and see how mellow their mind will be out there. It helped pass the time and kept us laughing. Irreverent humor at this level was always fun, and there was a lot of it! We had no sympathy for them.

We also knew there were people out there that truly wanted us back home. They felt we'd spent enough of our national treasure, living and otherwise, on a war that just kept drying up the well. It was now an attrition war, who could hang in there the longest before the citizens rebelled. It appeared that time was getting close for the U.S.

The guys that really ground our gears, were the privileged. They hid behind their father's political associations, used school as an exemption, left home and hid in Canada, or just used a bit of cash to avoid service. If they claimed they didn't want to kill people, a combat medic job would have been perfect for them. There was always a need. Since 90% of the people over here were support people, there were a lot of jobs here that could help us. Using morality was a cop-out. The war was immoral? Show me a war that wasn't.

What it all came down to was they felt their lives were more important than ours to serve. They enjoyed all the privileges of living in the U.S. but didn't feel compelled to protect what they had. I knew about the Communist's "Domino Theory," how they would invade one country after another until they were at the front door of America, but I felt the idea of Russia invading the U.S. was ridiculous. Nuke us into the Stone Age was a viable plan, but not before several million tons of nuclear power fell on their heads too. It was a lose/lose proposition, which was the cornerstone of the whole Cold War. But these guys claiming some lame reason for not joining us in the R.V.N.- pricks one and all!

The one thing that always nagged me was that I felt the war wasn't being managed like it should have been. I felt a lot of energy was being wasted, as well as a lot of manpower. What I was seeing about Vietnamization and what was coming from the press were two different animals. We were swimming in an ever-enlarging gray area and I started wondering if the job would ever be over, if we'd ever win. I came here out of patriotism, and came back for another adventure, period. But politics was stinking the whole thing up like a jalapeno turd. It was getting real ugly and I began wondering if some of the folk's back home protesting were right, and that shook me right to the bone.

I realize that there wasn't a front line trooper in any of the previous historic battles through the centuries that didn't wonder at some time if their leaders were working with all their oars in the water. It was the old, typical grunt experience. Our eyes were seeing something the high command wasn't They were seeing the big picture, we were seeing the ground in front of us in a low crawl. Neither part ever seemed to get together. It was an ancient story, and will probably never change. But I was being directly effected by their choices. Fraggings of officers by their own men were becoming more common. It made you wonder.

We had our own little race riot in Vinh Long. I was never sure just what happened, but one of our crew chiefs took exception to what a black trooper said and they went at it. Our crew chief got hit in the mouth with a hammer and lost a few teeth. The black troopers seem to be separating themselves from the whites. They have their own multi-movements hand shake and appear more distant than when I arrived. I think the crap in the States is starting to affect us over here. We're suppose to be on the same side, but sometimes it doesn't look like it anymore.

Denny came back from "last light" one evening and he was pale as a ghost. He'd had a real scare put into him by the evening's events. He was so shaken he could hardly speak; so I let him calm down before he told me what happened.

His LOH had been low leveling outside our perimeter and was peeking under the bushes when they scared up a couple of V.C. in the grass. One of the guys in the grass popped up and fired a burst at the LOH, hitting the pilot in the leg. Apparently things got real interesting in the cockpit. The pilot lost pedal control and the observer on the left wasn't sure if he should suppress fire or help with the ship. The LOH was bobbing around like a cork in the ocean, so Denny stepped out on the runner and killed the bastard under the LOH. The wing took out the other V.C.

It was a close call and nobody could tell the story and evoke the mental and physical realities of the event, even those involved. I helped talk Denny down and sympathized. I'd been there too. The dry, coppery mouth, the clenched teeth, the tight asshole, bad memories, fried brain pan, I had them all at one time or another. But it was the adrenaline that put our asses back in the seat the next day. I can't account for it, I just knew it worked for me. Going back out, day after day, putting your ass on the line was something that happened a lot. Nobody wants to fly an unarmed, dustoff chopper into heavy enemy fire, but guys were doing it every day. The Navy Seals, the SOG guys, the tunnel rats, the LRRP's, even the reliable grunt kept going back, "Doin' the Danger." The pilots hitting the targets amid horrendous AAA, day after day, the men of the "Jolly Greens" rescuing pilots shot down in North Vietnam. Of all these combat jobs, I'm sure duty and honor play a big part, but the adrenaline rush plays the biggest part of all. Putting oneself or one's machine against another man is exciting stuff. You get to shoot powerful weapons and

## Charlie Palek

blow things up. Your riding hard on all the schoolyard fantasies you had when you were a kid.

This doesn't apply to everybody, and it certainly doesn't make you less of a man. There are guys out there that would rather be anywhere than combat, but they continue to stay and do their job. That takes even more courage, in my book.

When the bullets started flying, it was good to have the fire-eaters and the cool dudes with you. You needed that combination of support. And what happens when the fighting is over? The upper staff officers would rather these warriors fade off into the unknown until they are needed again lest they embarrass somebody with their pirate-like behavior, their lack of military decorum or their just plain rudeness and black sense of humor. It went with the territory! They gave us no-fire zones and rules during Tet; we gave them the raspberries!

A few days before the end of April, we found out what the build-up was all about. We were going to run across the Cambodian border and kick some ass, get some payback, and have some fun! It was going to be a major offensive operation, using U.S. and Arvin units, hitting two primary targets; the Fishhook area N.W. of An Koc, and the Parrot's Beak S.W. of Tay Ninh. This was going to be a biggy, and our preparations went into high gear. We re-stocked, re-armed and reassured ourselves that this mission was going to make a big difference to the war effort. At least that's what I thought. How little I knew.

As luck would have it, I was due to go to Hong Kong on R & R on the last day of April. Our platoon sergeant came up to me in the company area a couple days before I was set to leave. He put his hand on my shoulder, like a father talking to his son, and asks me if I'd consider giving up my R & R, so I'd be able to fly the mission into Cambodia. We were desperately short of trained Oscars and since the lead ships would be carrying two observers each, that stretched our manpower even more.

I had been thinking about this since I heard where we were going. I had let my R & R drift closer and closer to my Deros date. Now it looked like if I didn't take my R & R, I'd never get another chance. I'd be going home before the next allocation.

The other option was a doozy. Miss the mother-of-all-invasions into the sacred-no fire- no chase area of the war. The country that had frustrated every soldier in this conflict that operated close to the Cambodian border. We were going to piss fire right into their comfy little hooches, blow up their supplies and descend like black angels until nothing was left but a scorched hole and a pile of bodies. There was absolutely no fucking way I was going to miss this! This was history in the making and I wanted to experience the whole thing.

    I told Sgt. Conley that I would absolutely be flying into Cambodia and I would like to fly the backseat with Mr. Willis and Denny. He smiled and said "No problem, it was already scheduled that way." He knew I would go, the bastard. He was smiling as he walked away. Jesus, was I that predictable, or just stupid! The next few days would tell.

    The end of April saw everybody in the troop, as well as the other troops in our Brigade, gearing up. We were making our C4/frag superfrags, double checking our mini-guns and M-60's, trying to stuff another several hundred rounds of ammo somewhere in the LOH, and filling every available leftover space with grenades. The LOH was going to be fully loaded, I only hoped it could fly.

    Our lift platoon was preparing the Hueys to ferry out to our A.O. all the stuff needed to keep our Cobras humming along. Belts of mini-gun ammo and 40mm grenades, 2.75-inch rockets, food, fuel, and toilet paper. There was an air of excitement all over the flight line. The crews knew this was going to be a biggy, and nobody wanted to be the first to screw up. We tried to keep the conversation light, but we also suspected we could be sticking our dicks right into the jaws of the dragon.

    Everybody worked his ass off on the last day of April 1970. At beer call that night, speculation and assumptions were running wild. Pretty much everybody expected to see some heavy action tomorrow. We were going to attack a huge base camp across the border and unless the N.V.A. got word we were coming, every enemy soldier we found there would be armed. We expected to see a lot of well-trained N.V.A. out there and there was little hope of surprising them, not with the security in this country. I thought about the possibility of being shot down, as did a few others, but I tucked that little bastard way into the back of the attic. Didn't want to see that again!

    I slept about 2 minutes that night. I just couldn't shut my brain down — the neurons were firing a thousand times a minute while I tried to sleep. It never happened.

    Up bright and early the next morning, well before sunup. I drug my ass out of my bunk after a firm 60 seconds worth of sleep, kicked Denny's bunk to roust him up and dressed.

## Charlie Palek

Despite my lack of sleep, I was pumped up. I ate some of my goodies for breakfast and headed to the flight line early. By the time the rest of the guys got there, I was ready to roll. I double checked everything, laid in some extra grenades, and put plenty of spare ammo in the back compartment.

We were to stage out of Moc Hoa, just south of the Parrot's Beak. Our mission was to fly across the border and check out a base camp a few klicks inside Cambodia. The rules of engagement were simple; we couldn't fire at anybody or anything until we were fired at first. Once we took fire, all rules went out the door. We'd be in the biggest free fire zone ever. No rules! If things went as discussed, we were going to be hungry hawks in a large mass of field mice. There would be no stopping us unless we ran out of fuel, ammo, or blood.

We flew to Moc Hoa right at sunrise. We had two teams of three Cobras for this operation. It was the first time each LOH team had worked with 3 Cobras above our rotors. H.Q. must be expecting a lot of shooting down there. The more the merrier, I always say. We could never have enough 2.75-inch rockets above our heads. Boy, was I wired up!

We were scheduled to be the first team in, so we landed at Moc Hoa, refueled, and went back up again, leaving team 2 to play the waiting game. We grabbed some altitude and flew lazy circles just east of the Cambodian border.

We were waiting to get the word to go, so as we flew around, I was listening to AFVN. Jimmy Hendrix was wailing on his guitar when we got the word. We did a hard right and flew right to ground level, crossed the border and as we flew over the imaginary line, I thought this whole event was going to be so rock & roll funky! Hendrix was leading the way, and I thought that was pretty damned appropriate. Rock & Roll had kept the fighting man's spirits up in this fuck-fest since the beginning. Except for those Country and Western wienies. The Motown sounds, Stones, Fogarty, the Doors, and the Beatles, they all contributed to our mental stability, such as it was. We'd sit in our rooms and play the same old taped albums over and over again. It mellowed us out and took our minds off the situation we would be facing the next day. Music soothed the savage beast. We would rather have had the music soothe the savage breasts, but girls were hard to come by.

I switched my radio off of AFVN and onto the combat net as we low leveled into Cambodia. We were running low over a tree line. Less than

1,000 meters into Cambodia, we popped over the trees and directly to our front was a huge base camp and it looked like we had snuck up on them! As hard as it was to believe, we had orders to shoot only if we were fired on first. It's a good thing those orders weren't given to the troops on Omaha Beach. Rules of engagement during an invasion — those buttheads at H.Q. really knew how to fight a war!

It must have been too early for these guys, 'cause hardly anything was moving. We hovered around like bees, flitting from hooch to hooch, peeking into doors and windows, looking for the N.V.A. I was positively baffled that nobody was even sticking their heads out the door to check out the chopper flying around in their compound! They appeared to be completely confident about their sanctuary; there wasn't even any security around the base. Boy, were they going to get a wake-up call today!

Our every emotion was in a fever pitch, every nerve and muscle ready to explode in anticipation. We dicked around for about 10 minutes when a helmetless N.V.A. soldier walked out of a hooch, his step jaunty and his AK over his shoulder. The internal chatter in our LOH was of three mystified crewmen wondering what the hell was going on?

The ground was hard packed mud and looked like the base had been around a long time. There were a lot of hooches, sheds, and bunkers around, a few smoking, cooking fires, but to me it looked like a peacetime jungle base camp. The N.V.A. had screwed the pooch on this one! It felt good to really be on the offensive this time.

I was watching our early-riser out my door, as he arrived at the shitter (a three-holer I guessed,) and as he opened the door he gave me a little wave! I stopped myself from waving back, this was so absurd! I started laughing to myself while we continued to scout the area. This was not at all what I expected.

Suddenly our wing reported taking fire from one of the hooches. Some idiot stuck a rifle out the window and plinked a couple shots at our wingship. Oh, baby! Things turned wild in the blink of an eye!

The gunfire rousted people from their comfy bunks and they started running out into the morning sun, and we were waiting for them. All of a sudden, we were in the middle of a "target-rich environment." There were guys running everywhere, some with and without weapons.

We had never run into so many targets before, Denny and I were yelling at Mr. Willis about the targets on our side of the ship and Mr. Willis was trying to put us on the people he was seeing to his front! We started firing, engaging, anything that was moving out our particular door. We were receiving fire now, but it was sporadic. Frankly, I was too busy pounding away with my 60 to notice. Denny was hammering away on the other side and we were leaving a bunch of bodies in our wake, brand new Russian weapons at their side. We passed the shitter a couple times, but I was reluctant to riddle it. I was hoping our Sad Sack was hiding in there and finishing his business. Maybe he'd make it through this. If he had any sense, he'd stay where he was.

Mr. Willis was setting us up for frag runs on the buildings and our 60 ammo was running down fast. There were too many targets running at one time, and I had to force myself to concentrate on one N.V.A. at a time — take him out and go to the next one. It was a madhouse! It reminded me of the times at Shubert's dairy farm. We'd head down to the barn about 10 p.m., flick on the light where the stanchions were, and the concrete floor would be black with roaches. We'd jump in and scoop them up by the handfuls, drop them in jars and keep at it until they were gone. Fish bait for tomorrow. The base camp was just a bigger version. We were shooting up equipment as well as people, and targets were plentiful.

The Cobras were eager to get down and dirty, but since we were receiving very little fire, we had no reason to call them. They were repeatedly requesting some rocket time, so we tossed a few smokes into some hooches, climbed to altitude and reorganized while our three Cobras unlimbered their rockets.

We watched the Snakes roll in one right behind the other, blasting hooches to bits and generally creating hell on earth. While they rearranged the buildings in the base camp, we took stock of our stores.

My 60 ammo was down to about 300 rounds, as was Denny's. Half our mini-gun ammo was gone, as were the grenades in my stockpile, except for the smokers. We had enough firepower for one more short mission before we were relieved. From our altitude we could see people running into the trees or piling into ditches, searching for cover. The guns expended about 2/3 of their ordnance, leaving enough to cover us if we were taken down.

As they climbed into the sky, we dropped back out of it and continued the search. We were finding N.V.A. hiding behind every bush and tree it seemed like. We hunted them down until we ran out of ammo; I even resorted to firing my .38 after I fired all my shotgun ammo.

Our other team came on station in a nick of time and proceeded to kick ass and wreak havoc! We headed back to Moc Hoa, refueled and found a parking spot. Everybody piled out with one thing in mind — rearm as soon as possible and get back over the border. Our troop had brought along some of our grunts to hump rockets to rearm the Cobras. While they did that, we drug a couple hundred pounds of 60 ammo into our LOH, refilling the mini-gun box then piling in as much as I had room for, for my 60. Denny was on the other side cramming grenades in his pod. Mr. Willis checked the ship for holes, and found none!

This was the most intense hour and a half I had spent in my life and we had come out of our first mission unscathed! The conversation among our crew and wing was a breathless rewind of the weird shit that had gone on while we were on our first mission. The wing Oscar had nailed a few N.V.A. himself, the pilot keeping an eye on us while he searched for targets of opportunity. We chatted like old maids at a quilting bee while we rearmed the LOH with more explosives. There was no fear; we were living on the pure adrenaline coursing through our veins. Confidence was high and we were ready to go back.

We switched on the radio to hear how our 2nd team was doing, and they were flying around, finding targets aplenty. Doug was the backseat in the second lead LOH and actually hit an N.V.A. soldier running down a trail with an M-79 round. He hit the guy right in the back of the neck and the head shot off the body like a cork leaving a bottle. This was the second time he had nailed a guy with an M-79. Awesome shooting.

Once we had rearmed, we got a few minutes rest when our C & C gave us the word to mount up. The 2nd team was going through their ammo supply as fast as we had, so we were due to relieve them.

We lit the boilers and heard the familiar whine of the turbine coming to life; the blades sounding like the baseball card in the bicycle spokes.

In very little time, we were back on station. Team 2 giving us a rundown of what was happening. They said they were finding that a lot of soldiers were leaving the base camp and heading for the jungle and grasslands around the base, so that's where we should hunt. We could tell by the voices on the radio that they had seen a lot of action, and again, very little fire.

So Team 2 climbed, we dropped down, hearing our guns proclaim themselves ready to cover us again. There were more hooches burning, the stench of burning grass, cordite and hot earth heavy in the air. The base looked deserted again, bodies lying all over the ground, looking like miniatures on a diorama.

We started running low and slow over the grass, keeping one eye on the base camp area. We found N.V.A. hiding in clumps of grass, ditches, shallow bunkers, anywhere they thought was safe. We started throwing our frags at them when possible, keeping our 60 ammo for the runners.

We passed over a clump of grass and I saw a couple guys lying in the weeds. We did a hard right and I saw a total of 8 guys in the grass, all lying perfectly still, brand new AK's next to them. They were wearing N.V.A. uniforms, soft caps, and web gear. The AK's were equipped with the knife bayonet, a trophy the Navy guys would trade a night with Farrah Fawcett for.

Since I was on them during our turn, I got the honor of blowing all of them to N.V.A. heaven. I made sure all the kills were head shots so I could talk Mr. Willis into putting me on the ground and gathering up their weapons and web gear.

After the deed was done, I again marveled how these guys lied there while we hovered over them, ready to kill them. This had to be something they were taught, but it seemed so improbable. Those 8 guys could have stood up while we were lining up on them, bringing all eight AK's to bear and we'd have been in a world of hurt. They could have perforated every square foot of the LOH and our hides as well, but they didn't. I just found this behavior too weird, and for the third time.

While we skimmed the grass tops, checking the bodies, I ask Mr. Willis about putting me on the ground and gathering up the AK's. He looked at me over his right shoulder and gave me one of those "NO WAY" looks I had seen before. I told him it would only take a minute to gather up those fine trophies, but he said no. I begged, I pleaded, I hopped up and down on my seat. Nothing helped! I threw as much of a tantrum as I could and still maintain my dignity. I never got there. We hovered around for another minute, shooting up the AK's, then left. It broke my heart.

Ten minutes later, we came across a 12 foot dike about 100 yards long with a line of bushes growing half-way up the base slope. I thought I saw a flash of white behind one of the bushes so I told Willis to swing around and try a little recon by fire. He lined the LOH on a parallel course with the dike out my door and I took apart the bush and a body rolled out, complete with a weapon. I continued strafing along the line of vegetation and a couple more guys rolled out dead. We got to the end and Denny worked the bushes over as we doubled back. A couple more guys tumbled out. This was unbelievable! We took out twelve or thirteen guys in that one tree line. These guys were wearing a mix of black pajamas and street clothes, their weapons ranged from M-1 carbines, SKS's, and old Chi Com bolt actions. It looked like we were dealing with N.V.A. trainees and cadre.

By the time we had run the course and gotten low on fuel, we had found several other N.V.A. hiding in the grass and banana groves. The targets were getting more scarce, finding hiding places as far from the base camp as possible. Team 2 came back up in a nick of time and started spreading the search pattern further out. We headed back to Moc Hoa, our hearts still racing.

Once we got back to our staging area, there was less of a frenzy to reload even though we began immediately. The grunts were humping rockets to the Cobras, a steady line of trooper's running back and forth from the ammo pile to the ships. Our five team members got together again, hands and arms waving in the air describing the last 1 ½ hours of flying. We were still high about our experiences, and still excited about going back out one more time. A three mission day for a team was a rarity, but chances were good today that we'd be going out again one more time and still make it to Vinh Long by dark.

We all had a few minutes rest, but the adrenaline was still in the blood, keeping us sharp. I finally had time to clean the empty brass casings out of the cargo area. I didn't have time after our first mission and adding the second mission to that, I had about 3 inches of brass over the floor of the cargo area. I scooped them out with my hands, the brass tinkling like a wind chime as they fell at my feet. I had just finished tidying up my cubbyhole when we got the call again. One more mission and we'd be done for the day.

We cranked up and headed north again. The countryside was looking more familiar every time we passed over. Team 2 told us when we got on station that there were still people out there, but by now they had found better camouflaged positions and were getting harder to find.

Team 2 climbed, we dropped, and the whole process started again. The other team was right, after about seven hours of us being on station, the N.V.A. had dispersed and were hiding like rats in a ship. We managed to nail a few more guys before we got low on fuel, but we had to really look for them. We were checking under the canal water, banana leaves, anything a person could cover himself with. We managed to find a few more soldiers that for some reason decided to stick around. Bad choice on their part.

Our third mission over for the day, we headed back to Moc Hoa to refuel and shutdown. Everybody was talking about our day, excitement still present in our voices. Before we left for home, one of our gun pilots took a picture of our two LOH teams. Participants were: SP/4 Crummey, Capt. Metzner, Mr. Willis, Sgt. Workman, Sgt. Summerhill, Mr. Falcon, SP/4 Nyberg, Mr. Parker, and Sgt. Houston. Our total KBA's for the day were 165. The Scouts got 92 of them. My total for the day was 29; Houston's was 35. Not a bad day. We felt we had hurt them bad and things would probably get even more interesting in the next few days.

The flight back was kind of quiet; everybody lost in his own thoughts. I sat back in my hole, letting the cool air wash over me. I didn't realize how tired I was. All of a sudden my body felt like it had been put through a wringer. We'd had a full day of tense, adrenaline pumping action and we were feeling the after effects. But we had nailed their asses good and I hoped the other units that invaded had the same success without any casualties.

The next couple days we staged out of Moc Hoa again, widening our search more and more. I didn't know where everybody went, but they had disappeared like yesterday's news. We managed to find a few guys, but it wasn't like the first day.

We flew over the 8 guys I nailed in the weeds and their bodies were still there, but they had green plastic around them like some kind of coffin/cocoon. After three days in the sun, the bodies had swelled up and the plastic stretched across the bodies like a sausage casing. The busted up weapons were gone, and I assumed the web gear was too. I passed on asking Mr. Willis to set me down and check it out.

While we were sitting around in Moc Hoa, we saw an Arvin truck convoy that had rolled across the border and stopped close to our staging area. I got curious and walked over to one of the trucks and saw a whole 2 ½ ton truck full of brand new SKS's, trussed up in groups of ten. Excellent trophies. I went to grab a rifle and an Arvin in the truck pointed his carbine at me! By this time our LOH team arrived and thought a few of the rifles would make good trophies or trading items. The Arvins still refused to allow us the rifles and finally a U.S. officer advising the Arvins came over and told us he couldn't let us have any because they belonged to the Arvins. What a bummer. We knew they'd be back in the hands of the V.C. in short order. Reports from the other units that entered the Parrot's Beak and the Fishhook areas had found caches of weapons, rice, ammo, and medical supplies. They were being hauled out or destroyed in place, and the troops were finding tons of the stuff. For the first time I could remember, I applauded Nixon's decision to let us go into Cambodia.

A couple of days later, we actually staged inside Cambodia. Our unit flew to Neak Leung, on the coast of Cambodia. It was called "the Ferry" and since the bright, shiny new Premier of Cambodia, Lon Nol had invited us into this country, we grabbed at the chance.

Cambodia was a beautiful country; no bomb craters or burned out villages in this part of the country. The greens of the tree lines seemed more intense, their pagodas masterfully carved and decorated with bold colors — and the women, well they were gorgeous. They stood about the same height as the Vietnamese women, but they were darker with more rounded bodies. More curves, huge brown eyes, their wrap-around skirts and jet-black hair. They were certainly different. Exotic to the extreme!

We crossed the border to our staging area and did a little hovering around, checking out the area. We had crossed a river and saw a contingent of Arvins bathing and washing their clothes in the coffee-colored river. We circled a beautiful pagoda, several beauties working in a small garden, and then I saw it. A beautiful Cambodian flag laid out on a bush drying. Apparently an Arvin had washed it out and draped it over the bush to dry.

This flag was a worthy trophy and I imagined every Scout flying over this area had their eye on this little beauty. But I had a couple advantages. Since we would be the first LOH on the ground, I'd get a leg up on the rest of the guys. 2nd, I could unstrap and be on the ground a lot quicker than Denny or Mr. Willis. So by the time we were about 10 feet above the ground, I was unstrapped, had my helmet and flak gear off and standing on the skid when we kissed the ground. I was well on my way to the bush before the LOH engine was turned off.

I strolled, as nonchalantly as I could, over to the bush holding the flag. I checked around, confident that the Arvins were not watching. I grabbed the flag and stuffed it under my shirt and strolled back to the LOH. About half way back, I run into Denny heading for the bushes. I asked him where he was going and he told me about this great Cambodian flag hanging on a bush. I pulled the flag out of my shirt and said, "You mean this one?" His mouth went a little slack before calling me a son-of-a-bitch! He saw it flying in too, but I was faster getting out. He took it well, the fortunes of war and all that!

The word had finally gotten around; the bad guys were getting tougher to find. They headed straight away from the border. After our first mission, I wandered down to the river and still found some Arvins bathing and laundering in the vile river water. I also noticed clumps of clothing along the riverbanks and once in a while a clump would come floating by in the river. Upon closer inspection, I realized they were bodies, in various forms of decomposition. There were a half dozen bodies that I could see from my position, down stream from the Arvins. The thing that really tightened my colon was the Arvins were actually bathing in this putrid water with bodies floating in it!

The wind was with me as I wandered back to the LOH's. Knowing how foul a human body can smell after lying in the tropical sun for a few days, I knew how lucky I was not to have to have the wind wafting my way. I got back to the LOH with a coppery taste in my mouth. Somewhere in Cambodia families are wondering what happened to their son, daughter, husband, or wife. Some of them were lying in the mud on the bank of a river, slowly rotting away in the hot sun.

We spent the day cruising over some grasslands without seeing shit. We were to be very careful about our targets — the Cambodian government was having a problem with opposing factions and we had to be careful about sending the wrong people to meet the Grim Reaper. Most of the Cambodes were using Commie weapons. Carrying an AK or SKS didn't make you an N.V.A. around here. We had to check with our C & C before we fired.

We got back to home base early that day, and the hot topic was Kent State. One group of guys was sitting in the traditional circle, discussing the details of the whole incident. Seems the Ohio National Guard, while providing campus security on May 4th, fired live ammo into a crowd and killed four students and wounded 10 more. The discussion got hot and heavy, with some interesting perspectives. It should be noted that war protesters carrying signs with "Baby Killer" or "Support the N.V.A." were not looked upon fondly by the troopers over here. It was hard to find true sympathy from anyone.

One of the fellas grunted and asked "Is that all they killed, just 4? Fuckin' NG's." Another trooper piped up and wondered what kind of an idiot would throw rocks at people carrying loaded rifles. It was hard for me to tell just what actually happened, but now this war was causing the deaths of students living in the supposedly safe and secure World. It was confusing and I didn't feel good about what was happening, but as I had stated earlier, we had our own problems here. The bull session lasted another hour, with nothing accomplished. The general consensus was against the students. They were protesting the war by bombarding N.G. troops with rocks. If they were so eager to do that, why didn't they join up and learn to use a real weapon and help out here! Things were getting crazy back in the World. Maybe we were safer here!

We staged out of Takeo a day later, much farther into the interior than we ever had gone. Our sweeps were becoming more confusing because of all the factions fighting one another and when we flew we saw very little movement anymore. We did see more of the country and I thought I would have enjoyed playing tourist in Cambodia for a couple of weeks, but the political system was as shaky as an alcoholic's hand. It was certainly a beautiful country; I hated to think about the bomb craters marching over the landscape as in Vietnam.

The sweeps became like cruises, and we were bored. The pilots would find a suspicious hooch and tear it down with the chopper's skids, going from corner to the other and collapsing the hooch in on itself. A lot of white flags were flying over hooches we passed over. Whether they were friendlies or not, who knew. We left them alone.

Cambodian armor was making its presence known as we overflew Takeo. When we landed, we checked out the government troopers just down the road. They all were young, and full of juice, displaying the mock-heroics all young soldiers eventually do. I felt like an old man next to them. They were using Communist weapons and web gear and seemed well fed and cared for. The stink of death wafting across this country would be a reality, and not too far away either.

Our Cambodian missions were terminated in the middle of May. We received 2 new observers one day, both E-5's with infantry experience. They were oriented to their new jobs, and scheduled to fly a day later. Get them in the seat, as soon as possible that was our motto. We all needed some down time after Cambodia. We'll put the newbies in the LOH's so we could get some beauty sleep!

Charlie Palek

The first day they were to fly, Doug Houston found them smoking pot on the flight line, one hour before they were to go up. Doug went back and reported them, and our C.O. bounced their sorry asses right out of the Scouts. I applauded Doug's decision. I wouldn't have felt safe being covered by an idiot high on drugs, with a machine gun in his hand that could put out 2,000 rounds a minute. That kind of help we didn't need.

We were in mid-May now; my DERO's date was 2 days shorter because of a drop. I'd be going home the same time as Denny, hopefully on the same plane. My flying days were over, unless an emergency required my services.

I spent the next week getting my shit together and just loafing around. I spent a lot of time reading and writing letters in the flight line hooch. The REMF's were making barracks living a hell on earth with their little details and they were always looking for E-5' to do the deed. So I snuck over to the line hooch, cleaned a gun or two to pass the time until day's end.

The thought of going home, for good this time, was becoming a much-anticipated event. Once I had mustered out, I was going to see an uncle in Seattle for a few days, buy some civvies, and chill out. No more army bullshit, edible food, clean sheets, and no reveille. Paradise at last.

Before I left, we had an awards ceremony for our Cambodian incursion. These awards we called "Impact Awards" because they were pushed through quicker than your average run of the mill medals. No red tape, no reviews, none of the usual REMF bullshit and award nominations that one typically has to go through. The lead Oscar each got a "Distinguished Flying Cross," which was a real surprise to me. Our guys plus the gun pilots stood in formation with Cav hats on (I think I looked ridiculous in a Cav hat) and received our medals. Our C.O. said a few kind words about duty, honor, and our exceptional ability to kill our fellow man, and it was over. Another day, another piaster.

MURPHY'S LAW OF COMBAT
#3
"A sucking chest wound is nature's way of telling you to slow down."

I was ready to go home, but after our last LOH got nailed I felt some regrets about leaving again. There was obviously a lot of work to be done, but I was going to leave it to the newbies. I hoped everybody I left behind made it back to the States with all their fingers and toes.

    The Scouts threw a party for Denny and me a few days before we left. We incinerated more steaks, had plenty of whiskey and beer (a bottle of wine showed up sometime during the party, but no one would admit to bringing it, drinking with our little pinky up took too much effort.) It was a great send off and a good time to say goodbye to everybody. The party lasted into the night and everybody was dead to the world by the time we got back to the barracks. It was a down day in the morning, so that was good for all those pumpkin heads out there, struggling to get their boots off before they passed out on their bunks. Oh, the horror!

    I left the unit with 90 KBA's, 12 less than Doug had. This morbid little contest had to be conceded to Doug, but he was a good observer. He had a few more weeks to go and I never found out what his tally was. I hoped he nailed a bunch more of the little bastards.

    The day finally came for Denny and me to leave. We packed our duffels, I grabbed the old bolt action rifle I was bringing home, we checked out of the Apache H.Q. and we were on our way. We hitched a ride to Long Binh and checked into the 90th Replacement Battalion, the III Corp. newbie/oldie cattle drive. This was the place I'd visited three times before, the tent city that sends men to their new assignments or gets them on the Freedom Bird. Denny and I were going in the right direction, but there were plenty of guys with cherry-red skin, dumbfounded looks and squeaky clean, dark green (in other words "new") fatigues that were going in to meet the dragon. We wished them luck. Christ we were happy to be going home. 364 and a wakeup — fuck me!

    We checked in and were told we'd be flying out in two days, maybe! What the hell was maybe? The Army, in its infinite sense of the diabolical, continued to screw with us two days before going home! Big surprise! We wandered back to one of the holding tents, found a couple of bunks and cooled our heels. There wasn't much to do but hit the typical clubs for a cold one and that's about it. I found a book lying on the floor, picked it up and dove in for lack of something better to do.

    The next day, the staff got our flight together and had us open our bags and lay stuff out. We were told that a few items we were not allowed to take home — explosives, C-4, live ammo of any kind, automatic weapons, unregistered weapons, knives and bayonets, enemy ears or other body parts, drugs, and anything else that would be considered military property.

## Charlie Palek

I had a bracelet made from the rear rotor chain of a LOH wired on my wrist. As the E-7 walked around, inspecting our stuff, I held up my wrist when he walked by. He looked at me for a millisecond and told me "take it off." I calmly told him this chain was unusable and was actually taken out of the chopper junkyard. He stuck his nose up against mine and said — "Would you like to have a seat on the plane tomorrow?" He grinned like a skull, and I knew exactly what he meant — Keep the bracelet, lose your seat. They held that shit over our heads every hour. I took the bracelet off and threw it on the pile, which I knew the REMF's would go through later and end up taking some of our stuff home with them. Army bullshit! Hard to avoid!

After we all had a chance to turn in our ill-gotten gains, he told us there would be a thorough inspection of our bags. If anything was confiscated from the aforementioned list we could kiss our Freedom Flight goodbye for a few weeks. Everybody passed the inspection. He and his brown noser only spot-checked a half dozen suitcases. PRICKS! These guys really enjoyed the power they had over us, and it irritated everybody, but we were at their mercy. Little Hitlers with their own little kingdoms. HOORAWH!

The afternoon arrived and we were called out of our comfy little tents and stood in formation. One of the dipsticks in charge told us our hair had to be trimmed above the ears and military length on top before our flight out.

Now, most of us had worked on getting our hair just the right length before leaving for home. We let it grow, had it carefully trimmed, this process going on until our DERO's date arrived. The idea was to have any kind of hair length that would pass inspection without it looking like a military cut. Nobody wanted to go home with "Whitewalls," except for those LRRP maniacs.

So we bent over one more time and gave another pony ride to the powers that be. We were told it was our call if we felt our hair was regulation, but if it didn't cut the mustard before boarding the plane, we'd be pulled out of line and would receive a haircut that would allow you to catch the next plane, in a few days! I had my hair cut before I left a Vinh Long, and Denny's was close to being unreg, but he was always fucking with their minds anyway. He wasn't worried.

Our last night in-country was uneventful and sleepless for me. Morning, however, didn't come soon enough. We dressed in our khaki's,

*Tattletale*

complete with our cunt caps and salad dressing and waited for our flight to be called, which was about mid-morning. We were bused to Tan Son Nhut, checked our bags, and got a look at our Bird. She was beautiful, and I felt the urge to run out and make sure there were no popped rivets on her skin and that all four engines weren't overburdened with hours. We sat around for an hour or so, then got the word to board. Den and I walked up the ramp, grabbed a couple seats close to the beer wagon, and let out a long sigh. In less than an hour we were over the water and a cheer went up from all aboard. Beers were passed out by real curvy, round-eyed, women that were brave enough to fly with a fuselage full of horny, young, intoxicants ready to party! I remember finishing the beer and laying my head back — and I don't remember another thing about the flight. Not a damned thing!

We flew into California and were taken to Oakland for out-processing. We were all given half-assed physicals and dental checkups. The dentist showed up about 1½ hours late, pissed about having to check our group out. I think our exam pulled him off the golf course because he was really surly and in a big rush. He had each of us sit in his chair and he stuck his mirror in our mouth for about 2 seconds then called for the next guy. He gave our group of 30 men a "complete dental checkup" in 45 minutes. The Army takin' care of business. We got through this goat-fuck as quick as possible, had our Class A greens inspected for unauthorized insignias, and signed our release papers. I had to take the "Mobile Riverine Force" badge off my uniform, but that was no big deal. I was free!

I had left Denny before when I arrived at Oakland. He told me he was thinking of re-upping, which shocked me down to my socks! When he said possibly for 6 years, I kind of freaked out. I ask him why in the name of all that is grotesque would he want to do that. He didn't say much, but I think he enjoyed being in the Army and being good at what he did. We shook hands and wished each other well. The Army certainly needed more guys like him.

We were offered a free steak dinner before we left, but I blew that off, anxious to get out of the tentacles of the Green Machine. Me and a couple of other boys grabbed a cab and headed for the airport. While I was riding in the cab, I noticed that one of my teeth, a Vietnamese rebuild, was a little loose. I started working it with my tongue and it fell right out. I couldn't believe it! The tooth had been partially cracked off during a "touch" football game between the grunts and the Scouts about a month after I got to Vinh Long. I caught an elbow in the jaw and the tooth split, one corner of a canine disappearing down my gullet. I had it rebuilt by a Viet dentist that worked on base. Apparently, the warranty was only good until I was back in the States. Timing is everything! I had it repaired by a real dentist in Seattle when I visited an aunt and uncle. The dentist told me I was lucky the material had held up as long as it had. Inferior dental material, apparently. I felt the expiration date on that filling was cutting it a bit too close.

I bought new duds while in Seattle and had my first real restaurant meal. My uncle took me to a seafood restaurant and bought me a plate of prawns that was piled 3 fish high. I ate two of them with some cole slaw and puked my guts out 20 minutes later. I guess my stomach wasn't used to rich, satisfying real food. I took it a little easier after that.

A couple days later, I had recovered from my first two days back in the World to catch a flight from Seattle non-stop to St. Louis. I called Mom and Pop and gave them my flight time and number. They guaranteed they would be there with bells on.

Sometimes when I was a kid, Dad and I would just drive to the St. Louis airport and watch the planes land and takeoff. Dad loved it, and his enthusiasm passed straight to me. Once in awhile we'd catch a military jet from McDonnell/Douglas next door. That was considered a real treat. Catching an old piston-engine WWII vintage was Nirvana! I knew the family would get there early so Pop could watch the planes.

I was able to carry my Chi Com rifle on board the flight from Seattle. They stored it in a compartment between coach and 1st class. The flight to St. Louis, no way. They insisted I check the rifle into baggage and I protested. I could see it disappearing before the baggage ever made it to the plane. But the company staff was insistent so I reluctantly let them have it, and half-heartedly kissed it goodbye. I sat next to an older fellow who looked at my ribbons and said "see some action?" I told him "A lot of action." He just smiled, laid his head back and went to sleep. Once we hit the friendly skies, I did the same. The flight home was uneventful.

Coming into Illinois and seeing St. Louis from the air was exciting and cleansing. Soon I'd be back in the bosom of my family, enjoying my favorite foods, being pampered and congratulated by people glad to see me back. The pilot sat our plane down like an old Caribon pilot, slamming it down and hitting the brakes hard. Now I truly was close to home.

## Tattletale

When I got off the plane and walked into the terminal, Mom, Dad, and all the little Paleks standing there like good little soldiers. Mom and Dad got big hugs, as well as Donna. She was old enough to know what was going on. Ann and the twins, another story. Terry had a big ol' grin on his face, impressed with the uniform. Ann looked at me with a smile on her face and a little fear in her heart. She wasn't sure about me. Sherry on the other hand, knew I was a wacko and her nervousness showed! She kind of hid behind Dad, peeking out like a puppy in trouble.

We headed for baggage claim and miracles of miracles; my rifle actually made it home. I got a few sideways glances walking though the terminal with a rifle, but I cared not. Terry thought it was pretty cool. While we were standing at the baggage claim, an Army Colonel stepped up, waiting for his bags. Terry looked up at him and asked Dad if he was a Sergeant too. The "bird" looked down at Terry like a cockroach had just crawled out of his ham and beans. It was beautiful. One last zinger to the Army officer corp.

We loaded up in the Chevy and headed home, stopping for lunch in Belleville. Everybody was having a good time, eating out being a treat for the family. After we were done our waitress came over and asked me if I was back from Vietnam. I told her I was and she told me her brother was over there and kept hoping he was o.k. I wished her my best, and she told me lunch was on her. She was glad I made it back. I was floored by this after all the stories we had heard about vets being mistreated from the airport to home. Renewed my faith in people. I thanked her profusely, and told her to continue writing to him — word and support from home was crucial. She promised she would.

The final leg of my trip home, I felt better than I had in a long time. Even though coming home was going to be great, there was an underlying bitterness I couldn't shake again. Things weren't finished over there, and I spent a lot of time in the summer of 1970 watching the news every night to see how things were going, and the news wasn't very good. After being there for two years I found it amazing that the military minds of the day could think they could contain a guerrilla force that could infiltrate just about every square foot of border there was. The U.S.A. had kicked ass so much I guess we thought we were invincible, but I worried about this one. Same old feeling seeping deeper into my brain.

I speeded over to Roxy's on my motorcycle as soon as I got home. She met me in the driveway and did she feel good to hug! Lordy, it had been a long time. We went into the house where her parents were waiting. Her father, Lawrence, gave me one of his patented, seesaw handshakes and his huge smile. Roxy's Mom gave me a hug, but I sensed she was a little afraid of me. I had been killing people the last year I was there, and that habit would be hard to shake, she thought. Later I found out from Roxy that she feared I'd become violent and do some real damage sometime after returning home. It was happening elsewhere to other Vets, and she expected the same from me. Psychos running around in the town square mowing down the citizens with the illegally obtained AK-47 he sent from the war zone. I was going to have to win her trust again.

My gleeful homecoming lasted about a week before Dad and I had it out over the award certificates that he had hanging on the wall. I insisted he take them down and he refused, claiming he was proud of them, and I should be too. Harsh words were spoken by me that I immediately regretted, but I was a butthead about this and the argument never should have happened if my shit was together. About three weeks later I was given a dinner by a group of Dairy Producers that included a lot of men friends of the family. Pop wanted me to wear my uniform, and I refused. It was another senseless argument I could have avoided. I knew he was very proud of my service record but I didn't want to hear it. I wore civvies to the dinner.

The capper was at a party thrown by my high school buds. I got a bit tanked up, said some things I shouldn't have and left the party with Roxy in tow, flat-ass embarrassed about the whole thing. We went to her house, she read me the riot act in her usually soft, forgiving way, and I ended the night throwing up from the alcohol and a chip dip that I didn't realize was clam. While I was standing in the back yard of the House house, I realized I was going to have to get it together. All my family and friends had put up with my almost whimsical desire to put myself in harm's way and I was being an ass after I'd come home. I was going to clean up my act and get back to normal, if there was such a thing.

The next day, I resolved to stop being a dickhead and get back to being civilized, at least mostly civilized. I started helping out around the house again, and tried cleaning up my language. The "F" word was still cropping up in my casual conversations and the kids got an earful when I wasn't careful. I especially had to be good when I spoke to a couple of the city's women's clubs. Since I couldn't tell them how our LOH's swooped out of the sky, machine gunning the poor bastards carrying a weapon, I discussed the culture, the people, and some of the positive things that happened, and tried not to say the "F" word and offend their delicate sensibilities.

Everybody I met was great to me. My favorite biology teacher, Ron Brown, wrote an editorial about me that would have made George Patton blush. Nashville citizenry wanted to give me a parade, but I begged off, ceremony not one of my favorite things. Somehow a parade wouldn't have felt right. Suffice to say, the good people of Southern Illinois received me with warm hearts and honest thankfulness. They were happy I was back, and not like some of the other sons that returned in a coffin. That was worth a lot to everybody, especially me! I had nightmares for about 8 months, then they quit. I found myself under the bed once in a while yelling "incoming!" but that eventually stopped too. I had been purged.

But I had a lot to learn about civilian life. I decided to go to Southern Illinois University, use my V.A. education money and study still photography. While I was down there, one of my high school buds took me to his fraternity, hoping I'd consider joining. The first two frat brothers I ran into changed that notion in a hurry. They were cocky, know-it-all butt holes and they both had handshakes like a woman's. They proceeded to tell me how their initiation ceremony would proceed. The shortest guy, looked me right in the eye and told me they would paddle my bare ass until it was a bright, cherry red, then he grinned like a Cheshire cat.

I looked at him, envisioning how he'd look with an M-60 round between his eyes. Habit. I decided then and there that I wasn't going to join a frat full of low-life draft dodgers who thought they were hot shit. I could smell confrontation with these guys a mile away. Thus ended my frat phase.

About mid-June, after I had registered at SIU, I started looking for a job. The day before I was to check out working for the County Highway Department, the father of one of my high school friends came to the house and ask me if I wanted a job. The Haege cattle farm was a big operation west of town. I said yes in a second. He was a good man and the thought of farming and dealing with cattle instead of packing groceries or picking up road kill was a no-brainer to me.

Dean Haege had been a Marine in WWII, seeing action on Iwo Jima. He still suffered from the effects of malaria he caught somewhere in the Pacific. He had a good crew working for him and I fit in easily. I got to spend a lot of time outside, got dirty, and enjoyed the job immensely. I worked weekends and summer all through college. I left about the time I graduated, and none too soon. They bought a herd of dairy cows and started milking. Not what I wanted to do!

College was a real eye-opener. I'm not sure what I expected, but everybody seemed unconcerned about the fighting. When somebody would comment about my tan, and I told them where I had been, it got a shrug of indifference, and that was all. People in college were too damned smug and comfortable. I didn't feel like I fit in. I didn't join any organizations, kept to myself, and did my work. My life revolved around Roxy and my family.

In '71, I married Roxy, deciding I was not going to let her get away. She had offered me tons of support with her letters and shipments of food, and it was something I would never forget. She was a true gem and I was lucky she agreed to be my wife. 30 years later and my thinking hasn't changed.

In the summer of 1970, I found myself back on the Shubert farm. Dwight and I loaded up a couple of .22 rifles and walked the pasture where we fought so many battles so many years ago. I told him the things I brought back from Vietnam were: a healthy cynicism for our government, which hasn't changed in 30 years, a slightly dinged up body, a healthy respect for all the grunts in all the services that do the dirty work, and an experience I wouldn't trade for all the rice in the Delta. I went over to Vietnam for the adventure and to test myself. I was satisfied with my performance and can honestly say Vietnam was a positive experience for me. But it wasn't all milk and cookies. War is like that.

I go to some of the local schools and talk to the kids about my experiences. I never had a problem talking about this so it is easy for me. I hope I can bring a message to them that will make them think about why our country is enjoying a white-hot economy now. They can thank the veterans of all the wars, police actions, classified intrusions and secret missions. No parades, ceremonies or presentations. A simple "Thank you" will suffice.

As for Mr. Murphy, he followed me home and has been hanging around me for 30 years. After 26 years in the photography business, he's the reason I still carry 3 complete camera systems to every job I go on. Backup to backup my backup. If nothing else, Murphy does tend to keep one honest. Finally…

There is not a week that goes by that I don't think about some aspect of my two tours. I've tried getting in touch with some of my mates but they still don't want to talk about it. I fear Vietnam will always be considered a dark time in our country's history, and I hope our services will have learned some lessons from it's hard experiences. For myself, I saw typically heroic American battlefield conduct. The men that faced the bullets everyday whether they were on the ground, on the water or in the air did a damned fine job and I hope they never forget that. If anything is true, it's that to really know about it, you had to be there.

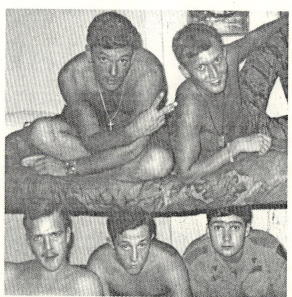

The "Filthy Five", taken one night before Honker left. <u>Top:</u> Denny Workman, myself. <u>Bottom:</u> Tom Stradley, Joe Harrell, and Tom Russell.

Three of my five E-5 buddies at Tra Vihn. Stradley, "Honker" Harrell, and Self without the shirt.

That is good ol' Hook, the grunts truck driver peeking into our room and finding out to believe some of the things he reads.

A group shot of one of the raunchiest groups in the Delta – The Apache Scouts.

*Charlie Palek*

That is Mac, our Line Chief. As you can see, he is not too fond of snakes.

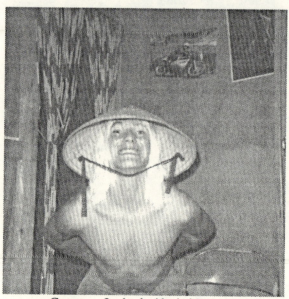

Cosmo – Isn't she/ he/ "it" cute?

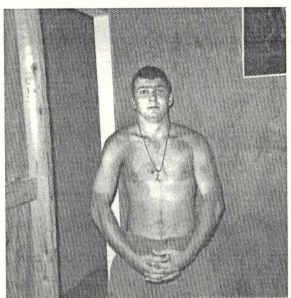

This one is Mr. August. It wouldn't be bad except for the Firestone wide oval around his belly.

A couple of ice cream salesman at Tra Vihn. They start smoking fairly early.

*Charlie Palek*

The Arvin A-Cavs busting through to a cache.

An old Papasan we found fishing at Chau Duc.

*Tattletale*

Getting ready to sling 274 out of Thoi Binh.

Our wing landing on a Navy barge for refueling. Those two Charlie model gunships belong to the Navy's Seawolves, who operate off the barge.

This is a result of a Cobra pilot low leveling, misjudging the height of a rice paddy dike, and hitting the dike with a skid. Needless to say, the gunner in the front seat of this Cobra got pretty messed up.

Not much left, even for a re-built.

What is left of 559, our C&C ship that had a booby trap explode inside of it, killing four people and wounding three.

Me and 274, sitting in our maintenance yard.

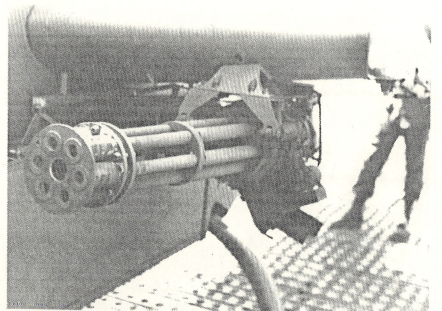

The big daddy of the minigun, the 20-mm mounted on a Cobra. This jewel will put out 2000 r.p.m.

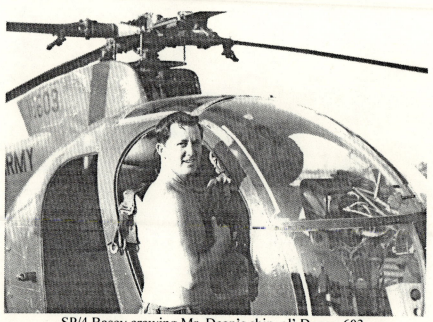

SP/4 Basey crewing Mr. Dean's ship, ol' Doggy 603.

*Tattletale*

Mr. Sorenson (Wild Bill), Mr. Willis (Chatty Randy), Mr. Dicresce (Balls) and Mr. Dean (J.D.) with a Russian flag taken off a Cong that "Wild Bill" had greased with his mini.

Threatening to throw a frag at Wil.

Charlie Palek

Lt. Sprague and I with gravestones I got out and picked up. All are NVA.

A V.C. tombstone that one of our observers scarfed out of a V.C. graveyard.

This is one of the most outstanding aerial shots that I have taken.

Me and my good buddy "Red Dog" Landry, an old 9$^{th}$ Division man. He had helped himself to my crackers and jam.

Charlie Palek

The terrible twosome!

Mr. Dicresce and Wil ready to go to the AO at Chi Lang.

Our new setup, no minigun but a backseat to cover the pilot's side of the ship. The backseat is a little cramped, but not as bad as it may look. That is SP/4 Doug Houston in back with "Wild Bill" Sorenson flying.

Trailing smoke in an echelon right over Vihn Long Airfield. Notice Chalk One is breaking hard left.

*Charlie Palek*

My cubbyhole with all of my tools.

Taken at Moc Hoa, 2 May 1970. Troop got 165 kills, 92 of them were ours. <u>Back Row</u>: Sp/4 Crummey, Capt. Metzner, Mr. Willis, Sgt. Workman, Sgt. Summerhill. <u>Front Row</u>: Mr. Falcon, SP/4 Nyberg, Mr. Parker, me, and Sgt. Houston.

Denny, Mr. Willis and myself prior to our first mission in Cambodia.

Mr. Willis and myself in my backseat slot, working in Cambodia from Dom Phuc. I've got my faithful M60 and 12 gauge with me.

# Chapter 6
# MY FAMILY'S MEMORIES

*Sherry's thoughts:*

I was 4 years old when my brother Charlie went to Vietnam. I don't have a lot of vivid memories, only a few that have stayed with me throughout the years.

I hear stories now from my family, especially my parents, of what a scary and unsettling time this was for everyone. I remember praying for Charlie and all the other soldiers to be safe and to come home soon. I don't ever remember any tears or negative feelings that he wouldn't come home safe.

My parents had my brother Terry and I relate to Vietnam by focusing on the children there. Most of them had lost their families and their homes. We were always sending them toys and making them cookies. I envied those kids because they got to spend time with Charlie — something I never really had a chance to do. He was kind of a mysterious celebrity to me at the time, and even though I was scared to death of him, I still wanted to be around him. My image of him was a man who was far away shooting people. To me that's what the news on TV depicted everyone in Vietnam to be.

I didn't know any other kids who had family members in Vietnam, so they didn't understand why I reacted so strangely when a plane would fly over and I would press myself as close to a tree as possible so it wouldn't see me and shoot me. In the meantime my brother Terry would be on the other side of the yard playing Army and bragging about his big brother in Vietnam. We reacted totally different during this time.

The day we went to pick Charlie up for the last time was bigger than any Christmas I can remember. On the way to the airport I was anxious and scared. When he was making his rounds of hugs and kisses I remember peeking around Dad and looking up at him, and he winked at me. All I kept thinking was "please God, don't make me have to sit by him on the way home!"

I remember going in his room one morning and staring at him sleeping. I can still remember the smell of his clothes and duffel bag. It was a very earthy scent that if I try, I can still smell.

*I eventually warmed up to Charlie and grew up with a big brother that teased me, told me ghost stories and laughed at the crushes I had on his friends.*

*Today, I have a hard time watching movies about Vietnam, which is strange, because Charlie loves them. He tells us stories about the fun times he had there, the friends he made, and even some of the bad things he went through.*

*Even though he still teases me, still tells me ghost stories scaring me to death, I will always respect him for the person he is today and what he and countless other soldiers have endured. I'm so very proud of him for writing this book.*

*Charlie thought I saw him as a "wacko" when he came home from Vietnam. Well, today I still think he is kind of a "wacko" – – but a very lovable one!*

> *I love you big Brother,*
> *Sherry*


Terry's thoughts:

Disclaimer: *I was pretty little when you were over in Southeast Asia, so I'm not 100% sure that my recollection of some events are "real" or just the active imagination of a kid who watched too many "Johnny Quest" cartoons. Likewise, I'm not sure about times and dates. Nevertheless, here are my recollections:*

• *I remember sitting at the kitchen table in the old house. I was seated at the southwest corner and Dad was catty cornered across the table and Sherry was in the TV room (I guess that's what you call the room with the TV?). Mom was standing at the ironing board that was positioned between the 2 rooms. I haven't a clue as to where Donna or Ann was. Mom had set a small, black reel-to-reel tape recorder on the ironing board and we were listening to tapes that you had sent. I remember you mentioning that the kids didn't have toys and it made me feel sad. So mom sent you a care*

Charlie Palek

*package and I stuck in a blue car I got from a cereal box (it was 3 pieces...body, front wheels, back wheels.) Later, I remember you sending us a picture of some little kid, about my age, with the car. I remember feeling jealous as hell that this kid was getting presents from you! Sad one minute and jealous the next!*

• *I thought that Vietnam was a big camping trip. You were all sleeping in tents and cooking dinner over a fire. I don't think I ever thought about people shooting at one another or that you may never come back. You were gone someplace hot and far away playing dress up and would be home when you were finished.*

The biggest "event" I suppose I remember was going to the airport to pick you up when you came home the last time. We were all in Dad's blue Chevy. I remember Ann getting carsick and hoping she would puke so we could make fun of her. I can't remember if it was the way there or the way home. I don't really remember much at the airport but I remember the ride home (I guess because it involved food.) Stopping at some place and eating and you getting your food free! I remember riding home and it was the 3 "men" in the front seat. I remember you teasing me about something and you grabbed my shirt with your right hand and I noticed a silver ring that you were wearing. It had some kind of a black stone in it like onyx or something (is this right?). I never remember seeing a ring like that again. Oh well, that's what I remember. Anyway, when we got home, I remember seeing you, in uniform, kick starting your blue Honda 350. It wouldn't start, but finally you got it going and took off for Roxy's. I also think that it was on the way home that we told you that you were going to be in Mary Beth's wedding!

• *I remember eating dinner at Hargan's across the street one day and Mr. Hargan asking me something about my brother in NAM (rhymes with YAM) whereupon I quickly corrected him and said it was pronounced Vietnam (rhymes with BOMB).*

• *I remember thinking that there were huge trees that were really a network of secret passages. You would pull on a limb and a secret door would open up and it would allow you to go up into the housing area or down underground into the work area. The work area had all kinds of secret, high-tech computers with rows and rows of blinking lights (this was also about the time I was introduced to James Bond...can you tell?) When I asked you if you ever slept in trees and you said that "sometimes" it solidified into my brain that there were sleeping quarters up in the trees!*

*Tattletale*

- I remember the night you got home from Texas on your motorcycle. It was nighttime, and instead of driving down Bryan Street, you turned on Adams and drove through the backyard. I also remember that you said you tied a pair of wet socks to the luggage rack to dry and they blew away.
- I remember some story you told in the kitchen. You were on the south end of the table in the old house. The story was about some Vietnamese guy running, and at the same time, looking back at you over his shoulder. He failed to see the stop sign that was in front of him and ran smack into it. I remember this story because you were wearing a white tee shirt and you bent backwards over the back of the chair to show how the guy looked when he hit the sign. I also remember thinking "what is a stop sign doing in the middle of a campground?"
- I'm not sure of the time of this, but I think it was while you were home on leave. You and I were sitting on the couch watching a movie in the old house. The couch was green vinyl. You were wearing jeans and a white tee shirt. You were cleaning a rifle of some kind. I had gotten a double barrel dart gun as a gift for something. I grabbed it and a white rag (probably one of Dad's good handkerchiefs) sat next to you and cleaned my gun too. I remember you leaning over and putting some gun oil from a brown can onto my plastic shotgun and telling me to rub it in.
- I remember you spit shining my black boots for me and then not wanting to wear them. I finally did and eventually scuffed them up. Then I tried to spit shine them myself. Mom abruptly put an end to that when she saw me ladling on the black shoe polish and hacking loogies all over the place.
- I remember the story you told about getting the rifle with the bayonet. It seems like you "hooked" it somehow from a guy while you were in your helicopter and that it was put together from several other guns because it had several serial numbers and none of them matched.
- I remember wanting to wear a white tee shirt and black boots like you did all the time. I would have to pull the tee shirt out of the dirty clothes (how many white tee shirts can a 5-year-old have?) I also remember wearing my wristwatch upside down like you. A picture of all of us at the dinner table confirmed this little tidbit. Yours truly has his hand up and the watch is upside down.

*Terry*

Charlie Palek

*Ann's thoughts:*

When asked to write what I remembered of Charlie's tours in Vietnam, I hesitated because I don't remember much. Being between the ages of 10 – 12 years old then, I knew that he was in Nam, fighting in a war, but not understanding why. I don't remember any kids at school making remarks about him being in Nam so therefore, I didn't experience the negativism that my older sister probably received from her schoolmates. So my memories are entirely good or bad memories, through the eyes of a 4th – 6th grader.

I remember... being in the 4th grade. Our Weekly Reader had short articles about the war in Vietnam, not necessarily what was going on, but rather maps and lessons in geography and Social Studies. I do remember pointing to the Mekong Delta on a map and sharing with my class that that was the area my brother was in. I also found an English to Vietnamese translating dictionary in our school library. I checked it out and wrote to Charlie with a few simple words that I found in the book that I thought we could share, like "hi," "bye," and "water buffalo." He said we'd sharpen our Vietnamese language skills and when he came home we'd have secret conversations and no one would know what we were talking about. I can't remember any of those words now, but it really doesn't matter. I don't think water buffalo would be involved in many of our conversations!

I remember all the letters and tapes and pictures we received from Charlie. Now that I'm older and I talk to co-workers and others who had a loved one in the war, I realize we were very lucky to have him write as often as he did. Many soldiers didn't write to their families and vice versa. But we did and he responded to all our letters. The pictures were great! I remember mom taking time from her busy schedule to sit down with them and put them in an album, carefully copying the caption of the photo Charlie had provided on the back of the photo. When we received a letter from Charlie, especially with pictures — everything would stop and we'd read and look them over. We tease Mom now that once she was reading a letter from Charlie while in the big easy chair in our living room, when we experienced a mild earthquake. When my older sister frantically asked what was going on, mom's calm reply was "Oh, it's just an earthquake." The house could have fallen in on top of her and when they would have dug her out she'd still be looking at those pictures and reading that letter.

I remember how thoughtful he was sending us gifts at Christmas... a 98 piece of china from Japan for mom, a reel to reel tape recorder for dad, a portable TV for Donna and me (Sorry, twins, I don't remember what he sent you, probably 2 big sticks). But not just at Christmas and not just for us... flowers for mom and Mrs. House at Mother's Day, birthday presents (a painting of a tiger on black velvet was one of my favorites) and many gifts for Roxy. We also sent him home made cookies and candy, as did my grandma and aunts. One Christmas we made home made taffy while Roxy played Christmas carols on the piano. We carefully cut it into pieces and wrapped each piece and sent the can over to him, however he never received it. I'm sure someone enjoyed our taffy. He'd write back saying how he'd share his cookies with the others and by the time he'd get the can back, all the cookies would be gone. He said many of the other troops didn't get goodies from their families...how sad.

I remember...the 2-week period when we got no mail from him. I'm not sure whether it was in the 1st or 2nd tour but regardless; it was an awful 2 weeks. He was evidently in an area that wasn't able to get mail in or out. We were so used to getting at least 2 letters a week from him; we'd expect it all the time. I remember hearing my mom tell dad that she feared having a knock on the door and opening it to a representative from the Army telling her Chas had been killed. The anguish they went through.

I remember...watching Bob Hope on TV at Christmas time, scanning the many thousands of soldiers on TV thinking that maybe we'd see Charlie. Well, we never did and Charlie didn't get to see Bob Hope until he got back to the states. Those shows sure made us miss him more, but I really admire Bob Hope for brightening the holidays for all those troops for so many years.

I remember...the absolute worst time, when he called to tell us he was going back to Nam for a 2nd tour. How upset my parents were, especially mom. I'll never forget that night. Like I said before I didn't understand why he was going back but I sure didn't want to go through another year of fear and uncertainty. I was old enough to remember that.

I remember...the best time — the day of his discharge. Mom made us go to bed at 8:00 that night in June so we'd be able to get up at 3am to go to the airport in St. Louis. It was still light outside! She had tried to convince us to stay home that morning because it was so early, but we had insisted on going...knowing we'd never have to put him on another plane to go to war again! I don't think any of us slept that night...we were too excited. Going to the airport was always exciting, but this was the ultimate trip. Dad borrowed a friend's movie camera to tape the homecoming (what I would have given for a video recorder and camera 25 years ago.) We waited impatiently for the big jet to pull up as we peered through the large glass windows hoping to be the first to see him coming down the plane's steps. When he did, all decked out in his uniform with ribbons and medals, I was so proud! Dad said he looked like a Christmas tree, all decorated up. The tears that flowed! When we retrieved his suitcase he had a small sign on it stating HOMEWARD BOUND FROM VIETNAM. My dad asked him for it when we got home. The last time I checked, it was still taped to dad's workbench.

I remember...all the people that stopped by to see Charlie and welcome him home. I remember the pills he had to take to keep him from getting malaria. I remember Terry dressing exactly like him. If Charlie wore jeans and a white tee shirt, so did Ter. Charlie would purposefully walk from room to room, around furniture with Terry 3 steps behind him? Terry even ate liver because Charlie did (in my opinion that was a little extreme!) I know for a fact that admiration from little brother to big brother still exists. I remember that cute red Camaro he bought when he got back. We all thought it was the coolest (especially mom...she'd always drive it instead of the family car, although she may deny it now!) Too bad I was too young to drive, but he did pay me to wash it.

Reflecting back over the past 25 years, these 3 things amaze me:

#1 – That his wife Roxy, who was his girlfriend at the time of his tours in Vietnam, was able to remain faithful to him and vice versa. I think a relationship like theirs was a very special gift then and more so now. We are sure glad you decided to stick with him Roxy. You are one in a million and we are very blessed to have you in our family!

#2 – That my parents were able to remain sane during his tours and continue to raise their other 4 children in a normal household routine. Being a mom myself now, I can't imagine what they felt each time they put him on that plane, off to fight in a war. One never knows what will happen day to day, and one never knows if we will see a loved one again when we say goodbye, but the constant fear they lived with day to day is beyond my imagination. These 2 people are such an inspiration to not only my siblings and me but to many, many other people I know. I think their love and devotion to one another was the key to keeping their family together during this time. Mom and dad, we all love you very much.

#3 – The fact that Charlie came back from not one tour, but two tours physically healthy, and more importantly, emotionally sound. I've talked to several men involved in the war and to know that he did two of the most dangerous jobs in Vietnam, a door gunner and a radio operator, and coming home alive makes me so very thankful. I didn't realize the importance of his duties while there until these last few years. Sure there are things he'll share with us and things we'll never know. To know he shares many of these experiences with high school classes now, that he has attended several reunions with his platoons and that he feels the need to write this book makes me realize that he has come to accept his position in Vietnam and makes me all the more proud of him. I just wish every sister who had a big brother in Vietnam could feel this way. While looking over his medals and memorabilia of Nam one day made me realize that my big brother is a Vietnam hero. But in my personal life, he's always been a hero to me and always will be.

*I love you, Charlie!*
*Annie*

*Donna's thoughts:*

This is my personal account of life at home during the two years that my brother, Charles Palek, spent in Vietnam. The years are from 1967 – 1970. Charlie left for the Army seven days before my 14th birthday and came home from Nam the last time, the week of my 17th birthday. I was just starting high school at the time and about to enter the worst, most emotional years of my life simply because I was trying to grow up and was not doing a very good job of it. I had braces, was skinny, I had no self-esteem, was flunking Algebra 1 and worst of all, I had no dates. So add this to the stress the war put on the family, and you can imagine my state of being. (Poor mom).

The following are memories in categories of family members and how this time in history affected them in their day to day lives.

Charlie Palek

## MOM

- She was determined to lose some weight and this she did. I can remember her taking 5" off of her dresses and I was never sure if it was the diet that did it or the worry over Charlie and what he was going through. I have just recently learned that the possibility of him becoming a POW was her biggest fear, whereas a vain teenager my concern was the chance of him being maimed or of loss of limb.
- Mom did literally go gray while he was away. I can't remember that much gray in her hair before he left.
- When Charlie's letters came, which was every day or so, they usually contained pictures of where he was and men in his company. She literally devoured these letters and all life at home came to a stand still until she was finished. Once we had an earthquake on a Saturday morning and mom was sitting in this stuffed chair engrossed in some of Charlie's pictures. While I was trying to get out of my upstairs room with everything swaying around, and the twins were watching TV as it walked across the floor, I came running down the staircase screaming, "earthquake, earthquake!" Mom, not missing a beat or looking up from those pictures, calmly says, "I know." I always joked that if the house had caved in we would have found her under the rubble still looking at those pictures.
- A good example of how quickly the mood of the house could change was when I came home with a dress that I had meticulously labored over in Home-Ec. I was bound and determined to get an A on that garment, and surprise mom with my fine sewing skills. I managed to get that A, and literally ran home to show mom the teacher's great comments on my project. She was sitting in a lawn chair in the backyard reading something when I arrived home. I rushed up and said, "Mom, look at my dress...I got an..." to which mom interrupted me with this terrible look on her face, and said in a tiny voice, "Charlie's been wounded." There went the great moment, the excitement, and the praise. It was a very quiet dinner that night for the adults at the table.
- Charlie asked mom to mount all of his Nam pictures into scrapbooks. I'm sure it was a labor of love because she spent many, many, hours writing in white ink underneath each picture describing in detail what Charlie had inscribed on the back of each photograph. If memory serves me there were three albums total.

## FAMILY

• Each night we sat in the kitchen, at the table for dinner and watched the news on TV There was no talking or noise during the report of news from Vietnam. Charlie always told us not to believe the estimated body count numbers they gave, but only the total counts. That gave me a pretty good indication that we weren't being told the truth about this war, but I never asked if anyone else felt this way.

• We baked a lot of cookies and sent them to Charlie and always found out that he shared them with the guys. That always made me feel good to know that instead of hoarding the gifts from home he let others enjoy them too.

• Once we received a letter from a young man by the name of Angel Vasquez from New York City. He went on and on about the best cookies he had ever tasted, that were sent to Charlie from home. We decided to surprise Angel and send him some cookies of his very own. That started a wonderful exchange of letters and cookies to someone who really seemed to hunger for any correspondence from home. Later when we didn't hear from Angel anymore we learned that he and two other guys from Charlie's unit had been transferred to another unit and all three had died fighting on Hamburger Hill. Just as all was fine and we were enjoying life with a new friend, the war once again became a glaring reality right in our own home.

• One summer Washington County lost three Vietnam servicemen. Two of them I knew if I saw them, but one, Johnny Javorchik was a neighborhood friend who had grown up with us. I remember at his funeral there was a young man in uniform serving as his honor guard. Later I heard that Mrs. Keller, Johnny's mother, could have requested Charlie as the honor guard. She didn't and everyone seemed relieved that she hadn't. I never did understand that. My thinking was that if Charlie was home, in the air going and coming, at least he'd be out of harms way and we get to see him at least once more in case something happened to him. Again, I didn't question anyone's opinions.

•The impressions of the other members of our family at this time are that they were too young to really be affected by it. Ann was around nine years old at the time, and Terry and Sherry were three. Ann seemed to enjoy baking those cookies for him. Sherry was afraid of him when he'd first come home because she really didn't care for strangers. Terry was so very proud of him that he firmly believed that Sergeant ranked right under a Four Star General and the President. He once saw a Lieutenant Colonel at the airport and remarked "Boy, just look at the Sergeant, Dad!"

## ME

•*I felt closer to Charlie during this time than I had ever felt before. As a kid growing up, I was just a nuisance to him and he'd never look me in the eyes when he talked to me, which made me feel pretty worthless. But Vietnam offered me the opportunity to give him something he really needed and wanted...word from home. And that's what I did. I wrote during my study halls, on weekends and every chance I got I'd record the top 20 hits off of St. Louis station KXOK. This usually took all Saturday but it didn't matter because all the guys wanted to hear the latest tunes. I'd fill in with my personal news and news of mutual friends. This was the time that I started to really share my fears and dreams with Charlie and he gave me good council and advice. I didn't always agree with him, but he usually turned out to be right.*

• *On the day that he left for Vietnam the first time, we had an argument about a guy that I liked from school. Charlie told me I was wasting my time because he was a loser. I got so mad that I didn't go to the airport to see him off. Later in his next letter he stated that he had cried as he watched the plane taxi down the runway, and how it hit him that he might never see any of us again. My shame at that moment will never leave me. How full of pride I'd been and how wrong were my actions. I've tried to never skip a goodbye with anyone since that day.*

• *He brought all of us gifts from Asia. To mom he gave a 96-piece set of china that was absolutely beautiful. To me he gave a Petrie Racer 35mm camera. Sherry received a silk dress. Terry became the proud owner of a miniature GI fatigue set with cap and Palek on the chest. Ann was given a gorgeous black velvet painting of a tiger and for the life of me I can't recall if Dad got a gift.*

•*Charlie also provided me with material for my History classes. He sent me an Ace of Spades and told how this was seen as a symbol of bad luck and how they would drop them everywhere they could to spook Charlie Cong. He also sent me some pieces of propaganda, theirs and ours, and told me what they said and meant. That was one of the better* oral reports of my life. Once I opened an envelope up to have sticks and twigs fall out of it. The letter with it said that on a patrol one night he saw this foliage glowing in the dark. He thought I'd think that was neat, so he put some in his pocket and sent it to me. Naturally it wasn't glowing by the time I got it, but it was the thought that counted. I kept those twigs for a long time.

- I learned a lot about human relations in this time period. I still marvel at the faith and fidelity that Roxy held on to so firmly. I asked Charlie, the night before he left for Nam, if he had gotten his class ring back from Roxy as he was planning to do. He had a conscience about forcing her to be faithful with the future of his life so uncertain. He simply stated that, "No, he didn't get the ring back", that she wouldn't let him have it. She was one of the truest women I'd ever met. She not only wrote and sent things to Charlie but she included me in a lot of her plans. Many times I got to go to the show, shopping, or just got to hang around her and all of her friends. You have to realize that as a self-conscious, awkward, teenager it was quite a boost to my ego to hang out with college girls. I even got to take a trip up to U of I for an entire weekend, and I got there by train! I sometimes wonder if having me around made Charlie seem closer. Whatever the reason, Roxy helped me through a very difficult and surly time of my life.

- On the subject of my friends at the time, I remember them asking about Charlie but never once did I ever have to defend his actions for fighting in this war. He was always thought of as a hero and respected. There was one girl who never acted like she liked me at all and I could not figure out why, until someone remarked that my brother came home safe once, just to go back again, when her brother never came home from the first time. I never again mentioned Charlie's name when she was around.

- My first year of school I carried a clipboard from class to class. On the cover of the clipboard I had placed a cover sheet used for doodling. It said "Go Army," with Charlie's address and names of places in Vietnam. When he came home the first time, which we figured to be the last, I took the cover off my clipboard and threw it away. One guy in my classroom looked at it one day and said, " Oh good, now that your brother is home safe and sound, I guess your going to forget all about the war and the other guys still over there, right?" Well, I strongly denied his accusations when inside I knew he was right on target. We had even stopped watching the news during dinner each night. It was almost as if we were all saying "OK, we've had enough and we don't want to do this anymore!

• I also had a 5' x 3' map of Vietnam in my bedroom. I had constructed circles to denote a 25-mile and 60 mile radius. I always figured by his last letter, where within a 60-mile radius he was. The 25-mile circle was used to show where the heaviest fighting was, according to the news releases. That map came down too, the minute he called to tell us he was on U.S. soil.

• I remember the day he called to say he was going back to Nam. He had mentioned it and said that if he could get the red tape through he'd go back as a door gunner. I always expected him to go through with it, but sure hoped that he didn't. We were expecting the call and I was upstairs in my room when it came. I sat down on the top of the staircase and eavesdropped on mom's conversation. All I remember her saying is "Oh no Charlie, you didn't." That's when I went to my room to think about how I didn't want to go through this again with the family.

• The whole time Charlie was gone and getting wounded, I was quietly preparing for the worst. I figured mom wouldn't be able to cope, so being the eldest at home I might have to help dad in the event of a crisis. I had the funeral home picked out that mom and dad would want to use, I had a place for the kids to go during the funeral preparations, I'd have Mike Michaels play taps because he did at Johnny's funeral at the last moment, after having the foresight to bring his trumpet along in case. Our funeral would not have any of the bugs in it that Johnny's did. I had our clothes picked out and all confusion would hopefully be eliminated. There was nothing to do but wait for the school secretary to come get me out of class when those letters would stop coming for a week or more. That was the worst of the times. Waiting and knowing that he was hurt or worse, because Charlie always told us if he would not be able to write to us for awhile because of maneuvers.

## CHARLIE

• The first time Charlie came home from Nam we came back through Mascoutah, Illinois, and stopped for something to eat. After ordering, Charlie said he just had to play the jukebox. He went up to our waitress who looked to be about his age and asked for change to play some music.

She then asked if he was just coming home from Nam, and he answered yes. She reached into her tips pocket, got a handful of change out, handed it to him and said the music was on her and welcome home. This was the basic attitude of the people in the Midwest, one of support not one of condemnation.

- The first morning he was home, I went into his room to make his bed. Now understand this, mom always ironed the sheets so they had very deep creases in them. As before when Charlie slept, after a week on those sheets you could still see those creases. That first morning his bed was completely stripped of sheets, blankets, mattress pad, even the cases were off of the pillows! All bedclothes were lying on the floor. When I showed mom, all she said was, "Donna, we have no idea what he's been through."
- One day I sat and talked with him about Nam and got the courage to ask if he had killed anyone. When he asked me why I'd ever ask such a thing, I replied, "Because I don't ever want to find you hanging in the basement like your name sake." He talked for a little while and I never knew if he felt better, but I sure did, because uncle Charlie had never talked about World War II, and the memories caused him to take his own life, many years later.
- He always had vivid stories to tell of the children of Vietnam. I remember the twins collecting prizes out of cereal boxes and sending them to Charlie so he could take them to an orphanage. Many times he gave his c-rats utensils to village children who would gather around as the soldiers ate. He also sent home many pictures of children in the surrounding villages.
- We had a family across the street from us that had three of the most wonderful children I had ever met. Each time I babysat for them they would end the day with a prayer for Charlie's safe return. It didn't matter that they had moved in after he had left and didn't even know him, it was just something they did. When Charlie got home, Doug, the eldest son, all of five years old, came over, shook Charlie's hand and said how glad he was that he had come home safely. That was our whole neighborhood's attitude.
- When he got home, there was a pigment fungus that he had on his back. It literally ate the color pigment out of his skin. Where it should be dark tan it was white. I applied medicine to it each night after his shower and it took months to go away. Charlie told me terrible stories of what

## Charlie Palek

jungle rot looked like and that almost all the guys in the boonies got it sooner or later.

- There was a little friction in the house after he came home from Nam. Dad had hung all of Charlie's citations from his medals, which were pretty many, in the living room for all to see. I can recall Charlie getting very upset that they were up and immediately took all of them off the wall in front of Dad. Not being one for confrontations, I left the room and could not understand why Charlie was so upset. I too was as proud as dad of his honors. The only other time I can recall is when the V.F.W. asked Charlie to attend one of their meetings and dad was to come along. They really got into it over him wearing his uniform. Dad wanted it on and Charlie wanted to throw everything away.

- Years later after Nam, he and I were both attending S.I.U., Charlie told me to never, ever go out with a guy fresh from Nam. He said they were animals for a while and no sister of his should go out with one. I didn't understand but didn't argue either. Several weeks later a new guy in one of my classes started to ask me out. He was fresh from Nam, proud of it, told everyone who would listen, and was very persistent. He told me that I had to go out with him. When I asked him why I had to go out with him, he got right in my face and said, "Because I fought for our country in Nam and you owe it to me." I asked him if he had served one tour and he answered yes. So I told him that my brother had served two tours, listed Charlie's medals, and told him that my brother was more of a man than he'd ever be because he didn't treat people in such a rude way. He never bothered me again, and Charlie's advice turned out to be crystal clear from then on.

I always felt that God spared Charlie for something special, maybe this book is it. I learned from the Nam experience that no one is guaranteed tomorrow and each day should be treated as your last. Always say good-bye and show your love. And I was convinced that I'd try to marry someone in a nice safe profession, because the stress factor is so great. I've now been married to a cop for 20 years and I feel that the Nam experience made me see life as it is and in turn made me a good police officer's wife, because reality stares us all in the face every day, some see it, some don't. I do.

*Donna*

*Roxy's Thoughts:*

    *1. When we were dating in high school, I would occasionally ask about what your plans were for the future. They were always the same – a military career. And believe me, I tried to convince you otherwise. But I knew for sure in May, 1967, when you told me you had enlisted in the Army. Guess it didn't seem real to me until you told me that night in May.*

    *From that time on, I knew it would be different for us – separations and letter writing. But one thing I knew even then...I'd always be waiting for you . You weren't going to be over there alone – not with your family and me keeping you up on what was going on here. Your Mom was best – always making me a part of all their news, too. You are her #1 son, and she wasn't about to let you feel alone. One of my best memories was of making taffy to send overseas to you – that was one of the messiest and most fun times I had at your house! We all felt better doing something for you – sending cookies, food, or letters.*

    *2. The first time you were wounded and I got a letter that started, "Now honey, don't be upset, but..." Literally, scared me to death. I hated the fact that you were hurt and recuperating by yourself. That really upset me. I probably wrote 10 letters that week, instead of 7!*

    *3. The call I received from you at Illinois Wesleyan about your decision to return to Vietnam. Not a good day. I was fairly brave on the phone, but you should have seen me afterwards...cried all night. Couldn't understand that one – wish I had played more of a part in the decision. But we had no commitment at that time, and I realized that...but...it hit everybody almost harder than when you first enlisted. I remember being home not long after that. Uncle Larry and Dick were there visiting my folks. You came in to say goodbye to everybody. When you left, that was the 1st time I saw my relatives cry...and I was the one trying to make them feel better.*

    *4. I was always amazed at all the things you could see and remember when you were over there. The little kids really got to you – I think because the twins were so little, and you missed them so much. You were always talking about them. And how much you missed citrus fruits and food in general.*

    *5. I was at 2 colleges while you were gone and the sentiment was the same. Very anti-war – probably because the ones who were protesting were safe and secure living off the folks money and didn't have any other*

Charlie Palek

cause to make noise about. I remember a week of rioting on campus – with the song, "War" blaring away on stereos all across campus and torches down on the Quad. Pretty scary atmosphere...drugs and demonstrations are scary. The worst person I argued with was my roommate's boyfriend at the U of I. A typical pot-smoking, hippie-type with loaded parents. He went off one night on the war, and I couldn't take it anymore. Let him have it with both barrels about what a terrific guy you were and he couldn't begin to fill your shoes. Of course, I broke down in tears, but he got the point. Never said a thing to me after that.

6. Your homecoming was a much-anticipated event. I decided not to come to the airport. That trip was reserved for your family. Your folks deserved that 1st glimpse of you. But it sure was a wonderful sight – you in your uniform speeding over to my house on your motorcycle! What a hunk!

Love, Roxy

Mom's thoughts:

I didn't want Charlie to enlist, but it was his choice. It was a sad day for all of us when he left.

When we finally heard from him, we got a letter often. Sometimes every day, sometimes 4 or 5 letters at a time. When we didn't hear for a week, we knew something was wrong. He told me when he left if he was wounded, and possibly could, he would tell us, rather than someone else telling us. So whenever the letters didn't come we watched every newscast on TV because we knew what area he was in. What a wonderful relief when his letters came, yes he was wounded, but would be o.k. This happened 3 times while he was there.

Along with the letters he sent pictures with a caption on the back. That night I would put them in an album for him, writing the caption on the bottom of the picture.

Charlie's sisters Donna 14, Ann 10, and the twins Terry and Sherry 4, would save every small toy they saw or found in cereal boxes, because

Charlie said that they spent their spare time at an orphanage and would give the toys to the children there. Terry would lay in bed at night and worry about the children, because he and Sherry had lots of things to play with they played with snakes.

The girls enjoyed helping bake and pack cookies etc. to send to him. Sherry wanted to send a bowl of tapioca because Charlie liked it.

We were all very busy which made the time go faster and one more day closer to Charlie's return.

The 1st Christmas he was away, was a sad one. But the next year we all had a great time. He sent all of us some great gifts but the best one of all was him being home, and well. Roxy, his girlfriend from the next block came over. We had a wonderful Christmas.

Since that time the whole family still wants to be together on Christmas or any day we can. That is what Dad and I look forward to.

Charlie had an Uncle Charlie Palek, and now Terry has a little boy who is named after Charlie. His name is Charles Cooper Palek.

We all remember Charlie calling saying he was going back for his 2nd tour. I guess I was numb, but we knew he was so unhappy in Texas. He had nothing to do, and that is not like him. So we loved him and prayed for his safe return. And we were certainly blessed.

On his return home a neighbor (Bob Hargan) wanted to have a great homecoming, a real celebration. I told him I didn't think Charlie would like that, so instead they asked him to all the organization's suppers (The Lions Club, Legion etc.)

A friend Dean Haege offered Charlie a job when he returned home. Dean was a farmer and had feeder cattle. I think that was a wonderful thing Dean did and I will always be grateful that Charlie had plenty of work out there.

I never watched war movies then, and I still won't watch them, 23 years later.

Love, Mom

Dad's thoughts:

I was born on a farm in Oakdale Township near a little town called Elkton. When I was 6 months old my family moved to a farm 4 miles south of Okawville. We lived there 12 years, then moved to another farm 1 mile west of this farm for 3 years, and then we moved to a farm 1 mile northwest of Plum Hill where we lived until 1945.

I had 4 older brothers, and 2 sisters. With all these boys in the family my Dad never had to hire any outside help to get the farm work done. One by one my older brothers left for jobs they eventually found and when I was 13 it fell to me to help Dad do his farm work. We usually had 10 cows to milk, twice a day. We had chickens, and hogs for our meat to get us through the winter, and did all the farming with horses. We never did have a tractor.

As I grew older I had a lot of time to think, I always hoped for a military career. In fact, I built model airplanes out of everything I could get my hands on. My Dad always had a good workshop, and lot of tools and he never cared that I used his tools as long as I hung them back up in their place. I knew my Dad would never own his own farm, so I knew I would have to do something else besides farm work, so I fantasized about something in the military.

All the boys in the family were eligible to go to war, and I remember my mother began to cry because she knew some of her sons would have to go. Les was already in. He was drafted in August for a year, and then he spent 65 months in the Army.

Charlie was next. He was drafted in 1942, Buster Shubert, sister Betty's husband was next and then Helen's husband Rich was next. Uncle Bill was too old for the draft, and all the farmers around Okawville got up a petition to keep Joe in his job as a mechanic, rather than have him drafted. Well, he was deferred from military service, much against his will, and he never did have to go.

Then came little Don, I was deferred because if you had enough points to work on the farm, you were automatically deferred. This went on until April 1945. And every time I mentioned going into the Service, Dad would hang his head and Mom would start to cry Well, in August of 1945 the Hagebush brothers owned the farm we lived on, and decided to sell it. Dad said he was too old to start out on another farm so he sold all his farming tools, and live stock, and bought a little house in Okawville. So, then the way was clear for me to leave. After I helped my Mom and Dad get settled in their town house I went to the Draft Board and got released so I could enlist in the Merchant Marines. All my brothers and brothers-in-law told me to enlist in something beside the Army as they had too many men in there at that particular time, so it was the M.M. for me. You may ask, with my interest in airplanes why I didn't choose the Air Force. Well, we were all sent to Chicago in 1942 for a physical and I was O.K. in everything but my eyes. I had 20/20 in one and 20/30 in the other so that disqualified me for the Air Force.

But I'll tell you, Charlie, that my decision to go into the Merchant Marines was the right one. Of course I was lucky to be on some good ships, with good shipmates and that made the difference.

In 1942 on Easter Sunday night I had my first date with your Mom, and we were pretty much a twosome from then on. We both dated other guys and gals after that, but we always seemed to belong together.

When I left to go into the Service, I told her I would probably be gone a year before I came home, so she could date anybody that following year and if she still had feelings for me I would give her a ring when I came home.

Well, I was gone from August 1945 to May 1946 and she sent me her ring size before I came home. I came home for a month, gave her a diamond, and left again and was gone from June 1946 to August 1947.

I came home August 28, 1947 and we got married Oct 18, 1947.

So that brings us to the time you were born 16 months later. It was quite a surprise when you were born on my 27th birthday!

I always hoped you would choose the military, and I know how much I encouraged you. When you were big enough to build models, I think I bought you every model I could find to keep your interest in flying. I know I waved the flag in your face more than any father did at that time.

I was real happy when you enlisted in the Army, as I wanted you to make a career out of it. And do you remember, I told you to write to Roxy often because when you are in the service, mail from home is really important. You evidently took my advice, because look what happened.

When you left and had your basic training you said you were going to Ft. Gordon for Paratroop Training, I was once again happy because you were doing something with airplanes.

You wrote and told me they had put you in the Infantry. I was really pissed off, as I sure didn't care about you being a foot soldier.

I even made it a point, when I saw an Army recruiter in Centralia to tell him what I thought of the Army Recruiter system. I told him what had happened with you and he just shrugged his shoulders. I told him right there, that there would never be another Palek enlist in the Army.

## Charlie Palek

All the time you were in Vietnam, and especially the times you were wounded, I berated myself for having waved the flag in your face so many times.

When you came home after your first tour we were all so relieved that you were safe. Then you went down to Texas and then said you were riding your motorcycle home and going back to Vietnam.

Well, we weren't happy, but I told your Mom that you were old enough to know what you wanted to do. We didn't like it but we went along with your judgement. And after you were gone overseas, and told us you were an observer in a helicopter, I knew you had finally gotten what you wanted.

Of course, we did an awful lot of praying. We are not that religious, but we had to do something and that was all we could do.

Then we started getting all your certificates for all the citations so I got out my angle square box and started making frames for them and one by one I hung them on our wall.

The last time you were wounded, and then came home, our prayers were answered. When Dean Haege gave you a job we were real happy about things until you took all the citations down from the wall and put them in a box. That sort of ticked me off, as I was very proud of the record you made in Vietnam. I still have all those citations in the very box you put them in, so they are yours to keep.

Now that it's all in the past we can look back and wonder what was right.

It is all coming out now what a farce the war in Vietnam was and what a bunch of bungling fools our top men in Washington were. Every book that I read now about that war makes fun of the guys that could have won the war for us. So it is no secret, now what mistakes were made.

I read books, as many as I have time for, and they all, especially the authors, (most of them are Vietnam veterans) tell just what they think about how they were manipulated during the war, and they have no use for Johnson, or Kissinger — those damn fools. Everybody knows that war could have been won, but things were so bad on the home front that nobody wanted to talk about it.

All the young guys that went to Canada to escape the draft and all the things other guys did to get out of it. And guys like Quayle, his Dad bought his freedom, everybody knows that but he is so damn stupid he wouldn't have been any help to us anyway. And now we have a president who is a draft dodger. Boy, what next?

Charlie, I don't know if this letter is what you want, but I can truthfully say that we were all behind you all the time you were gone. And we still are. Every time Terry fails at something he is scared you will think he is a failure. Ha.

I hope you can find something in this letter that will help you.

We are all very proud of you, Charlie, for coming through the war and making such a good name for yourself, and being such a good big brother to Terry and your sisters.

I am sure Roxy had a lot to do with it so we thank her too. We think she is a real jewel.

*Love, Dad*

# About the Author

*Having had an interest in military history since I was 10, I felt the need to experience war for myself as an infantryman, the one true warrior. I graduated from high school in 1967, and Vietnam was heating up fast. I volunteered immediately for Army infantry and Vietnam service. My lottery number was above three hundred and my family and friends knew that I could probably "sit it out" if I wanted to, but I had to seek the adventure.*

Born in 1949 in Southern Illinois dairy country, I was always out in the fields, hunting groundhogs, fishing or plinking at starlings and blackbirds with my trusty 22. Schoolwork was a necessary evil, except for history. Sports were something I did not excel in and they were not a big part of my life.

After discharge from the Army in 1970, I received a degree in Still Photography from Southern Illinois and began my career in portraiture, making people happy with their own faces. Nature and wildlife photography was, and still is, my favorite pastime. I married Roxy, who wrote to me on the average of one letter every three days while I was in Vietnam, and we will celebrate our thirtieth anniversary in 2001.

I have photographed grizzlies in the wilds of Alaska, and have even done some parachuting, but nothing has given me an adrenaline rush like combat. She's a hard taskmaster, but completely unforgettable. I'm sure most combat veterans will agree.